Farm Fresh Forensics

Sheridan Rowe Langford

DEDICATION

For R.C. and Reba

CONTENTS

ACKNOWLEDGMENTS

Many people made this book possible. My Other Half deserves so much credit for lighting the fire under me to get this first book started. My mom has been both my greatest fan and my most honest critic. So much credit should go to my wizard, Stephanie Morgan, the talent behind Magic Beans Creations. I want to thank my buddy and cell mate, Fergus Fernandez, for not only putting up with me all those years, but for coming up with the Farm Fresh Forensics name. Father David, you cracked open the door and let in the light. Sue Givens, you are my Sheep Mother and my mentor. Joy Hall, you are my crack dealer leading me down the path to sheep, dairy goats, and Livestock Guardian Dogs. None of this would have been possible without the love and support of my website readers. I love you all.

"What you leave behind is not what is engraved in stone monuments, but what is woven into the lives of others."
Pericles

CHAPTER 1

THE PLUNGE

"Life was a funny thing that occurred on the way to the grave."

Quentin Crisp

I am so absorbed in the camera that it's easy to overlook the obvious. Straddling his body, the lens takes me closer than my nose wants to go. The newly dead soon give off a musty smell as the early stages of decomposition begin. This odor is a minor annoyance, like the fly landing on my shoulder as I play Twister over yet another dead man. I pause for a moment to consider the question that nibbles at my mind the way decay eats at the man beneath me. When did something so freaking abnormal become routine?

Like many new beginnings, mine started with a divorce. Through no fault on either side, we both just pulled the plug and it was time for a new start in life, so I took a transfer within the police department, and like Alice, dove headfirst down the rabbit hole into a twisted new Wonderland.

I stared at the printed words "Homicide Division" on the newly accepted transfer papers and walked with a spring in my step back to my truck, having no clue that I was about to peek underneath rocks which humanity keeps hidden for a good reason. I would later explain to courtroom juries that my job was to investigate all questionable deaths, from murders and suicides, to accidents and naturals that might be murders.

You do not simply dip your toe into a career like this to check the bathwater. It is a plunge, a total commitment. The gore alone causes most to balk, but a certain percentage of the population is blessed, or cursed, with the ability to see past that and let the dead talk. People who have this trait are not unaffected by what they see, but have the ability to table those emotions so they can go places others cannot. Later, when they do come up, gasping for the air of sanity, they must process what they've seen.

"But she, and Death, acquainted —

Meet tranquilly, as friends —

Salute and pass, without a Hint —

And there, the matter ends —"

Emily Dickinson

It takes a lot of dead men to train a crime scene investigator. There's no shortage of death in the Big City, and so every time the phone rings, I pack up my truck and roll out with an experienced CSI who is only too happy to teach me what he knows. The sooner I'm running calls on my own, the sooner his load will lighten. Training a crime scene investigator is a bit like cutting a precious gem. You start with a rough, uneven rock, then grind away the unnecessary parts and cut it at angles that best accent the stone. It's easy to fall into the trap of believing that being a crime scene investigator is all about photography, fingerprinting, collecting evidence, and report writing. If the student can master those tasks then he will be a good CSI. To this I say, "Horse Hockey."

These skills are merely different angles of the gemstone. The real trick to getting a beautiful gem is to cut it in such a way that the light passes through and enhances the stone. Just as light must pass through a gem to show its beauty, the skill of observation is what enhances the crime scene investigator. A CSI must become attuned to every nuance inside a scene. Observation is an art. To master this art one must first understand what is normal, only then can the eye pick out what is abnormal. And to know what is normal, a death investigator must stand over a lot of dead men. My life soon became a morbid Dr. Seuss rhyme.

Dead man with bad smell,

Dead man in motel,

Dead man with a fly,

Dead man with no eye,

Dead man on a train,

Dead man in the rain.

My day begins with murder. Actually, it begins with a frappuccino, it just moves to murder. This morning it's a dead guy on the railroad tracks. I've been on the job a couple of weeks and so I'm not just observing the experienced Crime Scene Unit investigator. Now I get to actively process the scene while he supervises. In order to get as many death investigations under my belt as possible, I go out every time the phone rings with the next CSU in the rotation. Today I'm rolling with the Old Fart.

Our job is to check the dead guy on the tracks and decide if we need to call in investigators and treat it like a murder. I slug my last gulp of mocha frappuccino down the hatch and pack my gear. Like me, the green dolly holding my assortment of toolboxes and tackle boxes is still new and shiny. A wad of dirty chewing gum stuck to one of the tires gives it an uneven wobble as I whack-whack across the parking garage to load the CSU truck. I load the boxes into the back of the truck and smile at Tigger.

In a moment of whimsy on my first week, I had slapped some Winnie-the-Pooh and Tigger stickers onto my new green tackle box which was filled with DNA collection kits, fingerprinting supplies, plastic baggies, and everything else a budding young CSI might need. Winnie-the-Pooh and Tigger would follow my entire career.

A ball of sweat rolls down my nose. Seven o'clock in the morning and already too humid to breathe. Another postcard day in Houston, the Bayou City. Another day, another lesson. On this day I learn you should never leave the house in anything you wouldn't want to be caught dead wearing. SpongeBob SquarePants pajamas. Grown man.

There are rules on a crime scene. As the crime scene investigator, the scene belongs to me, but the body belongs to the medical examiner, so I couldn't move it without her. Since she hasn't arrived yet, I busy myself taking scene photos. I can process the scene, take pictures, take a video, set out evidence markers and start a rough sketch to diagram the scene. The only thing I can't do is flip the body over to photograph him, so SpongeBob waits face down on the ballast rocks while I fumble around the scene trying to remember the order I'm supposed to do things.

It's clouding up fast. Looks like rain. SpongeBob might get wet. Time to speed things up. I load a tape into the video camera to film a short movie of the scene and pat myself on the back for remembering how to turn the camera on and find the red record button. My finger finds the focus lever and the sharp image of a blowfly zooms into view. Yuck. I trip over a railroad tie and step on SpongeBob.

"Oh! Excuse me!"

It will not be the last time I talk to a dead man.

After finishing the video it's time to take more photographs. I start at the intersection 500 feet west of SpongeBob because it's the closest place that will mark his location for future reference. Busy fiddling with my new lens, I completely forget CSU Rule#1 of crime scene investigation: *DO NOT BECOME SO FOCUSED IN THE CAMERA THAT YOU IGNORE YOUR SURROUNDINGS.*

The only warning I get is a soft whine and the quick grinding of pebbles on pavement. The whoosh of a fast-moving Chevy jostles past. I stumble into the ditch. The Laws of Physics clearly trump a police badge and a CSU uniform. Body intact but dignity in shambles, and with a better appreciation for Rule #1, I start snapping my way toward SpongeBob. I see Old Fart waving. With great excitement. At me.

I lower the camera to gawk. Old men like that rarely get excited about anything but fresh coffee and lunch. Then I see the train. Oh. Shit.

SpongeBob is about to become yellow hamburger. Behind the locomotive the sky is turning black and Old

Fart is waving like a windmill in a hurricane. Snapping away, I stumble down the ballast rock lining the tracks as I run toward my dead man. If SpongeBob is going to be a Union Pacific hood ornament then at least we should get the pictures. CSU Rule #2: *DOCUMENT EVERYTHING.*

Much to my relief, and maybe a twinge of disappointment, the train is on another track and has already stopped. Old Fart had his panties in a wad over the thunder cloud. A large raindrop lands and bursts like an egg on my notepad. SpongeBob doesn't have a lot more planned for his day, but I do, and it doesn't include wearing a wet uniform for the next six hours. Old Fart saves himself and climbs into the truck. That leaves just me and SpongeBob. And he's getting wet. CSU Rule #3: PRESERVE THE EVIDENCE.

I grab the most fragile items before the rain can wash the blood away and then trot to the truck for an umbrella. The joy of auto-focus on a camera is that it allows you to continue shooting a scene while holding an umbrella. I pat myself on the back again. A CSI is all about flexibility. It rained. Document it. Note the time in your report. It's as easy as that. Maybe. Hopefully.

It's a short shower and just as it stops the party gets started. Everyone arrives. Homicide Investigators, Railroad Investigators, and the Medical Examiner's Office Investigator all begin climbing their way across ballast rocks to meet a slightly soggy SpongeBob.

By the time we're bagging him up, the sun is back and we are in the sauna that is Houston after a rain. It is now noon and I'm hungry. Never one to suffer in silence, as the bag is zipped on SpongeBob I inform Old Fart that this Princess is hungry. Approaching "hangry". Since he allows as how he could eat too, the next order of business is deciding where. Barbecue. Had SpongeBob been hit by the train, we would still be having barbecue. Not much affects the appetite of a crime scene investigator. This trait tends to separate us from those who can't eat Chinese take-out after flicking maggots off evidence. CSU Rule #4: SHIFTS ARE LONG. ACCESS TO FOOD IS UNPREDICTABLE. TAKE CARE OF YOURSELF.

It's a good thing we take the time to eat. No sooner do Old Fart and I get back to the office than the phone rings again. Stinker in Apartment.

Decomposition is ugly business. With bellies full of barbecue, Old Fart and I are now forced to climb stairs. Flies buzz at the windows to announce what we already know. We have a Stinker. In the bloating stage of decomposition a build-up of gases in the body will cause the skin to expand to gigantic proportions and the deceased will resemble a ghastly Michelin Man. I expect that. I've seen it before. What I don't expect is the sound. The creaking. The groaning.

Imagine a wooden ship at sea rocking gently in the waves, its lines taunt then slack. Its boards creaking. Imagine Rice Krispies in milk. A tea kettle beginning the slow whine of a whistle.

"Is that him?"

Old Fart nods.

"What. The. Hell?"

"He's about to burst. You don't want to be here when he does. Make it quick." He covers his nose and he backs out of the bedroom.

"That old bastard just left me here!" I tell Michelin Man. He is unsympathetic.

Old Fart's footsteps rattle the metal stairs outside as he climbs down. The truck engine roars to attention with the promise of air-conditioning. While I stand there staring in disbelief at a rotting dead man, Old Fart sits in the comfort of cold, clean air.

I shake off thoughts of committing homicide myself and

get to business. Hide behind the camera. CSU Rule #5: WHEN THINGS GET BAD, LOOK THROUGH THE CAMERA.

Psychologists might call this displacement, where the mind substitutes something new for a situation that is unacceptable. I don't care what it's called. I only care that it works. I retreat into my other world behind the lens and snap pictures. The questions gnaw at me.

What happens when he bursts? Does he explode? Does he leak? Will decomp fluid shoot across the room? If so, how far will it go? I back up some more. It's important for a CSI to have a good lens. It takes you places you really don't want to go.

And so it goes. Focus. Shoot. Whistle. Whine. Focus. Shoot. Creak. A fly lands on my head. His tiny little feet walk through my hair. The skin on my scalp crawls. I finish the roll of film, turn my back on the Michelin Man, stomp down the stairs, stalk across the parking lot and rip open the door to the truck. Old Fart giggles. I plop into the seat with a glare. He informs me that my odor is unpleasant.

Later as the medical examiner and body car attendants are hoisting the large red body bag down the stairs, Old Fart and I sit in the truck and thank everything holy that we don't have to package up and carry the Michelin Man. They have abandoned the stretcher and are slowly bumping him down the stairs, one step at a time. The body has popped. The bag is now filled with body fluids and is behaving accordingly. It sloshes with each bump down the staircase. The M.E. guys are turning green. I turn a sympathetic shade of green too as I watch the slosh and sway inside the bag. The barbecue gurgles in the back of my throat.

My next lesson is on dignity. I have barely arrived at the office the next day when the phone rings and we are rolling out on a suicide. This deceased is a 77-year old cancer patient who has just signed up for hospice. His wife was washing dishes when she heard the gunshot.

When we arrive the first thing I notice is that except for the gaping hole in his head, our complainant is immaculate. There is no nursing home smell, and the house speaks of a lifetime of care. The walls bear evidence of better days. Proud smiles gaze down at me from old photographs, but it is the single item on his dresser that says the most. Propped open so that our old gentlemen can still read it, is a card: Happy Anniversary, 50 years.

The oxygen tank stands like a silent sentry beside the bed, a necessary, but unwelcome visitor. A partially filled urine container whispers a reminder of the cruel injustices that come with aging. His room tells a story, but with a bit of gentle probing it yields even more.

The bullet blew a gigantic hole through his fragile temple and exited out the back to lodge in the pillow behind him. The blood spatter on his hand leaves little doubt that he fired the gun he still clutches.

I offer to call someone for his wife. Even though there is a granddaughter, the wife doesn't want her to see him like this, so she patiently waits until we're finished. She bears her grief alone but with quiet dignity.

Every time I walk into someone's home, it speaks for them. This home spoke of a life well-lived, with love, care, and dignity.

My next call is to the jail to process a suspect in a sexual assault of a child case. I need DNA cheek swabs and hair samples. Hair from everywhere. Everywhere.

To collect these hairs your suspect must stand naked on a sheet of white butcher paper. The samples must be taken from five different spots on the scalp and groin. To do this, you inform him that either he can pluck the samples himself or you will pluck them for him. This is more effective if you're holding a pair of pliers.

My suspect is cooperative. Nasty and a little arrogant, but cooperative. No one has bothered to tell him that he's staring at a life sentence. As I fold dark curly hairs into evidence bags, I ponder how different he is from the old man who shot himself and I wonder what this man's home looks like.

Call after call, each time the phone rings, it signals another dead man marching forward. I am learning fast, but a bit at a time, one chink of the chisel with each phone call, I'm changing.

Standing in the rain battling a camera lens which keeps fogging up, I watch as the tiny chunks of melted mozzarella cheese that were his brains sweep across the street, into the gutter, and down the drain. I curse the sky. Rain respects no murder scene and so I can choose to splash along the gutter, scooping up brain matter with a spoon, or I can snatch up the wooden post that bashed his skull in hopes that it contains the killer's DNA. I opt for the wooden fence post.

It's the right thing to do but as rivulets of rain course through my hair and down my face to cascade off my nose like a waterfall, it seems disrespectful to allow his entire third grade education to float into the gutter. Peering through tendrils of soaked hair, I pause to follow the journey of a larger chunk as it bubbles along its concrete path, taking leaves, pine needles, and my sense of decency with it.

In time the novelty of death wears off. Although every scene is still different, the steps to process the scenes are the same, so I am able to settle into a familiar routine. This makes the occasional surprise all the more unexpected.

She stares at me with unseeing eyes. I ignore her and continue to work. Letting the camera guide me, I shoot my way into the scene. The sycamore leaves above us rattle in the wind. It's cold and I don't want to be here. Another victim of the drug war, she lays curled on the pavement with a backpack by her side. In our business we must distance ourselves from the dead; it's the only way to survive. As cruel as it sounds, while the camera snaps away, she is a piece of furniture, another dead prostitute. I ignore her empty eyes as she watches me.

Her dirty fingers still clutch the strap of a stained and dusty backpack. I gently tug it free. The zipper snags as I pull it open. Even as I go through the contents, my mind is elsewhere. With just a touch I can identify each item before I pull it out. People who live on the streets carry the same things: a toothbrush, a disposable razor, a dirty hairbrush, a tiny bar of soap wrapped in toilet paper. None of this interests me but then I feel it.

Inside a plastic shopping bag, inside a plastic bread bag, covered with a blue bandana, is something that makes me pause. It has a bit of heft to it. I carefully peel away the wrappings to reveal this thing that was so precious to her, this thing that she went to such trouble to protect — and it humbles me.

As the plastic bags fall to the pavement, she becomes a person. No longer a piece of furniture, she is a young woman, a victim of society, a victim of circumstance. I stand over her and for a moment, I stare into her unseeing eyes. Who was she? What were her hopes? Her dreams?

The wind whistles through the sycamore leaves as I carefully place a battered copy of Webster's Dictionary into the evidence bag.

And so it is that my case files grow, each tragedy is stamped and filed in a plain brown folder. They soon fill cardboard boxes underneath my desk. In time memories of the dead are like signposts marking my way across the city.

As I drive down the street, I hear the crack of gun fire. Months earlier, maybe a year, who knows, the images begin to blur, I walked this same street, piecing together the chase. They started shooting at him here. He lost control of his car here. There is still a gouge in the pavement where his truck flipped. He died here. I pass it on my way to another dead man so I give this one a salute and drive on.

I see dead people. Long after the bodies are gone, their images remain in my head. The average commuter in this fine city never sees them, but as I crisscross the freeways, the blocks, and the neighborhoods, they wave to me.

Those two died at that intersection — young victims of gang violence.

She hanged herself there when her husband wanted a divorce.

He shot himself in that luxury apartment when he got the doctor's report.

She was raped and strangled behind those steps.

Street by street, the faces go on. I arrive at my destination and the figurative lingering becomes physical. I smell him long before I find his body. I've smelled worse but he's bad enough to get my attention. We get him packaged up and on his way to the morgue, but the odor lingers. It's in my clothes. In my nose. I have questions that won't be answered until autopsy but that isn't what's on my mind as I drive. He's in my hair. In the morning my hair smelled of Japanese cherry blossoms. By night it smells like decomposition and maggots.

The skyline of the city dances in my rearview mirror on the drive home — and he's still there, clutching my shirt, clinging to my hair, lingering on my mind.

CHAPTER 2

RED WOOSTER & THE WARRIOR GODDESS

My tires crunch along the gravel and come to a silent stop in the driveway. The moon is high, backlighting the Batman ears of the shepherd who greets me with a panting welcome at the back gate. I unlace my boots and kick them off on the patio. The dogs sniff each boot. This saves us the discussion of how my shift went, so I shovel out three bowls of kibble before placing the boots on their shelf outside where they will patiently wait until tomorrow.

The dogs wait at the foot of the tub as the water runs down my head, taking the lingering stench down the drain with it. The smell is out of my hair now, but not out of my mind as stubborn images crawl like maggots through my brain. I wrap the dirty uniform in a wet towel, pad across the stone floor in bare feet, and dump the whole lot of it in the washer. A cold blast of air from the refrigerator is a welcoming refreshment as I pour a glass of cold wine. Then I snatch up a sunken brownie from the microwave and head back into the moonlight.

The bricked path to the barn is striped in shadows from

the wooden beams above it. Grapevines drape across the trellis that covers the path. The moon peeps through the leaves and lights my way. A muffled whinny greets me.

With a flip of the light switch, eager eyes squint as I toss hay into their stalls. I share the brownie with the dogs and finish my wine as the patient grinding of teeth slowly smooths away the rough edges of the day. I set the empty wineglass on a dusty shelf and step into the stall with the big gray horse. Montoya greets me and I lay my head against his loin, deeply inhaling the heavenly aroma. It is a comforting blanket that wraps itself over my shoulders and tucks into my soul. He pauses in his chewing and turns to sniff me and I wonder if he smells Japanese cherry blossoms or maggots. He turns back to his hay. I run my fingers through the dark gray tendrils of his heavy mane and the maggots crawl away.

Divorce is a double-edged sword which slices evenly, leaving pieces which you must decide whether or not to gather, or leave on the ground to rot like fallen fruit. Even an amicable split pulls your life apart, and ours was no different. After the dust had settled and the tears had dried it was time for a new beginning. He took enough money to start over again, and left me with the farm and the animals on it. I considered it a more than fair trade.

My empty living room now has one large cushioned chair with an ottoman, a trunk, and a lamp. It is a bit sparse, but now I watch what I want to watch on television, I eat what I want, when I want, and answer to no one. If I want spaghetti for breakfast, or Raisin Bran for supper, no one cares. I am the master of my fate, the captain of my soul. I spend the first month re-painting the interior of the house in Tuscan colors of warm butter, salmon, and olive green. No one has to approve these colors but me. It is quite liberating.

The upside to being the master of your fate and captain of your soul is that you are your own boss. The down side is that when something goes wrong, you're in charge. As I start painting the house it soon becomes apparent there is a major foundation problem. Several rooms have large cracks crawling across the walls. I consider embracing the flaws and painting the cracks with vines and flowers but lack of time and artistic skill prevents that. Instead, I glob more paint in the cracks and call it good. I have more pressing problems than a cracked foundation.

We are well into a wet winter and the horse barn is flooding with each hard rain. Although I clean the gutters regularly, each downpour brings a river into the stable which fills the stalls with standing water. Some nights all I can do is watch the sky and cry. I can't stop the rain, or the flooding, or the senseless death that comes every night at work.

To top it off, the water well goes out. I find myself standing in mud over my ankles, but don't have running water in the house. God is surely laughing at me. The cherry on the sundae of my life is when my homeowner's insurance company sends a nastygram stating that the roof on my house is over 20 years old and if I don't replace it, they will no longer insure my home.

For all practical purposes I have no paper money, but I do have a farm, a job, and a retirement account which I vaguely recall someone saying we could borrow money against. I call the retirement office and inform the man that I need a new well and a new roof and I want to borrow against my own money. He laughs at me.

When you're ankle-deep in mud and dead men, you get short on humor and so I am less than amused. Perhaps sensing that I am one step toward homicide, he clarifies himself. Although we could use my retirement money, for the paltry amount that I need, I'm better off taking out a short-term loan with the police credit union. In no way, shape, or form, is a new water well and a new roof, a paltry sum of money in my book but I take his advice and call the credit union. And it quits raining.

The first hopeful rays of sunshine come out when the banker explains that the payments for a short-term loan can be taken right from my paycheck. Bottom line. What's the bottom line? How much money comes out of my check and for how long?

She gives me a ridiculously low figure to end my suffering. I question it. She taps on the computer keyboard and gives the same figure again. Just to make sure it is in terms I can understand, I ask, "So you mean to tell me, that for the amount of money I earn for working just one murder every two weeks, I can have a new roof and a new well?"

She assures me that yes, for one overtime murder a pay period I can have a new roof and a new well.

Well, sign me up.

One of the frustrating realities of my new job is that while nothing might happen all shift, at the very last hour, sometimes the last thirty minutes, the phone can ring and you will find yourself working a murder for the next six hours on overtime. Since this happens fairly often, paid overtime is a guarantee in my job. The dead may keep right on marching in but at least now they are paying the bills.

Red Wooster was the meanest sonofabitch in three counties and he should have been killed a lot sooner. With an ego indirectly proportional to his size, Wooster thought he was a ladies' man. I guess maybe he was handsome if you were okay with skinny legs and beady eyes. Perhaps it was his short stature that led to a fiery temperament which held the entire neighborhood hostage. Regardless, the only reason he was still alive was the fact that my mother was so fond of him.

My mom lives in a little clapboard gingerbread house on a lot that used to be one of my pastures. Our houses shared the same water well at that time and a portion of the rather large pump house had been converted to a coop for her free-range flock of chickens. Although they had plenty of pasture for themselves her birds crossed the field daily to play scratch and sniff with fresh horse poop in my barnyard.

Apparently my name on the deed was too blurry for Wooster's beady little eyes because he and I had more than a few barn dances with a rake. On this particular morning, however, Wooster is off picking bar fights with someone else while I stand in the pump house staring at the water well man and tilting my head like a cow looking at a new gate. It does not promise to be a good day.

Water soaks through a pinhole in the toe of my rubber boots as the water well man explains that I have to take the roof off the pump house before repairs can begin on the well. As he trudges back to his truck to leave, I slosh to the barn and wonder how I will get the sheets of tin off the pump house roof.

Wuzband, my ex-husband, is an accomplished carpenter. I call him Wuzband, because he was my husband and it sounds so much more civilized than calling him my Ex. It doesn't take long to discover that Wuzband put the sheets of tin on with screws instead of nails. This is a plus because it means I can just screw them off. The hitch is that I don't have the tools I need to unscrew the tin. One cannot fault him for this since in a divorce spouses often overlook little things, like leaving the other person silverware and power tools.

A fruitless search in the barn doesn't turn up the doohickey that I need to attach to my drill but the upside is that it also doesn't turn up any rats, so I call it even and go across the street to ask the neighbor. Being a master carpenter, he has the attachment I need. With the precious doohickey now safely in my pocket, I drag a ladder through ankle deep mud to the back side of the pump house and start my climb.

If you are a crime scene investigator you know a thousand ways to die. Nine Hundred of these ways will be flitting through your head as you climb any ladder. While falling off the ladder is the most obvious, do not rule out electrocution if you are mixing power tools and water. This is why I'm a big fan of cordless power tools when I can remember to charge the battery. I am soon climbing the ladder with the doohickey in my pocket and a drill with enough ass to do the job. I hope.

With each step up the ladder the water in my boot sloshes from heel to toe, draining across the blister on my heel. It is a curious fact of life that height is a relative thing. When one is standing on the ground, the top of a pump house doesn't look very high, but when one is perched at the top of a ladder in muddy boots, and one must take a leap of faith off the ladder and onto said roof, well then, suddenly the tin appears to be a much farther distance from the ground than originally estimated.

Being the master of my fate there is no one around to do it but me, so I suck it up and make that stretch. Muddy boots are not your friend in this situation. With copious amounts of stretching, sliding, and cussing, I make it onto the roof. With a bit more stretching, sliding, and cussing, I remove several sheets of tin and drop them to the ground. Sunlight floods the pump house. Repairmen can now reach the well from above. My job is done. Well, not really. I still have to get down.

It is another curious fact of life that stepping from a firm surface of height, back onto a ladder which is shifting in the mud can rival any thrill ride at an amusement park.

Not being a fan of such, I stare at the ladder that is standing lopsided in the mud. Decision made. Those sheets of tin can just stay right there on the ground. I will not be making plans to ride that ladder in either direction again.

With that behind me, I start slogging my way back through the mud to the house. Already deep in thought, I step into deeper trouble when my foot sinks into sucking mud and comes out of the boot. Par for the course. Cold mud squishes between my toes.

I hurl a cuss word, step back into my boot and try to jerk my foot loose. This results in an awkward sliding split which ends with one booted foot pointing east as the other points west. My feet are an uncomfortable distance apart and are creeping.

I pause to assess my predicament. With my back to him, he launches an attack. Over my years in law enforcement, I can tell you that most murders can be tracked down to one of three motives: sex, money, or drugs. While most killings come down to this trio, with my feet firmly anchored in the mud as that beady-eyed little shit ran at me with his wings spread and beak open, I will gladly offer up to you a fourth motive for murder – pure blind rage.

There is no faster route from pacifist to murderer than being attacked by a chicken in your own yard. Having neither stick nor dog, I reach into the mud, snatch out my boot, and smash the little bastard in the face as he bears down on me in feathered fury.

Nothing says worthy adversary like being smacked in the face with a muddy boot. Wooster shakes his feathers, squints at me in rage and makes another rush. I swing. And miss.

It's enough to get some respect. Wooster lands and runs a few steps then whirls back to have another go at it. I glance around for a weapon. There by the fence. A stack of metal t-posts. Brandishing my boot low, I start backing in that direction. The rooster darts in to attack.

Happiness can be a lot of things but few things in life bring true satisfaction like the feel of a cold steel post in your hands when a rooster is flapping your way. Wooster feels the power shift as soon as I do. No longer backing up in a crouch, I stand straight like Babe Ruth and let that Louisville Slugger sing.

Wooster sees that first one coming down the pipes when I make the mistake of telegraphing my intentions. Perhaps it is me shouting, "I'm gonna kill you, you stupid f@#*ing bird!"

He trips over himself as he runs and flies with fits of flight, dodging the blows I rain down upon him as my rage chases a chicken in bare feet through a muddy pasture. My anger does not care that he is my mother's bird. I will gladly beat him to death with a t-post and then hand her his body and a muddy $20 bill. Such is the nature of homicide.

The rooster becomes every assault on my happiness. He is the rain. He is the flooding barn. He is the old roof. He is broken well. He is Death poking at me every night that I put on a uniform. In bare feet, I slosh through the pasture swinging a metal post in vain as my target dances away, just out of reach.

Fortunately for Wooster, his date with death will wait for another day. Handicapped by the mud, my murder attempts are largely unproductive but the message is received. Wooster squawks and taunts me from a safe distance but gives up his attempts at an attack as I squish my way back to the house, dragging my t-post sword at my side. It is not my finest hour.

Life on a farm can be tough for a single woman, and each chore accomplished is a major victory. The chore for the day is the feed room door. With all the rain, the barn has shifted and the door isn't locking. The latch hole needs to be a little bigger. Since the cordless drill is out of juice, the hunt is on for the plug-in drill. I poke around on dusty shelves and am quickly rewarded. With drill located, I pat myself on the back for knowing that I now need drill bits. A bit more poking around and I find those too. A gold star is earned for figuring out how to attach them to the drill. Plug in drill. Push the button. The bit turns. Ah ha! Victory is at hand. Apply drill to wood. The bit chews into the door frame. Success! The hole is off-center, but who cares? I close the door. The latch locks. This is shamefully satisfying. "Woo hooo! I am Woman! Hear me roar! I am Captain of my ship!"

There is much fist pumping in the air. I am the warrior goddess! I am deep in the throes of my tribal dance when the rat falls from the ceiling. He plummets to the shelf below.

The warrior goddess screams. "Ah! Rat! Rat! Get it!"

This is a 911 call to dogs. The rat lands on a 2x4 wall brace near my shoulder and runs along the back shelf of the room. Like a tiny monster truck, he motors over jars filled with screws, nails, and pipe fittings. Until that moment I did not fully appreciate that rats are equipped with four-wheel drive. The dogs climb on top of each other, making wild snatches at the rodent on the shelf.

As fast as it started, it stops. The rat hides behind plastic jugs on the shelf. Standing on their back legs, the dogs look to me. I stare back. Mouth slack. "I'm not gonna pick up those jugs!"

The dogs turn to the rat and then back to me. They have voted. I am clearly the tallest one in the room and I have the thumbs. I have been elected me to move the jugs. Sometimes democracy sucks. I lift the first jug. Nothing. The second. Still nothing. And so on. As predicted, behind the last jug — the rat falls out.

A fairly large room will shrink rapidly when there is a rat at your feet. Another round of the Rat Dance begins. The dogs snap and snatch. The rat slips through a hole in the base of the wall. The four of us are left panting and gasping. Five. Five of us. I'm confident the rat is also gasping.

The dogs sniff at the hole while I lean against a feed bin to breathe. They return to reassure me that, "Sector 12 is clear," and I am safe from rodents as long as they are on duty. You simply can't run a farm without a good dog, or two, or three. We all have different talents that work together to get the job done. They're not afraid of rats; I'm not afraid of vacuum cleaners, so it all evens out.

Being the master of my fate I can now vacuum at daybreak or paint at midnight and I spend many happy hours painting the house while *CSI* blares on television. Until becoming a crime scene investigator, I'd never seen the show. Now I am ordered to watch it by Fergus Fernandez, my buddy who shares the cubicle beside me. His argument is valid. The public is watching *CSI*. It's important for us to know what the public believes we can do. This is coined "The *CSI* Effect" and will forever color the field of forensics. I liken the television show to frozen pizza. It isn't real pizza, but it's still enjoyable.

CHAPTER 3

DOWN THE RABBIT HOLE
WITH
THE FLIP-FLOP CROWD

"All the masterpieces of art contain both light and shadow."
Billy Graham

The bell chimes to signal that I have arrived at my destination. The elevator door slides open to the parking garage and I step out pulling my still shiny, but slightly dented, green dolly. By now more and more gear has been heaped upon the dolly because you never knew what you may need at a crime scene. As my experience grows, so too does the load on the dolly.

I slow-roll across the parking garage toward my truck, just me and my dolly. I've been cut loose to run calls on my own now. No trainer. No umbilical cord. Just a cell phone. It's my lifeline, my "dial a friend." If you need help, call. Otherwise everyone is too busy with their own dead men to worry about yours.

Winnie-the-Pooh and Tigger wave at me as I lift the green tackle box and heave it into the CSU truck. The edges of the stickers are a little worn now and at quick glance it seems they are not stickers at all, but part of the original box. They fit seamlessly, as if the tackle box is part of their Hundred Acre Wood, with Pooh and Tigger traipsing through it from one adventure to the next.

I tuck the green tackle box into its spot beside the others and slam the tailgate. Then I climb into the front seat by myself, check the map for directions and drive to my call. By now the cadence of death marching forward is familiar and the lessons are sprinkled in them like seasoning in a bad stew.

The sun rises on my birthday as we drive to a skull in a creek. Fergus and I have volunteered for this assignment before our shift. This means a double shift for us but being newly divorced, what else am I going to do on my birthday? I have since learned that one does not tempt Fate with such questions. CSU Rule#6: NEVER WORK ON YOUR BIRTHDAY.

In addition to the regular nasty things that show up on crime scenes, such as blood and dead people, other disturbing items have a way of popping in too. Our body is in a marshy stream which runs under the street by way of a large, concrete culvert. Because the body is lying in the water at the mouth of the tunnel, I have the bright idea to take some artsy-fartsy photographs from inside the tunnel.

The afternoon sun shines through the culvert and nicely illuminates body. I fancy myself a professional photographer. Wouldn't it make a great picture if I could shoot through the tunnel on one side and focus on the body at the other side? Yes. Yes, it would.

I slide down the creek bank like a drunken snowboarder. I wade through the water to get into the culvert and pause at the mouth. It looks a lot longer from this angle. Oh well, in for a penny, in for a pound. I thread my way through dead branches that are stuck in the tunnel. There! That's the shot I want. I move a bit closer. Is that a snake?

It is quite possible the snake and I both scream. The snake races toward the opposite end of the tunnel. In a rare moment of clarity I extrapolate what will happen when a three-foot long black snake plummets out of a tunnel onto a dead body surrounded by investigators. Maybe I should warn them. My shout of "SNAKE" echoes in the tunnel. If it is at all possible for the snake to move any faster, he does.

The medical examiner hears my muffled echoing shout and steps into the mouth of the tunnel. She sees the snake. He sees her. Apparently there is a sliding scale on the "What Freaks People Out" continuum and even though this woman makes a living working with dead bodies, finding a snake hurling himself in her direction tips her scale. She screams. Loudly. The snake does an about-face and races back toward me. Fast. One wouldn't think snakes could move that fast. This tips my scale. Retreat! With camera swinging around my neck, I turn and splash like Quasimodo out of the tunnel.

The Hunchback of Notre Dame has nothing on a woman running from a snake. It is a curious fact of life that fear can make you forget that you're wearing a gun. The upside to this is that bullets pinging off the concrete walls of a tunnel will probably not hit the snake anyway, but will most certainly piss off the people on the other end of the tunnel.

As if having to run from a snake on your birthday is not bad enough, Fergus and I discover yet another reason for the Thou Shall Not Work on Thine Date of Birth rule. It is another little considered fact of life that bodies in culverts must be carried back up the hill. These bodies tend to be wet, decomposing, and are sometimes falling apart. CSU Rule #7: WHEN CARRYING A BODY UPHILL, ALWAYS BE THE FIRST PERSON UP THE HILL.

If this rule causes confusion, consider that when a body falls apart, gravity dictates that it will fall downward, thus Fergus and I need a shower before our next shift.

As the bodies stacked up and my case files grew thicker, I no longer lived in the moment and looked at each scene with fresh eyes. Instead, I stepped into a new scene carrying the experiences and baggage from the scenes before it. The lessons learned from each case were like spices used to flavor a poor cut of tough meat. You can cook tough meat for hours but without the seasonings, you are still left with the unsavory taste of bad meat. To make it something you want for dinner, you need to add a dash of this and a sprinkle of that. A recipe is simply a set of ingredients and instructions that take you to your goal. The same is true of the beef stew we call a crime scene. Follow the instructions.

Step One: Look through the camera.

As I got more familiar with the job, processing the scene became second nature. While on the surface this was a good thing, not having to focus so sharply on the complexities of scene investigation allowed my mind the time to get snagged in the emotion behind each tragedy. More and more I retreated into the camera. The lens was both my guide and my protector.

~

"Poverty is no disgrace, but it's a great inconvenience."

Commuters, hustling like ants crawling back and forth to the colony, sit in air-conditioned comfort, oblivious to the fact that a rotting, maggot-ridden corpse is within spitting distance of their tinted windows. A city worker reported him. He died as he had lived, a shadow of society, ignored by the general populace, a resident of the streets.

I angle my way along the steep grade leading to his body. There he is, under a freeway overpass, like a boy in a treehouse, overlooking the worker bees of this world. His bed is a sheet of plywood crammed into the angle of the overpass. A few boards, a sleeping bag, home sweet home. As I follow my nose I can't help but admire his ingenuity. That admiration lasts only as long as it takes me to realize that someone will have to crawl under those boards and into this little fort with a rotting body. That someone is me. The sun is still up as I duck underneath the heavy beam and step into his world.

Once under the beam there is just enough room for me to stand up. As I carefully rise, my eyes adjust to the darkness and he comes into focus. I notice the movement first. Maggots. They crawl in and out of empty sockets mere feet from my face. I'm used to maggots but this is a little close for comfort so I bring the camera up to remove myself.

I'm not really here. I'm actually sitting on the couch, safe in my living room, exploring all this on the television screen. Looking through the lens takes me away from the horror, but it can do little for the smell. I snap and inch my way through the darkness. In a high-rise cave. In the middle of the city. Trying not to breathe. After a few minutes, I lower the camera and accept my fate.

It is time to closely examine the scene before me without the lens as my shield. So here we are, me and a rotting body, in a fort, over a freeway. I take a deep breath, and get to the business of finding the man behind the monster — to finding out how he lived, to finding out how he died.

After a while I take a moment to watch the commuters

below me, to imagine them as he saw them. It wasn't hard. They drive past, heading home for the day, concerned only about why the cops have the freeway shut down at rush hour.

~

I name her Rose. He tried to cut off her head. As fate would have it, however, the blade was dull, and he was drunk, so he was forced to leave her, raped and murdered, her body intact, but not her dignity. He left her posed as he undoubtedly saw her in his mind's eye. And that's how I find her.

I crouch over #791, just the two of us. The afternoon sun breaks through the dusty glass to warm her blood-stained cheek one last time. With a long, tired sigh I ask her, "What happened? What can I do here?"

Her eyes just stare back, as vacant as the house around me. I stand up and take a moment to watch the sun. Had #791 seen it rise? I look back at her, at curled fingers that reach toward me. No. She had not seen the sun rise. I turn back to the sun and give silent thanks for the warmth on my own cheek. Then I lift the camera.

The lens catches details that are often missed by the naked eye, and there's an art to looking at the world, to looking at Life and Death, through that lens. I walk through the house, letting the camera guide me, and this same house, where the boots of so many had already tromped, gives up her secret for the camera.

A sheet of plywood on milk crates stands in the corner of a bare bedroom. On top of that is a dirty mattress. Dingy blankets drape to the floor. I study the room through the camera, one square at a time. And there it is. Peeking out from under the plywood bed is the handle of a machete. The camera has found what so many human eyes had missed.

She was probably in her 40s, with auburn hair, and the

tattoo of a rose between her breasts. I see this and declare that she should no longer be called #791, but that her name will now be "Rose." The Homicide Investigator and the Medical Examiner agree that until we discover her true name, we will call her "Rose."

Warmth creeps over my own back and I turn to see the sun sinking over the trees. I move out of the window so that for one last time, Rose will have the sun on her back. Then they zip up her bag and take her away.

Step Two: Look past the flies.

I didn't need the crime scene tape. My nose led the way. As if the smell couldn't tell me, a flurry of flies announced that I had arrived. She'd been hidden there in the tall grass until Decomposition pointed an ugly finger in her direction.

In this neighborhood, people are quick to recognize the smell for what it is — death. Hers was a particularly ugly, violent death. Decomposition is never kind, but her insect activity suggested many wounds. I stood over her, ignored the gore, and let the maggots talk. Gobs of rice-like inchworms clung and crawled thick in isolated areas of her arms, belly, and side. Bugs always hit the openings in the skin first, and she must have had a lot of openings. Waves of maggots rippled across her face, giving the surreal impression that she was moving.

At first glance she was a monster, a maggot-ridden Medusa, but as my eyes moved across her body, I looked past the maggots, past the bloating, past the smell, and I saw her fingers. Although they were slightly mummified, baking in the sunlight was a fresh manicure. On a base of bright pink thumbnails, tiny painted flowers proudly waved at me. She was wearing one tennis shoe. A dirty sock dangled from her other foot. There, peeking from beneath the sock, another flower waved at me from the pink base of a toe. A maggot inched his way across the toe but the manicured flower continued to shine.

This was no monster. This creature at my feet had been a living, breathing woman, who not long ago, sat in a chair, picked out her color and chose flowers for her toes. I stood there, taking it all in. A wildflower struggling to grow in the barren soil by the dumpster caught my eye. It swayed in the breeze and dipped a salute at the painted toenail. For a moment, I looked past the gore and sighed. Then I lifted my camera and began.

Step Three: Ignore the crowd.

I would argue that the most gruesome part of a crime scene is not the body, but the throngs of spectators who hang on our every move like citizens in the Colosseum demanding to be entertained.

~

Last month they stood in the front yard and screamed at each other. She threw a beer bottle at him. He slapped her. And the neighbors stared. Last week he kicked over the barbecue grill. Juggling a crying baby on her hip, she tossed a plate of hamburgers on the lawn. He kicked a tricycle across the yard. And the neighbors stared.

Today he shot her. Then he shot himself. Blood oozed around leaves on the driveway and stained the towels that sprawled from the overturned laundry basket. The chrome bumper of his pickup truck reflected her bloody image as she laid, her outstretched hand still clutching car keys.

He slumped against the garage. A red peacock fan of blood had misted the wall behind his head. I stood there for a moment, taking it all in. And the neighbors stared.

~

Blood oozed along grout paths in the tile, forming a network of red highways on the floor. The advancing red tide was beginning to dry at the edges but gravity still pulled the slow trickle toward the doorway. A steady drip dropped onto the sidewalk forming an ever-widening puddle on the stoop. Each new drop plummeted into the crimson depths and caused a splash which misted the step above.

As I played yet another round of Twister to get across the body and through the doorway he caught my eye. The little fella was about four years old, barefoot, with a dirty blue shorts and a red t-shirt. His eyes widened when he saw that I had noticed him. There he was, playing in the gray powdered sand, not forty feet from a dead man. Where were his parents?

I didn't bother to look. The courtyard was filled with the Flip-Flop Crowd. These people had stood in the hot sun for at least four hours watching my every move. It was evening now and I was prime time television. Watching blood dry is about as entertaining as watching paint dry but it captured the imagination of this sea of dirty feet in sandals. They brought their children. With babies on their hips, women shifted back and forth on weary feet but refused to go inside to the air-conditioning, inside to cook dinner, inside to their own lives. Nothing on reality television was as entertaining as watching a real CSI play Twister over a dead neighbor.

I passed the little boy again on one of my many trips back to the truck. He smiled and gave a tentative wave. I waved back and his smile broadened all the way to his toes. He was waiting as I walked back by. Another smile. Another wave. More children crept closer. Wow. Celebrity status. I was a celebrity. What bizarre world is this where a morbid game of Twister makes me a celebrity? In what bizarre world do parents let their children stare at a bloody dead man? I gazed into his innocent face and wondered how much of this he understood. And as I looked through the camera I saw the white sheet over a dead man reflected in the boy's eyes.

~

My disdain for the Flip-Flop crowd grew and was only exceeded by my disgust of the media who fed on the suffering of family members. Anything for a story. They wanted sound bites and video at the scene. Bonus points for evidence and blood. Reporters were shameless in their pursuit of any detail which could be used to rivet the viewer to the television screen. If it bleeds, it leads. If they succeeded in making the viewer in his recliner wish he were standing on the hot pavement in flip-flops, their job was complete.

Step Four: Just keep swimming.

With each trip back and forth through the crime scene tape, we became unwilling participants in the five o'clock show at the Circus Maximus. It was a spectacle devoured by the beasts who feed on pain. The suffering of the family is a darkness that grabs you like a drowning swimmer if you're not careful. You want to help. To ease their pain. But if you are not cautious you will get swept away in the current. In time I learned to spot the early warning signs and flee before getting caught in the crashing waves.
CSU Rule #8: DON'T LET THE DROWNING SWIMMER PULL YOU DOWN. You cannot help them if you are crying on the floor too.

~

They carried his body down the steep hill, one careful step at a time. I walked ahead to block the view. No family wants to see this, but they were straining for the first glimpse of what they have waited hours to see. How can he possibly be dead? Maybe there was a mistake. There's no mistake. By the time I'm called in, everyone is sure, and whenever I arrive, it removes any doubt. The words printed on my truck serve as a death notification. Crime Scene Unit. Even the Flip-Flop crowd knows that means someone is dead. So we slowly bumped down the hill together, a somber parade. We reached the bottom and I braced the gurney as they slid his body onto it. A son, a husband, a brother, now a shrouded figure in a white plastic bag. I doubt the family noticed the magic marker scribble on the side of the bag. His number is a silent tally of how many deaths this year.

They strapped his body onto the gurney with seat belts. It doesn't help the picture any. I tried to shield this, to spare them. They don't want to remember him this way. I understand this, but they don't. Her quiet sobs that had been muffled by her husband's shoulder grew louder. Without looking I knew she no longer had her head buried in his chest but was watching everything we did. My heart went out to her. A mother doesn't want to outlive her child.

A heavy black cover was placed over the seatbelted white figure. It helped the presentation. A bit. Not much. Since there was nothing more we could do, I stepped back to allow them to roll him toward the body car. As I followed behind the gurney, the sobs grew louder. Their nightmare just became a reality. I sneaked a peek as we passed and for a moment was captured in their grief. Just as quickly I looked away, angry at myself for getting emotionally involved even for that brief second. I felt her pain but there was work to do. I couldn't allow myself to grieve for her. Or with her. Instead I held the stubborn tear back and looked to the business of getting his body into the truck. His mother let out one brief wail before it was muffled into her husband's chest. The door closed on her son and he rolled away.

Step Five: Find out everything you can, but not too much.

Sometimes the key to dealing with suffering is to just not see it. It is a case of what you don't know won't hurt you, because the more you know, the more you wish you knew less. Sometimes, less is best. I was standing over the badly decomposed body of a woman. This was a dump scene. She'd been murdered somewhere else and dumped here. It was easy for me to be clinical and unemotional until the Texas Ranger gave me the details of her death. That's when I learned that less is sometimes best.

I didn't want to hear how she fought to live. I didn't want to hear how she died. I didn't want to hear how he drove her here and dumped her. It is one thing to let the evidence speak, to let the victim tell you her tale. Then you are her ally, her final shot at justice. Somehow hearing her story from the killer's point of view makes it all the more vulgar and violent. And it bugged me. It bugged me. Sometimes the less you know, the better.

How do we value life? I have mulled this over and come to the conclusion that we tend to place a higher value on a life that is familiar to us. It hit me one afternoon when I was working the death of a young woman. I looked around her home and it was hard to remain detached. When I stepped into her apartment I could have been walking into the home of a friend. Her books were familiar. Her hobbies were familiar. Right down to the canine nose prints left on the sliding glass door, this woman's life was familiar. One glance around the home and I knew her. As I photographed her death, six feet away, her dogs peered through the glass door at me. They barked their frustration and confusion. It bothered me. I stared through the camera at her life and her death, and it bothered me. As investigators, we emotionally distance ourselves from our work but from time to time, a death steps up and becomes something more because of something small. In my case, it was stepping on a rubber dog bone. I looked down at the bone under my boot, a toys so like half a dozen at my own home. Then I lowered the camera and took a long look at the dogs on the other side of the glass. Their confusion gave rise to my grief. And for brief moment, I mourned a woman that I didn't even know. Or maybe I did.

Step Six: Fall down the rabbit hole.

Mundane things that the rest of the world doesn't give a second thought to take on new meaning for anyone involved in death investigation. Bizarre images soon become paired with the ordinary.

She had turned her back on this world, and that's how I found her, with her back to the door. As the hall light fell into the room, she gave every appearance of a woman asleep. I stared at her for a moment, almost expecting to see the rise and fall of her breathing. But as my eyes adjusted to the darkness, her pretense of slumber was betrayed by the light spray of blood spatter on the wall.

I flicked on the light and ugly reality flooded the room. Mingled with blood were the familiar flecks of runny mozzarella cheese - brain matter. I scanned what was likely her entire high school education plastered on the wall.

Why? What moved her to this? She left few clues. On the

dresser was an envelope addressed to the maid. In it was a hundred dollars and a note that read, "For your trouble."

The questions buzzed in my head even as I tackled the more pressing issue before me - where was the gun? The dark pool of blood had congealed into a thick mass of cranberry sauce on the bed beside her. There, nestled in the protective crook of her crossed arms, like a snake in a bush, was the weapon. Even with the lights on, it was hidden. My flashlight beam prodded it from its hiding place and the beast grunted to life. Unlike the woman, who gave the appearance of being alive while not, the gun gave the appearance of being dead, and yet, it was very much alive. With the hammer cocked back, it was ready to fire again. This was a familiar problem - familiar, yet always a problem.

How does one remove a loaded gun, which is stuck in a jellied cranberry sauce of blood, from the protective custody of the dead? Very carefully.

Because the gun was so deeply buried in the pool of hardened blood, we were unable to determine if it would be affected when we moved her. Several scenarios flashed through my head.

1) We move her. The hardened blood pulls the trigger. I get shot.
2) We move her. The hardened blood pulls the trigger. The medical examiner gets shot.
3) We move her. The hardened blood pulls the trigger. The dead woman gets shot again.
4) We move her. The hardened blood pulls the trigger. The bed gets shot.
5) We move her. The body pulls away from the cranberry sauce. Nothing happens.
6) We leave her here and go get a frappuccino while we think about this some more.

Although #6 was clearly our best choice it apparently was not an option for us, so after a quick check to make sure the barrel of the gun was pointed away from the living, the medical examiner gingerly lifted an arm. A large chunk of cranberry sauce came off with the hand. She carefully moved the arm back and forth in an effort to get the blood to fall back onto the bed. It stubbornly refused. Instead, it flapped in the breeze like a giant crimson pancake. The medical examiner continued her futile attempts to flick it off. I found this vastly amusing in a macabre fashion. In fact, it was quite funny until the moment I realized that although she had to handle the body, I was the person who had to remove the locked and loaded gun which was also embedded in cranberry sauce. Option #6 was suddenly looking far more appealing. When it was over, I took a moment to ponder holidays, cranberry sauce, and suicide. Back in a more innocent day I never associated the three, but I am older, wiser, and a bit wistful now, and I shall never quite think of cranberry sauce the same way again.

Even in the dim light, the wallpaper stood out. Blood with brain matter. It misted the room, leaving a fine coating on the walls, the ceiling, and the hardwood floors. I checked for a ceiling fan before I flipped on the light switch. A ceiling fan coated in brain matter is not what you want rotating over your head. The Old Timers tell the story of turning on a fan to find an eyeball stuck to one of the blades. Apparently the sight of the eye staring back at them as it slowly spun around the room left an impression.

In the light the pink mist was more obvious. I slowly mapped it out before entering, making mental note of the large chunks. Small pieces of skull, the largest slightly over a square inch, dotted the large room. As my eye scanned for anything out of the ordinary, occasionally my mind would land on a thought that bordered on the absurd and like Alice down the rabbit hole, I would indulge that idea.

A large chunk of pink mozzarella brain matter sat on the bar. Was this his education in Algebra or could this be the part of his brain that housed his love of music? I considered the puzzle even as I continued more important investigations.

The greasy smack-smack of my boots on the hardwood floor reminded me that it too was misted in brain matter and blood. I should have put on paper booties. What essence of who this man was would I bring home tonight on my soles? Were these his memories? I pushed the thought aside and continued on my way. It is what it is.

Later, our investigation over, the medical examiner was collecting the larger chunks of brain and bits of skull to accompany his body to the morgue. Once again my mind wandered down the rabbit hole because it seemed like his search was just a twisted Easter egg hunt. I pondered this for a moment then turned back to my own business. Busy with other things, I heard it before I saw it. Clink. Pause. Clink. Pause. Clink.

Like dominoes falling in a row, the thought raced through my mind until the final piece clinked into silence. The sound of skull fragments being placed in a bag with their counterparts sounded exactly like dominoes clinking against each other. The image intrigued and haunted me long after his body drove away. Perhaps that's why they call the game of dominoes, "playing bones." Maybe.

And so it is, that like cranberry sauce at Thanksgiving, the game of dominoes is now lost to me, just one more thing down the Rabbit Hole of bizarre associations.

Webster defines "epiphany" as a "moment in which you suddenly see or understand something in a new or very clear way." I had an epiphany when I stopped at the convenience store for a frappuccino on my way home from work. I was still in uniform and at that time, the crime scene investigators were wearing navy blue military pants and shirts. This uniform was professional, comfortable, and stood up to a lot of washing machine abuse. The shirts had police patches on the shoulders, a badge patch on the left breast, and a Crime Scene Unit patch on the right breast. As was often the case when the public saw my uniform, the convenience store clerk took the opportunity to read my patch when she took my cash. With her face scrunched up in disgust, she scanned my frappuccino and said, "Crime Scene Unit? CSI?"

"Yes, Ma'am."

"Oh, gross. How can you do that? I mean, really. That's just disgusting. How can you even do something like that?"

She said this as if I ate puppies. Careful not to touch my hand, the woman gave me change with the same air of disgust, as if the ability to swim with monsters somehow made me a monster. I was aghast. For the first time, I viewed myself and my job in a new light. Clearly I, and those like me, were freaking unusual, but were we monsters? I did what most women do, I called a girlfriend. At midnight. "Maggie, am I a monster?"

"Only after midnight."

I gave my old partner the fifty cent tour of the conversation and she enlightened me with a pearl of wisdom uncharacteristic of our normal after-midnight discussions. "We do what we do because we can and others cannot."

Interesting. Perhaps this was a gift. Or a curse. Maybe both. Our ability to wade into the violence. The blood and the maggots. Strange talents like these are necessary for society because people who can rub shoulders with monsters are a vital cog in the wheel. Crimes don't get solved if everyone decides they can't get out of the truck. I chewed on this along with a brownie as I sipped a glass of wine and swayed in the hammock under the moonlight.

"Normal is not something to aspire to, it's something to get away from."
Jodie Foster

CHAPTER 4

FALL OF THE JENGA BLOCKS

Two of the five flooded stalls in my barn had dried out enough that I was able to clean them and put in fresh shavings so I spent the afternoon cursing the rains that brought the flood while I hauled out the dried mud and dumped it in the pasture. I was already two hours into my task when I dumped a load of muck and noticed that my fence was lined with ripe blackberries. Well, look at that. Blackberries loved rain. And it just so happens that I love blackberry cobbler.

I grabbed a bucket and started picking. And picking. Since I'm not a big fan of snakes, I was cautious, but nature's bounty was tempting and I was soon thick in briars and berries. My bucket was filling fast — until I stepped on the cat and dropped it. The bucket. Not the cat.

Cats should not wait until you step on them before they announce their presence. It's a terrible waste of blackberries and not good for the heart. The cat decided that she should supervise the berry picking since I was obviously incompetent and so she accompanied me down the fence line.

In time the stallion decided that perhaps he should join us too so I handed him a berry. I'd had this animal for 21 years and to my knowledge he had never eaten a blackberry until that day. The stallion happily smacked his lips around the blackberry and announced then and there that stallions like blackberries — a lot. So I handed him another. This one was obviously even better than the first, so I gave him another. Soon his lips were blue. He followed me down the fence begging another berry. I gave him another and went back to filling my bucket. It was taking a lot longer this time since I had a cat and a gray stallion with blue lips following me.

A berry for the bucket. A berry for the horse with the blue lips. A berry for the bucket. A berry for the horse with the blue lips. A berry for the bucket. Trip over the cat. Cuss. Pick up loose berries. A berry for the horse with the blue lips.

I slipped through the fence into the mare's pasture. The horse with blue lips paced the fence line and shook his head at me. I gave in and took him a berry before I went back to pick a few more berries. The stallion stood at the fence smooching blue lips in my direction. I gave him another berry. The berries were disappearing faster than they were filling the bucket. Since there were still enough berries in the bucket to make a pie, I climbed through the fence to leave the pasture. The stallion with blue lips screamed at me so I went back and gave him another berry. How long would it take him to figure out how to pick the berries himself?

After berries have been picked, there is little use for a briar patch in your fence. Wuzband had been a big fan of chemical weed control. I was not, and since I was now captain of this ship, I was now the one loping this mule, and it was my decision. There would be no Round-up on this farm.

The weeds quickly took over.

With all the rain we had that spring, three horses couldn't keep up with the grass either. The fences had been overtaken with hedge thorns and one pen was full of waist-high briars.   Using a weed-eater was not an option. Mowing was not an option. I needed another solution. Ironically this turned out to be a choice that would change my life forever.

The answer was in the purchase of four scrubby white buck goats. I think perhaps God decided my life needed comic relief. I bought them from a friend who took one look at the cheap welded wire I had hastily tacked over my already existing fence and proclaimed, "That's not gonna work."

I think all goat people start here. We truly underestimate what it takes to confine the creatures. We run to the lumber store, buy cheap wire that can be tied onto an existing fence and then are shocked when goats stand on the wire and the welds break, leaving us with tangled metal spaghetti and goats all over the county. All goats get into trouble, it's just a matter of degree. There are meat goats and there are dairy goats. While dairy goats tend to be tame, delightful, dog-like creatures, meat goats lean toward semi-wild criminals that are controlled either by a bucket of feed or a dog, much like the carrot and the stick. Dairy goats can have you singing in a field like Julie Andrews in the *Sound of Music*. Meat goats can make Mother Teresa cuss. In their defense, part of the problem is that most meat goats aren't tame because people don't make pets out of something they plan to eat. The life cycle of meat goats is normally birth, to auction, to slaughter. Lucky ones spend some time as brush control goats in between these events. Really, really, lucky ones are show goats or breeding goats but the large majority are born to be eaten.

This, along with their near-constant escape attempts, often leads to an adversarial relationship between the rancher and the meat goat. My friend had prepared me for the fact that goats are bent on following their stomachs into trouble. Goats break out, not with intentions of escape, but with intentions to get to someplace else.

"The pen we're in is a goat paradise. It has weeds, shrubs and briars higher than our heads, but let's plan an elaborate prison escape so we can see what the neighbor planted in her flowerbed yesterday!"

I was unprepared for all this. After my friend drove off, the goats and I stared at each other, unaware this was the beginning of a new life.

Rip. Chew. Rip. Chew. Move on. Rip. Chew. Repeat. Time slowed as I stood in the pen full of hedge briars and listened to the goats browse. I stopped. To just be. There. In the moment.

Something moved inside me. An undefinable thing clicked into place like the piece of a puzzle I didn't know was missing. There was a peaceful rhythm to their chewing and for the first time I felt a connection as old as civilization itself. Countless shepherds before me had stood among their flocks and listened. I didn't know what it was, but it was important. There in the pasture with a flock of four scrubby billy goats, I became a shepherd. And I didn't even know what that meant. As the days stretched into weeks I found myself spending more time with the goats, getting in touch with a peace I never knew I needed. Suddenly vague passages about flocks of sheep in the Bible began to have meaning for me even as I shook my fist at God.

We all have things that push our buttons. For one of my co-workers, it was decomposing bodies. She was still in training and our first scene together was a soupy dead guy in the trunk of a car. She and the patrol officers were ready to toss their lunches but it didn't bother me. I was okay with stinkers. For me it was dead babies. With the confident assurance of someone new to death investigations, she said, "Oh, dead babies don't bother me at all!"

I gave her an already jaded smile and promised that "one day" she would get that "one too many." It's like a game of Jenga. Eventually you will pull out the wrong block and they'll all come tumbling down. That's the way it happens. One day you can handle it, and then a case pushes you over the edge. For me it was a series of dead children. I had my meltdown in Frozen Foods.

Her screams followed me around the grocery store. How could anyone ignore that? How could anyone not hear that baby screaming? Like Edgar Allen Poe's "The Tell-Tale Heart" the sound echoed in my head, growing louder and louder until I fled. I stomped past the vegetables into Dairy and her cries trailed behind me. In Bread I could still hear her. Finally I abandoned my shopping cart and stormed out of the store and into the bright sunlight of the parking lot. Into the heat. Into the Godforsaken baking heat.

How could anyone not hear that? How could they walk past as she desperately pushed her little socks off? How could they just walk on with their busy lives as a baby died in a hot car? How could they not hear her crying? How could God let it happen?

~

The little suit lay on the edge of the bed, pressed and ready for pictures. A navy blue pin stripe, with a bright red tie. His momma picked it out, and now here it was, waiting to join the family photos, to join the generations of faces that smiled from the walls.

I stared at the suit, taking it all in, and for a moment, like angry bees, the questions crowded my mind. But pondering on fairness in Life and Death is both pointless and agonizing so I brushed away an angry tear and picked up the camera again. His first suit and tie. He would, after all, get to wear them, but now he would wear the tiny new suit at his funeral.

~

She had been strangled with the remote control bed cord. For one long moment I stared at her frail body. They stole what they could carry and left her here, her vacant eyes staring at the picture of Jesus on the wall. Jesus held a lamb in his protective embrace. I stared at the trusting pen and ink lamb. I stared at a pen and ink Jesus. Then I looked back down at the lifeless, age-spotted hands which desperately clutched the bed frame, and an anger grew.

~

Anyone who walks closely with death will soon start asking the difficult questions and it isn't long before you start pointing a finger at God. Early in our careers the department spent a great deal of money on outside training for our entire unit. Fergus and Seamus were lucky enough to attend a Practical Homicide Investigation Workshop. This course was designed by legendary NYPD Homicide Investigator Vernon Geberth. They returned with loads of information, a treasure of a text book, and a slide which Seamus tacked to his cubicle which read: "Remember, we work for God."

I put a lot of thought into that sign. Because we worked in a major metropolitan city, we'd already stood over more dead men than most crime scene investigators see in their entire careers. After reading the text book it was clear the author was no naive "everybody join hands and sing"

Bible-thumper who imagined himself a murder investigator. He was the real deal with valid information that lined up with what we'd already seen on our own streets. This guy saw the same things we experienced on a nightly basis yet he put a different spin on it. The idea intrigued me even as I hurled accusations at God.

CHAPTER 5

ON GOD & BLIND GOLDFISH

Over my career I've given a lot of thought to the old wartime saying "There are no atheists in foxholes" and while the quote can be argued both ways, my own faith grew from my time in the foxhole. Before I started my job as a crime scene investigator, I came from the adrenalin-filled world of a police tactical team. Every night was a thrill ride of life and death, yet ironically, being that close to dying didn't draw me any closer to God.

One of the guys who trained me as a young CSI was a crusty bear of a man with no social skills. He hid behind a wall of crass humor, so the day he shared the emotional experience of starting his career as a crime scene investigator, I paid close attention. He said he almost didn't make it through the first year because he was so affected by the senseless suffering and man's inhumanity to man. Hearing those words in the twilight of his career as the sun rose on my career touched me and I repeated them to myself on many a cold and bloody night.

There is nothing quite like standing over dead children to make you question your faith and since mine was never solid to start with, the steady stream of injustice, cruelty and simple bad luck had me pondering questions I'd never asked before. This was not some monk-like academic exercise one indulged from the quiet solitude of a peaceful garden. It was an ugly birth through blood, tears, screams and accusations. It was a perpetual dark cloud draped over my shoulders like a funeral shroud. Death was my companion and I hated him.

By this time, I was truly no good company for anyone outside the world of Homicide Division. Our work separated us from normal people and I felt excluded from the world of sunshine and innocence. I lived in a dark shadowy place where bad things happen to good people and happy endings are elusive. Like a skier plummeting down a mountain, life was reaching a dizzy pace and each bump was a mogul which threatened to catapult me off my feet. My mogul turned out to be a goldfish.

In my dining room there was a large aquarium which housed several fancy goldfish. To better enrich both their environment and my own, I had placed an oversized piece of driftwood in the water and arranged vines and aquatic plants around it so the wood was both in and out of the water. This was what gave the artificial glass box an outdoor pond feel which appealed to me and seemed to agree with its occupants.

As I sprinkled fish flakes in the tank one morning, it came to my attention that a fish had gone blind. You cannot simply take a goldfish to the vet. Or maybe you can, but I couldn't afford a $150 vet bill for a 99 cent fish. Other than his blindness, he seemed fully functional. Perhaps we could work around it. With that in mind, every morning I tapped the glass beside the driftwood in the same place and sprinkled flakes out in the same place. Every morning the blind fish would follow his sighted companions and hoover at the top of the water like a blind vacuum cleaner. I made sure he got enough to eat. He was thriving and although I wasn't really a fish person, I started to look forward to our morning feedings. I may not be able to save the dead babies, doggone it, but I could help out this goldfish — until one morning.

One morning he simply wasn't there. I looked everywhere in the tank and he wasn't there. Like a crazy person, I muttered while hoisting wet rocks out of the tank. "Where's my fish? Where's my fish? WHERE'S MY FISH!?"

Nothing. He was gone. There was a damp spot on the kitchen tile so I searched the floor in case he had Peter Panned out of the tank. Nope. No fish. Dust bunnies, but no fish. My eyes landed on the cat. The barn cat was a large tabby and white fellow who had crept through the doggy door and was currently curled up on the kitchen counter watching me with great interest. It didn't take a crime scene investigator to figure out that murder. A blind fish that swims up to the driftwood for food would have been a Filet O'Fish Happy Meal for a barn cat. I lost it. Just as I had blamed God for the dead baby the night before, I blamed God for this too. The goldfish was the point where I went over the edge. He wouldn't even save a damned fish. God was on my shit list.

Webster defines the 'tipping point' as "the critical point in a situation beyond which a significant and often unstoppable effect or change takes place." For me, it was a drowned baby. Yet one more drowned baby. This one was the same as all the others. Dad left the baby alone in the tub for just a moment while he went for a clean towel. The only thing different about this case was that the baby was a twin. I have no idea why this fact grabbed my heart any more than the suffering of a father who beat himself with his own grief and guilt, but it did. One moment two little boys are playing in the tub and the next moment one confused baby is sitting with the floating body of his brother.

I suppose it's what drove me through the red doors of that church the next morning. I walked into a cavernous room of curious strangers. I didn't know them, or even care to know them, but something drove me to walk inside and make my way to an empty spot at the end of a pew in the middle. On the right.

I listened to the service like a stranger in a foreign land, as if the customs were vaguely familiar, perhaps something I'd seen on a *National Geographic* special. Everyone was welcome for communion so I followed the tide forward and received a cardboard cracker and what tasted like real wine. Real port. Not grape juice. I was indeed, a stranger in a foreign land.

Making my way back to my spot at the end of the pew, I settled down on my knees like everyone ahead of me, waiting for the crowd behind us to finish. We were supposed to be praying. I gave this some thought. Prayer seemed a bit pointless in my life. If you prayed, and events went your way, you praised God for his favor. If you prayed, and something didn't go your way, you praised God for his wisdom. Either way, God came out smelling like a rose, but the reality was that bad things still happened to good people and babies still died in tubs.

I wasn't about to pray for myself which seemed a bit selfish in light of dead babies and shattered lives but since everyone was supposed to be praying, it couldn't hurt to say a little prayer for the family from last night. For the father who would never forgive himself. For the mother, angry, shocked, devastated, who wants to throw blame but she can't today. Maybe tomorrow.

And the twin. The little confused boy who will grow up without his brother. The little boy who will feel that empty space beside him, in the tub, in the crib, when he learns to ride a bike, when he learns to throw a baseball. So I closed my eyes, bowed my head, and pretended to pray like everyone else. As I cautiously asked for blessings on that family, an incredible sadness moved into my empty heart and a slow tear squeezed its way out and down my cheek. I was past the point of being mortified. Everyone else was in their own world anyway so I doubted anyone noticed when the tears took over. I just lowered my face in prayer and tears and ignored the world.

Her cane announced her arrival. Its muffled thump and slide came to a stop beside me and the arms of a grandmother folded around my shoulders. She held me for a moment, kissed me on the top of the head, gave me another squeeze, and then thumped her way back to her seat. And in that moment, as sunlight filtered through the stained glass window beside me and warmed my wet cheek, I knew that God had not forgotten the family that lost the baby.

Good manners are an illusion. We politely conform to the rules out of respect for society and for the most part, out of respect for the feelings of others, but what happens when you stand up and snarl exactly what you think to the world? I suppose it shocks the neighbors and makes for interesting dinner table conversation between your friends, but I didn't care. I hurled curses at God and didn't care what happened. If I got struck by lightning at least it was some kind of answer.

I spent a while shaking my fist at Heaven. Surely no God would allow the things I'd seen. My shaky foundation of Christianity was crumbling as I reached out and lashed out at the people around me. I had deep spiritual discussions with friends who were Christian, Atheist, Pagan, and those who leaned towards the Eastern religions.

For all their arguments about cosmic accidents, I simply could not wrap my mind around the Atheist claims when I watched the sun bounce off a dragonfly as it skittered across the pond. There was too much beauty and order in this world for me to believe it was pure chance, yet I also wasn't ready to embrace the peaceful emotional distancing my Eastern friends practiced. It is hard to emotionally distance yourself when you're standing in blood. So I continued to lash out at a Christian God, even though I recognized the irony. You must actually believe in God to shake your fist at Him. Scratch me as an Atheist. I had to admit I was a disillusioned and very angry Christian.

One morning a Christian neighbor made the polite "How's work going?" inquiry at the mailbox. Instead of snarling a confrontational spat at her God, which would have horrified her to the core, and despite it all, I did still have a meager amount of social skills left, I gave her a filtered but honest answer. Rather than labeling me a godless sinner, she said something profound.

"Even David spent some time shaking his fist at God."

The words were freeing. They gave me the license to be angry. This cooled me off enough to explore the idea, so I did something I'd never done before. I sat down and actually read the whole book. Yes, The Book. I bought a Bible and studied it. The blind faith I saw in friends was still a bit puzzling but I passed it off as good people who had never truly seen the horrors this world has to offer. I was different though. I knew dark things. Was jaded. Tainted. A cloud of death followed me, staining the world with blood and the smell of maggots. And I was angry about it.

Then I met an Episcopal priest. I crossed through the red doors that changed my faith. Instead of responding with shocked indignation he fielded the tough questions I hurled at him with a quiet accepting patience. Perhaps he understood that he was God's surrogate and thus shouldered the brunt of my hostility. I couldn't sit across from God and throw accusations, but this Man of God would do just fine. Through him I could argue with the Lord. Sometimes he had no answers to my biting questions but he had enough respect not to blow smoke. I wasn't going to be satisfied by the smoke and mirrors or patronizing words that led to false faith.

After a while, I took a breath and looked past the suffering. Since I wasn't able to wrap my mind around the idea that there was no God, and there was no satisfying answer to the question of why God would allow such horror, my next issue was to address my own involvement in this play. On this stage of life, what was my role? The door to my faith slowly cracked open and the light flooded in.

I was wading into unspeakable pain but maybe there was a reason. Perhaps, just perhaps, God put me there because He wanted me in the middle of this chaos. Perhaps we are all tools in God's workshop. We have all been given certain talents and skills in this life. These gifts are not ours to squander. I was gifted with the remarkable ability to wade into the gore and the heartache, to look past the stench and seek the truth, but I was also cursed with a deep empathy for the suffering of others. Because of my gift, I was the voice of the victim who could no longer speak. But could my curse be someone else's blessing? I gave this some thought. Maybe it was time to embrace this painful curse.

With that new outlook I started to walk into each crime scene and ask, outside of the professional processing of the evidence, why does God have me here? In each case the answer was there behind the crime scene tape. Sometimes I was the sword of His justice but other times I was His hand of comfort to the victim's loved ones in what was arguably the worst day of their lives. I was there. On that horrible day. I was there to hold the woman who had lost a husband. I was there to lift up the father as he cried on the floor over a lost child. I was there for it all.

And that experience changed my faith. This wasn't about faith that keeps you safe in a foxhole while the battle rages outside. This was the faith that God still walks with bloody footsteps through the carnage outside the foxhole to find his sheep.

~

Some crimes are so heinous they are slap in the face of God. And so it was with the death of Gloria King. Estranged from her family, at 78 years old, Gloria lived on the streets, and the kindness of the church. A priest found her body hidden in an alcove beside the cathedral steps. Raped and strangled with her own rosary beads, she was left, partially clothed, hidden from the world, but not from the eyes of God. There are crimes, and then there are crimes that make the devil's own minions shudder. There would be Hell to pay for this one.

The homeless must travel light. Their meager belongings easily define them. Who was Gloria? The tiny bundle beside her was wrapped in an American flag bandana. As I carefully untied the knots, my rage smoldered and grew as each piece was revealed. Her Bible, tattered, torn, taped together, would later be described in trial as "well-worn." The Bible and two prayer books had carefully been placed in a plastic bread bag to protect them from the weather. This precious package had been tied inside another American flag. My mind was ablaze with questions. Who could do this? How could God let this happen? This godly woman. This helpless lamb. Why? I struggled to make sense of it. Emotion, faith, and doctrine all warred with the cold hard truth that lay before me. Frustration clawed, making the familiar clinical art of forensics a battle.

I tried to table the emotions, telling myself that I worked for God. I was His soldier. I was her voice. It didn't work. Like rising water from a heavy rain, the flooding tears were inevitable. There were simply too many questions and the cold stone bricks of the cathedral would not speak.

I wanted justice. I wanted answers. Only a monster would do this. Later I sat in the court room, staring into the eyes of that monster, her killer, and there were still no answers. At the trial he glared at me, his eyes bloodshot pits into his soul. I asked God for composure before I took the leap and boldly stared into the challenging eyes of Hell.

He was convicted.

I still got no answers. After the trial I discussed the case and my brush with Hell with a dear friend who shared her wise Native American words.

"You must do the Arapaho thing. Say 'It is finished' then turn and walk away."

Very sage advice.

"But ask the animals, and they will teach you."
Job 12:7

Shortly after the Goldfish Mogul, God saw fit to send me four kittens. They needed a home, and since there was no one around to tell me that I couldn't have four cats, I brought them home and tried to find four names. The calico runt was so small that we could only hope she would survive, so I named her, Hope. I named the girls Faith, Hope, and Love. I named the boy, Brother.

I'm not a cat person but was soon captivated by their antics and innocence. Each night after my shift I sat in a cushy chair with a glass of wine and watched the kittens play. It was better than television. When I wasn't home the kittens were locked in a spare bedroom to keep them safe. But as my job had so often taught me, safety is merely an illusion.

On that night I came home from work and opened the door to their room. Three kittens came bouncing out. Three, not four. Where was Hope? I called. No Hope. She'd given me this scare before so I started to search for a sleeping cat. And I found her.

Hanging on the back side of a chair. Swinging with a sickening sway. Hope had become tangled in the frayed upholstery fabric of the chair and hanged herself.

A darkness bloomed in my gut as I started to unravel the kitten. She was still warm. As I worked to untangle the corded fabric around her neck, I did something I didn't often do. I prayed. I prayed for God not to take my Hope. My gut was empty. I no longer had hope. There was no hope for anything. There was not one part of my life that Death wouldn't steal. But still. What if?

I yanked the last of the stubborn fabric away. Blew in her nose. Rubbed her back. Tapped her chest. There was nothing to lose. I continued CPR on a kitten that was small enough to fit in one hand.

She gasped. Then she opened her eyes. Paddled her tiny feet. I set her on the floor. Without so much as a backward glance, Hope toddled off to play. I sat back in the chair and sobbed.

The same God who hadn't saved a devout little old lady had spared a kitten. He had spared my hope. I had no idea what to make of that. Breathing life back into something was the most remarkable miracle I'd ever seen. It was an important lesson. When hope is gone, keep on trying anyway. God may just send you a miracle.

Too many nights I stood over the cold, hard evidence of what happens when hope is lost. Suicide comes in many forms but the common denominator is almost always a loss of hope. I share this short collection of stories because their stories mattered. Their lives mattered.

A Partridge in a Pear Tree

If the smell didn't do it, the flies on the windows were a dead giveaway. I made my path up the sidewalk and paused a moment by the opened front door. Like a sloppy flower arrangement, mail poked out of the box at every angle and spilled onto the porch below. It made sense; the mailman had called police.

I stepped inside and scanned the room as my eyes adjusted to the lower light. It was quiet. I was alone with him. The usual hustle and bustle of interest from patrol officers doesn't extend to decomps. No one wants to spend the rest of his shift smelling like a decomposing body, so they sat in the car with the heater on. I picked my way through the scene as I studied his life. There was a flutter near the Christmas tree.

Rabbit that I am, I froze. Every fiber aware. I strained to find the sound. Nothing. Silence once again rolled across the room like a fog. The angel atop the tree smugly gazed down at me with outstretched wings. I studied her a moment and then dismissed her.

Nostalgia tugged for my attention with a string of popcorn wrapped around the tree. Who strings popcorn anymore? I considered the man, sitting in front of his television, patiently putting popcorn on a thread. Was he thinking about killing himself then? I hope not. I would hope popcorn strings would take him back to happier times.

A thunder of feathers exploded beside my ear as the burst of green and blue erupted from the tree. Two parakeets landed on the bookcase while a third orbited the room twice before returning to the tree to rest beside the angel. He and the angel both glared down at me with disapproving eyes.

I stepped into a bowl of bird seed on the floor. A gray cockatiel was perched on a Wise Man's head, bulling his way into the Nativity scene on the mantel. My simple suicide just became far more interesting. I shut the front door to keep the birds from escaping into the December cold.

The first responding officers had failed to mention the birds. Most likely they didn't see them. They probably took one sniff, saw a gun by his side, and backed or ran out to gladly throw the responsibility at someone else. That someone was me. I poked around the house, gathering more information as I went from room to room, filling my basket of questions with answers. If one ignored the mess caused by the birds, and the insects spawned and encouraged by decomposition, the house was relatively clean. Six empty cages stared back at me behind opened doors. Large bowls of bird seed and water were in each room.

This was a planned death. Unsure of how long it would take before his body was found, he had released his birds. A white parakeet sat on the edge of his computer which still hummed in slumber. The bird fluttered away as I reached forward to bump the mouse. The screen popped to life to reveal his suicide note. It was nothing surprising. He did however, give an inventory of his birds. There were clearly more birds to find before I could leave the scene, so after a short call to the medical examiner, I found a towel and a bird cage and started toward the Christmas tree.

The Pearl

The door swung opened into another century. Antique furniture, polished and orderly, stood at attention as I entered the room. The frayed fabric on the old couch betrayed the ageless gleam of the dark mahogany. A place for everything and everything in its place.

I stood for a moment, lost in the time capsule. Sepia faces stared at me from behind dark picture frames. I pieced together the story of her life, preserved like a museum in the tiny apartment. She was a war bride. He brought her to this New World and then he died young. She was alone now. After all these years, there was no one on either continent.

I looked at the furniture around me. This old girl had once been wealthy but now she was trapped as the ghetto grew up around her, a pearl inside an oyster. I wondered if she'd been a prisoner in her own home, or if, like so many people blissfully unaware of the predators in their midst, she simply went about her day, unconcerned with the dangers that lurked so near.

The kitchen was the only evidence I was still in this century. I had been in these apartments so often that I was surprised to see white cabinets and appliances that gleamed. Clearly the nastiness of the ghetto I'd experienced in the past was less about poverty and more about the culture of cleanliness, for this lady had taken great care of everything in her tiny home.

A calendar on the pantry door gave me my first clue as to why I was here. She had a doctor's appointment yesterday. And today, as I rounded the corner into her bedroom, I saw her, backlit by the afternoon sun. Its warm glow welcomed me into the room but I stood in the doorway letting my eyes adjust to the change in light.

She sat beside the window, dressed as neatly as her home. At first glance the old girl appeared to be napping in the sunlight but my gaze followed the line from her dropped hand to the ancient revolver on the carpet beside her. And like everything else in this apartment, it had been well cared for, and was fully functional.

"Just the facts, Ma'am. Just the facts."

I was just here to gather facts, I wasn't here to assign blame. My only involvement in this case was to see if it was a suicide or a murder. The bare bones of the case were pretty clear cut. A man was being evicted. When police knocked on his door they heard a gunshot. They entered to find him dead. There was no one else in the home. The house was locked from the inside. The police gained entry with a key. The man appeared to have shot himself. On the surface, those were the facts.

Their eyes betrayed them. The constables shuffled their feet and looked away when they told me the story behind the story. I listened for a minute and then understood why they felt the cold fingers of blame pointing in their direction.

They had come to evict a 72 year old man from an apartment that he had lived in for 19 years. He'd had a stroke and was living on disability. Social Security benefits hadn't gone up in 2 years. The apartment complex had recently changed management and the rent had skyrocketed to well past what his meager income could afford. He could no longer live in his home and he had nowhere to go. So when the apartment complex filed eviction papers on him and the constables came to serve those papers, the proud and angry old man took the only route he could see.

The apartment was tidy except for the spray of blood spatter on the white wall. There was a bullet hole in the opposite wall. The helpless anger which powered him was gone and now the old man lay crumpled on the bloodstained carpet like a roadside advertising inflatable with no air.

The apartment manager plied for my support. She was the victim here. She had lived in fear of the old man's wrath. He kept falling short on his rent. I ignored her chatter as I stared at the drying blood on the old man's hand. Then I turned to look at her manicured fingers. With a long sigh, I stood up and addressed the woman who shouldn't have been standing in my crime scene. I took off my sunglasses and wiped the lens. "So why didn't you guys just grandfather the old guy in at the rent he'd been paying? He'd been living here for 19 damned years."

People who work with enough death begin to lose their social graces and mine were long gone. I didn't have a dog in this fight. I called it like I saw it. I was here because this was an In-Custody Death. Law Enforcement Officers were on the scene when the man shot himself. He may have pulled the trigger but the apartment management and the system killed him. It's not my job to make someone feel good about themselves. The constables were not at fault here. The old man was victim of a system that couldn't see past the almighty dollar.

She stammered, "Well, that's not our policy. It's not my fault. The new owners . . . . This is still a business . . . ."

I put my sunglasses back on and pointed her toward the opened door. It was time for her exit. It was time for me to start photographing the old man who had finally paid his last rent.

French Fries

As I walked across the breezeway to McDonald's, he wrote a note in his journal. The cashier handed me a burger and fries as he opened his patio door. The welcome scent of a warm meal perfumed the elevator on my ride back up. He opened the glass door and stood there, breathing in the city, taking in the skyline. I stood at my desk and opened the bag. He pulled a wicker table to the balcony wall. I pulled my chair to my desk. He peeked over the edge. I peeked into the bag. I pulled a fry out as he pulled himself onto the wall. And as the sweet, salty goodness of a warm French fry exploded in my mouth, he jumped off the 12th floor of his apartment building.

I finished my burger as the first police car arrived, a mere two blocks from my office. And thirty minutes later, I stood over his body and wondered what he was thinking as I was eating French fries.

The Class Clown

The ice had long since melted in his glass. The spiral note pad was almost full. Some people write suicide notes. He had written a suicide novel. It was a good read too. I wish I'd known him. I read his words again and wondered. I didn't wonder what he was thinking as he started that engine and sat back for one last ride, for he had written down every thought that rambled through his head while he sat in the car. And waited. I scanned his words again and savored the sheer originality. Once more, I wished I had known him. What a clever person.

As Death crept up the handwriting became more difficult to read. He went from a college student to a kindergartener, all over the page. But still, he was the Class

Clown. I stood over his body, read more of his note, and laughed at his humor. Such talent. Such waste. I don't judge any more. I have stood over far more suicides than I care to count and if I do my job right, I get to know each and every one. There are multitudes of reasons for choosing this course. There are multitudes of paths to take.

Ultimately I think it comes down to a sunrise. For some of us, the sun rises each morning bringing with it the hopes of a new day. Like Scarlett O'Hara, we have the confidence that no matter what happens today, "Tomorrow is another day!"

For some that sunrise doesn't bring hope. They have given up waiting, they have given up hoping. They have given up life. As we zipped up the bag on the Class Clown, once again his words played in my head. And once more I wondered. What if he had waited just one more day?

CHAPTER 6

REIGN OF THE BOOGEY BEAST

The goats soon cleared out the Briar Patch pen enough that I was able to turn that area into a chicken yard. My life pegged the meter on ludicrous the day Dora made her first appearance. Each morning after I fed the barn animals it was customary to take a nice long walk in the pasture with three dogs and my iced coffee. I enjoyed my time with nature while the critters read their pee-mail. Most of the time three or four half-grown kittens tagged along. After Montoya finished his breakfast, the horse joined us too. We must have been quite the spectacle.

On that day we had a new float attached to our little parade. One of my hens had discovered a hole the goats made in the bird pen so rather than waiting for me to deliver breakfast, she met me in the barn. I christened her, Dora the Explorer.

If you are on the bottom of the food chain, leaving the safety of the pen is not a good idea but Dora had other plans. She was coming on the walk with us. The brazen little hen clucked her way down the trail behind me while I kept an eye on dogs who were very much aware that a chicken was on the bottom rung of the food ladder. The kittens stalked and pounced at Dora who cackled and darted which made her even more tempting to dogs who hadn't had breakfast yet. Any attempts to shoo Dora back to the barn would have ended in disaster so I just let her come along. From time to time she'd drop behind and then run as fast as her little drumsticks could carry her to catch up with us. Clearly Dora enjoyed her morning walk with predators. For a chicken this must be the equivalent of swimming with Great White Sharks on the Barrier Reef.

Until I patched her hole, each morning would find Dora waiting in the barn with her goggles and scuba tank, eager for another dive in dangerous waters. Dora was the comedy I needed each morning.

Anyone who has goats soon learns everything there is to know about fixing fences. The first lesson is that cheap welded wire will need to be replaced with proper woven field fencing better suited to the rigors of livestock climbing it like a stepladder.

After I dumped the heavy roll of wire out of the truck, I was tasked with getting it to the pasture. Having neither a man nor a tractor, this became a slow, tedious roll, pausing from time to time to catch my breath and to shift the bundle in order to adjust the direction of travel both toward my destination and around dog turds. Once in place, the goal was to unroll the wire along the existing fence, cut off a length, and then tack it up. With years of building fences now behind me, I can tell you this is not the way to build a sturdy fence but at the time, I was a neophyte with a shiny new pair of fence pliers, making it up as I went. Fake it till you make it.

My first problem was that as soon as I cut my length of wire it rolled back up on itself, leaving me standing with pursed lips beside a springing wire beast which bounced and swayed and taunted me like a giant slinky. I solved this problem by cutting the wire and leaving the dog to sit on the end so it couldn't roll up on itself. While one dog sat on the end of the wire, the other dog fetched the bolt cutters I used to cut the length needed. My shiny new fence pliers then cut a piece of very expensive, yet pliable, aluminum electrical wire from a roll which was then used to tack the length of field fencing onto the existing fence. In this manner, foot by agonizing foot, I fenced in the front pasture to make a goat prison. It wasn't pretty, but I, the Captain of this ship, did it by myself. With two dogs. And a pair of new fence pliers.

It was during this time I reconnected with an old girlfriend who was a pro at ranching and she explained the main difference between men and women — their tools. Seriously. Unlike mine, Pam's fences were as high and tight as a marine's hairline. She shared this little bit of wisdom, "Work smarter. Not harder."

Apparently there are tools for all these jobs and the trick is learning what tool makes your life easier. This is why men spend endless hours trolling Home Depot. In reality it's not that men are gifted with innate skills that empower them with the ability to build things, it's that they possess the right tools and know how to use them. Since becoming a crime scene investigator I had already been spending a great deal of time in Home Depot acquiring tools I'd never needed before.

I was buying all kinds of things: a tool box to hold chisels for digging out bullets, saws for cutting up sheetrock (to dig out bullets), regular tape measures, electronic tape measures, rolling measuring wheels for diagramming murder scenes, construction flags for marking out bone locations, wooden dowels to use as bullet trajectory rods, orange paint for the wooden dowels, magnets on sticks and mirrors on poles. I had to buy the green dolly to haul the many boxes of gear that might be needed on just one crime scene.

Each week saw at least one new trip to Home Depot for mundane tools which could be used in rather unusual ways. Although the Home Depot salesman definitely had to stretch his imagination when I came calling, he clearly looked forward to our visits and pleas of "I need a tool for this . . ." Not only did it get his creative juices flowing, I'm sure it made for interesting dinner table conversation with the family.

Keeping the goats confined became a daily struggle as I matched wits with four young bucks who spent most of their waking hours either plotting escape, stuck with their head in the fence because their horns got caught, or raping their buddy who couldn't go anywhere because his horns were stuck in the fence.

Unneutered male goats are simply disgusting. There is no other way around it. They urinate on their front legs and faces in some misguided attempt to make themselves attractive, and when in rut, a buck will mount anything that'll stand still. This includes another male goat with his head stuck in a fence. So in addition to the "Your goats are out" phone calls that came in, I also received the "One of your goats has his head stuck in the fence and the others are raping him" calls.

In an effort to cut down on their criminal behavior while I was at work, I started confining the goats in the barn when I left. Since they tended to stay close to the barn at night, when I returned home after midnight, I'd release the goats to let them graze in the pasture. In hindsight, this was incredibly stupid on my part, but being a novice goat owner, I was unaware of the risks until the morning when I opened the stall door to feed and three somewhat rattled goats stood there — three, not four.

I peeked in the stall. Yep. Only three. If you have a farm, you are familiar with this exercise. You count the remaining animals again. And count them again. Since three is not a very high number, it was unlikely that I was miscounting, yet I continued this futile exercise as I walked around the barn with three high-stepping billy goats in tow. They stopped as I walked out in the pasture and found the first dead chicken.

And that's what it took before it finally sunk into my head that like chickens, goats are on the bottom of the food chain. I found what was left of Ken the Goat about 100 yards from the barn. It takes a lot to shock me but the condition of that goat did it. I'd turned them out at 12:30 a.m. and here I was at 7:30 a.m. staring at remains.

His head was intact but it was attached to a spine which had been picked clean of soft tissue. There was nothing left of that goat but a head, a spine, and four legs with some hide on them. Every bit of soft tissue had already been gnawed off of everything but the head. I found a dirty stomach and some intestines a few yards away from the primary scene. The mud around the remains was dotted with paw prints. My neighbor told me that it had to be stray dogs and I believed him at first, but now, after years of experience gained the hard way, it's clear that Ken the Goat was killed by a pack of coyotes.

There's no use crying over spilled milk or a dead goat, so Ken became a training tool for crime scene investigators. I pulled the camera out and documented the times and condition of Ken's remains, noting the arrival times of scavenging vultures and ants. When I got to the office that night we popped the digital photos into the computer and carefully studied the death of Ken the Goat. It was quite educational.

Had we happened upon a human body in that condition we might have erroneously assumed the time of death to be much earlier given the lack of soft tissue when in fact, we had a pretty clear 7 hour window of time the murder could have taken place. Each day thereafter I photographed and documented the condition of Ken's remains and we studied them in the office. So although Ken the Goat may have been a pain in the butt in life, Ken earned his CSU t-shirt in death by taking one for the team and contributing to the education of others in the field of forensics. Go Ken!

The problem with going into a feed store in the spring time is that all manner of things you don't need will be for sale, and without a spouse or a good friend beside you, there is no one to gently point out that you don't need five baby geese. So for no good reason whatsoever, one afternoon I walked into the feed store for something and walked out with five Brown Chinese goslings. I still don't know why.

Over the years I'd had a lot of chickens and I know chickens are certainly on the bottom of the food chain. Getting chickens is like turning on an All You Can Eat Buffet sign for predators. I know better than to get attached to a chicken. But geese. Oh my! Geese. I dubbed them the Apple Dumpling Gang.

Geese are like dogs with feathers. They are velociraptors with charm. Each morning I'd release them from the chicken coop and they'd run to their little blue plastic pool, climb the two steps up, and belly flop into the water like children at Splash Town. You simply cannot stay in a bad mood when watching geese play in the water and many happy hours were spent in a lawn chair with a book while lifeguarding geese. In addition to being feathered therapists, the other happy plus of having geese is that they are darned good weed-eaters.

Horses will not eat the grass that comes up around horse poop but geese have no such inhibitions. If you have geese and goats, you pretty much don't need a weed-eater. As gas prices were skyrocketing, I was discovering the beauty of using livestock to make my life easier. Goats cleared land and kept the fences clean. Horses did major bulk mowing. Geese did weed-eating. Chickens churned all manure into good soil and produced eggs. Time I would have spent mowing was spent instead supervising my yard crew as I read a book in a lawn chair. Money I would have spent on gas was spent on frappuccinos and books. It was there I read a book that would change my life, Barbara Kingsolver's *Animal, Vegetable, Miracle*.

This book details a family's journey of self-discovering during a year of trying to eat locally. The book is a best seller which inspired countless readers before me to take the plunge and turn their homes into farms. Straddling dead men might pay the bills but my passion was raising livestock. Although I'm a crappy gardener, as long as it can walk to water, I can pretty much raise anything on feet.

It is a truth universally acknowledged, that a woman in possession of a farm, must be in want of more animals, and just as Jane Austen's Mr. Darcy found his wife, I soon found myself being given more chickens. The son of a friend had found the birds dumped in the forest behind the Ag Barn at school. Apparently after the county fair, these birds were no longer needed and their wicked owner chose to simply abandon them to their fate. Being soft-hearted, my friend's son, scooped them up and brought them home to his mother, who immediately speed-dialed me at work.

I already had five chickens and didn't need any more but being a sucker for a hard luck story I agreed to let her drop the birds off in my coop. When I got home that night I crept out with a flashlight and got my first view of a Franken-chicken. These sleeping Buddha birds were twice as large as my adult hens and from the peeps they made when they woke up, it was clear they were still babies!

The next morning I called Dear Friend Kaye, my

biologist friend and neighbor. She gave me the straight skinny on these fat birds that were very likely a Cornish Cross referred to by many as Franken-chickens. Designed by the chicken industry to be a fast-growing bird with heavy thighs and breasts, they can grow 5 to 8 pounds in 8 to 10 weeks. They're bred to be butchered early. Those not butchered often die from a heart attack because their bodies cannot keep up with the rapid weight gain. Their heavy weight often leads to broken legs which cannot support such a large bird.

I had two choices. I could butcher them now or I could give them some kind of natural life before they either died or had to be euthanized because their bodies could no longer support them. I like fried chicken, barbecued chicken, chicken fajitas, and chicken salad. So I let them live. What the hell. I felt sorry for them. Sue me.

My older hens were ruthless and cruel to my Buddha Babies who couldn't even get out of the way so I removed them from the main chicken pen. The Bird Pen consisted of three sections, a large flight pen enclosed in field fencing and flight netting which contained a room-size chicken coop, and a smaller yard that was fenced but did not contain flight netting. Since the Franken-chickens couldn't possibly fly, placing them in this yard seemed safe enough, but then again, safety is just an illusion.

The Boogey Beast struck between 6:30 and 7:30 p.m. that night. I know this because I was across the street at a neighborhood barbecue. I left early to put my chickens up. The sun had not yet disappeared below the horizon as I was puzzling the great mystery as to why I saw only one Franken-chicken. She was still there, sound asleep, unaware that one by one her companions had been bird-napped and murdered. I found a pile of Franken-chicken bodies beside the fence. Apparently the Boogey Beast had snatched the first bird and carried it to the fence where it tried to climb up with its heavy load. Since the First Franken-chicken was so heavy, the Beast was forced to drop it there, go back and kill another chicken and try to get it over the fence. This act was repeated several times before the Boogey Beast found a bird small enough to drag over the fence, leaving a pile of fat friends who were unlucky enough to be sitting on the wrong side of the smaller bird.

This just left one lone, lucky Franken-chicken. I had no idea what to do with it. I couldn't leave her with the adult birds in the flight pen. They were so mean she'd end up getting pecked to death, so I moved her up to the house and left her in the foliage by the back gate where she'd be relatively protected by the proximity to the house and the housedogs. I named her Gladys because it sounded better and was shorter than Lucky-Bird-Who-Escaped-Death-Because-She-Was-Sitting-On-The-Left-Side-Of-The-Weight-Watchers-Bird.

The arrival of the Boogey Beast set off a full scale barnyard alarm. People think the problem with having a lot of animals is the responsibility of feeding them when in reality, the problem is that you care for them. You actually care. Albeit some more than others, but nevertheless, you care. And they die. Few things illustrate the Circle of Life better than a farm.

There are certain rules about farm animals. The ones you love the most will die. The prettiest ones will die. Your favorites will die. You cannot prepare yourself emotionally for it. You will simply be coasting along when The Big Bad will leap out and punch you in the gut, leaving you gasping for air in a fetal position. I know this, but nevertheless, I fight it tooth and nail.

So it was that I packed a dog crate into a little red wagon and stuffed five little geese into it. I could emotionally handle losing chickens. I couldn't handle losing those geese. They weren't just barnyard birds, they were smiles in an uncertain world. They were a bright spot of innocence that tipped the scale ever so slightly against the heavy weight of darkness.

Much of my life has been spent in an ongoing chess game with Death and the Boogey Beast. Death may be a part of life on a farm but my goal is to make the bastard work for it. This ends up being a lot of work on my part. I gave that a little thought as foot by bumpy foot, we slow-rolled in the dark toward the barn, just me and my wagonload of geese. The young goslings were set up in their own stall alongside the horses where the presence of the larger animals might discourage predators.

The sun rose the next morning as if a mass murder had never happened. This is a curious fact of life. It goes on. No matter what unspeakable evil occurs in the moonlight, the sun will rise, and the living will continue to peck out an existence, ignoring the scattered feathers of the unfortunate.

The geese continued to be a source of immense trouble and amusement. Each morning after I fed the horses and the goats, I released the geese from their stall and they waddled behind me as I led the way to the back yard where they browsed, chased bugs, and terrorized cats. I set up a tall chain link kennel outside the back door of the stall where I placed their little wading pool. This gave them a protected pool area underneath a porch and an interior stall. I gave them all that, and heaven forbid, I gave them names.

If you want a ticket for certain pain, name a bird. Getting birds for your farm is like opening a fast food restaurant for predators. Naming a bird merely announces the daily special.

"The daily special for Wednesday is Bernice!"

I know this and yet I still do it. To this day, God help me,

I still name farm animals. In the short run it helps me identify them in conversation. In the long run, I guess a name means they're more than just the daily special. Their lives, no matter how short, still have meaning. It's terribly egocentric to consider that an animal's life doesn't matter unless I've given it a name, but the reality is that you remember the ones with names. Their deaths hurt more.

Every morning I would stumble to the barn, with coffee in hand, to feed the horses and turn the geese out of their stall. No matter what happened the night before at work, the sun would rise and waddle out on happy little rubber feet. But one morning I turned around to count goslings and found myself short one bird. What the . . . ?

Perhaps she had just zigged when everyone zagged and was thus in another area of the barn. Nope. I ran back into the stall. No goose. No feathers. No blood. Nothing. Nothing but a single paw print the size of a bobcat. Damn that Boogey Beast!

This shook me. How could a bobcat be so bold as to come into the barn with the horses? Oh, how naive I was. Few things cure naivete faster than having birds on a farm. Suck it up, Buttercup. There was no point in crying over the loss of one bird since it was a guaran-damn-tee that the Boogey Beast would return for more geese when the sun went down.

I spent the day setting up another goose pen against the house along my bedroom window. With the idea that predators were discouraged by lighting, I strung Christmas lights all over the pen. The geese were most delighted when the sun went down and I plugged in that strand of lights. Like tiny Griswalds with rubber feet they stared in open mouthed amazement at the colors. Clearly this new security system met with their approval.

Red, green, yellow, and blue lights reflected off the white feathers of Gladys, the lone Franken-chicken, as she moved out of her fern foliage home to marvel at the neighbors' new lawn display. I gave no thought to what my own neighbors might think. Living at the end of a dead end street has its perks and being able to have Christmas lights year round was one of them. Besides, if you play Twister over dead men for a living, you get a wee short on social skills.

CHAPTER 7

THE COWBOY COP
& MY COMMITMENT TO CRAZY

When you live alone you can have a Christmas display for geese outside your bedroom window. You can also work all night and take naps in the middle of the day. This explains why I was dead asleep when the phone rang. I rolled over, glanced at the caller ID, and rolled back into bed. My life is way too complicated to answer unknown callers. If it's important, they'll leave a message. The phone chimed to alert me they'd left a message. Damn.

On the one hand I wanted to ignore it and go back to sleep. On the other hand it might be about a murder, in which case I needed time to wake up and remember the details of calls that were already beginning to blend into each other. So I listened to the message. Railroad Police? What the heck is that? I racked my brains trying to remember cases involving the railroad. Nada. Nothing. Not even any recent Hit by Train calls. Curiosity got the best of me, so I called him back.

The man who answered had a pleasant country accent with an air of self-confidence. Not quite cocky, just sure of himself. It was the voice of someone used to telling people what to do. Being surrounded by cops and lawyers myself, this alone did not impress me. It was what else he said.

He was a K9 officer and got my name from a mutual friend, who was a K9 Sergeant for my agency. This guy had rescued a Brittany Spaniel and needed help finding a home for the dog. The sergeant friend gave him my name and told him I might be some help. I was definitely not going to take on another dog, but to soften that news, I assured him that I would look at the dog and put some feelers out to help him get it placed. That should have ended the conversation. It didn't.

He talked. And he talked. And I found myself really liking this cop who was a cowboy who lived only twenty minutes from my house. This cowboy cop was a Special Agent for the railroad who hunted narcotics and illegal aliens with a German Shepherd. He also owned cattle and horses. He had my full attention. The man was practically a resume of my interests, so much so, in fact, that I started to wonder if this wasn't some joke played by someone who knew me really well. We talked longer in one phone call than I believe Wuzband and I talked the entire year of 2015. Ending the conversation with a promise to come scope out his rescue dog, I was left wide awake, excited, and slightly confused. Where the hell had this come from? I did what all women do. Dial a girlfriend.

Upon hearing the story, my friend assured me the entire conversation was not about a dog, but was actually about a man fishing for a date. A mutual friend knew we both lived in the same town, shared the same interests and were single, thus he gave the man my number. I was skeptical. Despite how interesting he sounded, I hadn't yet met the man in person. He might be an ogre. To this she replied, "Even if this guy has a third eye in the middle of his forehead, you need to go out on a date with him. You have too much in common not to go out with this man!"

Put that way, it did make sense. I'd dated a few guys

after my divorce but no one who matched my rather unique qualifications.

"Must Love Dogs" doesn't begin to describe the kind of man that I needed in my life. Must love dogs, and horses, and not be turned off by geese with Christmas lights or intimidated by a woman who could chase drug dealers over fences, or straddle dead men. I'm gonna be frank here. Those last two weed out a lot of normal guys.

Most men don't want a woman with more balls than they have. That's fine. I didn't want them either. This pretty much turned my dating pool into a wading pond. In my limited experience, all the average civilian man could see was a woman with a gun, and it either thrilled him or threatened him, and either way, I didn't want him.

But this Cowboy Cop was different. It was clear from the start that his interest in ranching and animals was not some ploy to get in my pants. He was single, not separated, not living with his mother, had a real job, was living in his own home, had two grown kids, dogs, horses, cows, two tom cats that needed to be neutered, a pickup truck, an old blue tractor and a Featherlite horse trailer. There was definitely something wrong with him. Perhaps there was a third eye.

Nevertheless, it was worth investigating, and besides, there was a dog that needed a home. So I put some feelers out and got a lukewarm response but enough of one to warrant calling the Cowboy Cop back a few days later and leaving him a message with the information. He returned the call while I was getting my toenails done.

I'm not a girly girl. Sometimes I wish I was, but it's just not me. I can't fake it. When I was younger I made an attempt but the older I get the more I just say, "Screw it. I can't wear make-up. A tan is about as good as it gets. I'm not that big into jewelry either. Sandals aren't practical. High heels are out of the question. My clothing is purchased on whether or not it can conceal a gun and dog hair. On that particular day however, I was wearing a white tank top, cargo pants, and flip flops, and just happened to look decent. My shoe choice was unusual, but then again, I was actually getting my toenails painted. Forty pounds lighter than I am right now, the picture wasn't half bad. And there was no goose poop on my flip-flops. That was a plus.

I wasn't expecting his call and I certainly wasn't expecting his invitation to come over. To see the dog. That's what he said. I mean, since my nail salon wasn't that far from his house anyway. Whatever.

So I followed his directions and easily found his place. And I was not impressed. First off, mow the damned yard. Second, the front yard is not a parking lot for farm equipment. He introduced me to his son and his cousin, the gravedigger. The Cowboy Cop's family owned the local cemetery. All three men were sweaty and muddy because they had just broken the cemetery tractor while attempting to dig a pond in his pasture. This was a major dilemma because not only was the pond unfinished, but you cannot dig graves without a working tractor.

With newly manicured toes I stood in muddy grass over my ankles and tried to find a way to leave. He insisted upon giving me the fifty cent tour. I met his dogs and his horses. The Brittany Spaniel was typical of her breed and if this home didn't pan out, I assured him the search would continue as long as he would foster her. That wasn't a problem. He was a sucker for any dog with a hard luck story.

When I was at work that evening my phone rang. The Cowboy Cop was inviting me to dinner. Tonight? I was on-duty. I'd already eaten. Well then, come drink a glass of sweet tea. I don't drink tea. He assured me that he'd buy whatever I wanted to drink. Okay, water then. Persistent fellow. Since I wasn't busy, I agreed to his invitation and met him in what was one of my favorite downtown restaurants. It was also one of his favorites. Again? Was the guy for real or was someone feeding him a list of my favorite things?

The man in the restaurant was not the sweaty, muddy creature who'd stood in an overgrown yard earlier. Cleaned up, he was a different cat altogether. And in uniform. It is a fact of life that most women love a man in uniform. Most women. Not all women. Police women are used to seeing men in uniform, so it really doesn't make our hearts beat any faster, but it was enough for me to drink a glass of water and carry on conversation. He was aware that my phone could ring and he'd be alone with his angel hair pasta while his date left to work a murder, and he was okay with that. And I was aware that his phone could ring and we'd have to box up his supper for his patrol dog.

Not long afterward he made his first farm visit to my house. Bling, one of my geese, took an instant liking to him and cuddled in his arms like they were the best of friends. The approval stamp of a goose is a pretty darned big endorsement. That certainly earned him enough credit to go horseback riding the following weekend.

He pulled up in my yard in his shiny aluminum 3-horse slant trailer with a 28 year old Quarter Horse. Men may not realize this fact, but if you're dating a country girl, your critters are your resume. Skip was an old cow horse who came off a respected ranch as a youngster. Over their years together the horse had worked cattle and raised his kids. At 28, the big red horse was still muscled up and looked about 8 years old.

I loaded Montoya in his trailer and we headed off to meet my girlfriends on the trail. The girls were already on horseback as we pulled up into the parking lot and they lost no time hustling over to check out this new man with the big red horse. As he competently saddled his own animal, one of them gave me a thumbs up.

We were soon on the way down the trail where I was better able to admire the man and the red horse. Thus far, both were passing with flying colors and it was an enjoyable evening ride up until the moment we looked across the other side of the canal and saw a park attendant closing the main gates. This would shut us in the park for the night. At that distance there was no way to get his attention.

This would not be a problem for the cowboy and the big red horse. As we girls continued our path down the bank, he galloped ahead, crossed two bridges, and alerted the park attendant. The man could handle his own horse. He earned another thumbs up and the respect of my tribe. That did it. We were officially a couple.

In every relationship, there is a part, past the "Wow! They like me too!", when the parties involved actually get to enjoy the companionship of being a couple. We had reached that point, where time off from work was spent together. We took our first day trip to explore the hill country where we did some sight-seeing and he introduced me to friends. It was very much a Bridget Jones version of 'holiday,' where I took a break from the responsibilities of life and just lived in the moment, having a country Cinderella kind of day.

The clock struck midnight and my carriage turned into a pumpkin, however, the moment I pulled back into my darkened driveway. A trail of white feathers across the yard pointed an accusing finger toward the canal, and was all that was left of Gladys the Lone Franken-chicken. The Boogey Beast had been bold enough to come right up to the house with the dogs beside the fence and snatch the bird from her home in the thick jungle of landscaped ferns, mints, and rose bushes. Yes, the clock had struck midnight, there I was standing over a trail of feathers, missing a glass slipper.

There's crazy, and then there's woman wearing rubber boots carrying a gun in the dark kind of crazy. I am the latter. It was days later when I was awakened by a loud thump against the side of the house, followed by the raucous honking of geese. The Boogey Beast was back and the sonofabitch just stole one of my geese! There are two kinds of women, those who cry over a goose, and those who grab a gun and dog and hunt down the bastard that stole it. I am the latter.

The Boogey Beast didn't have much of a head start so I slipped into a pair of cargo pants and rubber boots, grabbed my gun belt, and put the dog on a line. In very short time the dog and I were tracking the bandit through the night. Saving the goose was out of the question. This wasn't a rescue mission. It was a recovery mission. Blinded with rage, I was determined the Boogey Beast would not get to enjoy the fruits of his night.

As we crested the bank on the other side of the canal, a skunk squinted into my flashlight beam. Screech. Not only was he not the Boogey Beast, we didn't want to invite a skunk to our little party, so the dog and I eased off and let him pass.

A moment later we were back on the trail. I followed the dog down the canal and into the forest where we continued for quite some time before he finally indicated that our suspect had gone to the trees. I shined the flashlight but couldn't see any eyes glowing through the thick canopy above us. I was still scanning the trees when my phone rang.

As was his custom, the Cowboy Cop often called me in the middle of the night on his drive home from work. He was expecting another groggy conversation with a woman who'd already been in bed for a few hours. He was not expecting full blown, certified crazy. Since I'm a firm believer in full disclosure, it was as good a time as any to let the man in on what to expect in a long term relationship with me and so I told him what I was doing at the moment. To say that he was stunned was a bit of an understatement. I make no apologies for my special brand of crazy or my commitment to it.

Although I couldn't give him an exact location, I assured the Cowboy Cop that if I walked east I would eventually hit a major roadway. He told me to walk east and wait for him. Sure enough, not long after the dog and I reached the pavement, the headlights to his police truck glided into view. If you're not sure a man is serious about a relationship, put on a gun belt and rubber boots, clip a tracking line onto a dog, and trail a bobcat through the forest at 2 a.m. to retrieve the dead body of a goose. That kinda shit separates the real men from those kicking the tires.

I cannot help but wonder how many other people were moved to raise Bourbon Red turkeys after reading Barbara Kingsolver's book, *Animal, Vegetable, Miracle*, but Dear Friend Kaye and I had taken the plunge shortly after reading and re-reading it. This is not a book to be read once and then passed to a friend. No. It is a classic that has earned a permanent spot on the bookshelf. But I caution you, it will lead to raising vegetables, chickens, and turkeys. That said, shortly after reading the book, I convinced my mother to raise turkey poults from chicks to a size where I could move them in with my adult chickens. My long-suffering, but bird-loving, mother agreed and in short time I had a dozen young turkeys running in a flight pen with my chickens.

Each morning I fed the horses and goats and then hiked to the bird pen to admire my future holiday dinners. They were personable enough creatures, not as loveable as baby geese but then few things are. Geese are pretty intelligent, and domestic turkeys are not. My Dear Friend Kaye will argue this point.

It is good that I found them not quite as endearing because I have the most remarkable ability to make a pet out of pretty much anything and one shouldn't make a pet out of one's food. My interest in the turkeys was to provide the best quality of life I could for them until they were butchered. In essence, they would only have one bad day. In their case however, it was one bad night.

At daybreak I assessed the carnage in stunned silence. The bodies of eleven large turkeys were strewn all over the flight pen. Most were not even eaten. It was just a senseless Boogey Beast killing spree. These birds that had grown from spring to fall had all been wasted in a single night. There was one lone survivor. A single, shell-shocked, half-grown red turkey had survived. The Cowboy Cop and I made the decision to move this bird, along with my three remaining geese, to his farm. Score another one for the Boogey Beast.

If you live in the world of forensics, your definition of love may be skewed slightly more than a bubble past normal plumb. Because our shifts overlapped it was common for the Cowboy Cop and me to have a hurried dinner between calls. If I was working a call, he would often wait until I was finished and then meet me when I tagged my evidence at the Property Room. From there we could go eat together.

And so it was that I was standing at the Property Room counter with a pistol which had just been used in a suicide. The gun was found between the pillows and was soaked with warm blood. Normally a bloody item is not tagged in plastic but in this case we had used a clear plastic bag to transport the firearm safely to the Property Room where it could be properly processed and tagged. Because the gun had been completely submerged in the victim's blood there was little point in attempting to swab the firearm for DNA.

At that time, to properly tag a semi-automatic firearm, a plastic zip-tie was inserted which locked the slide opened thus allowing anyone to know at a glance that the firearm was safe. It's physically impossible for one person to pull the slide back on a bloody gun, and insert and lock a zip tie, without making a mess. This is an easy job for two people however. One person uses two gloved hands to lock back the slide while the other person uses two gloved hands to insert the zip-tie. Easy peasy.

In my defense, it's not like I asked for help at the local McDonald's counter. One would expect that a man working the Property Room counter at the police department of the 4th largest city in the country would have seen many things, each with its own story attached, and as such, would have been reasonably desensitized to all but the completely absurd. Such was not the case.

The young man at the counter visibly paled when I lifted the plastic bag containing the gun and explained that I'd need his help to properly get it zip-tied and placed in an appropriate cardboard gun box. It was a chilly night and the blood oozing from the crevices of the firearm had created a warm steam condensation on the sides of the bag's interior. He backed away from the counter and told me in no uncertain terms that even with gloves, he would not be touching that gun.

My head tilted like the RCA puppy listening to his master's voice in the phonograph. Really? It was a simple enough task and using gloves, he wouldn't even touch the blood. Negative, Ghost Rider, it wasn't gonna happen. The

Cowboy Cop was standing at the other end of the counter waiting for me to finish so we could go eat and was watching all this with wry amusement.

Like me, he was dumbfounded by the man's behavior. Again, this wasn't a complicated order at Burger King where you can have it your way. This was the Property Room of the 4th largest city in the country. Part of the man's job was packaging up evidence. We didn't get to pick and choose what we tagged. Nonetheless, he stood back from the counter, lest the bloody gun leap out of its bag and give him cooties.

The problem was solved when the Cowboy Cop swore at the guy with a taunt normally reserved for football team locker rooms, reached into the box on the counter, pulled out a pair of blue gloves and put them on his own hands. I reached down, gingerly lifted the gun, and tilted the barrel toward the bottom of the bag. A tiny crimson stream of blood dribbled out of the barrel. The young man behind the counter turned a lovely shade of green. After I locked the slide back, the Cowboy Cop inserted the zip-tie and locked it in place. We then put the pistol in a cardboard firearms box, sealed it, and plastered biohazard stickers on the outside. Then we peeled our gloves off and dropped them in the trashcan. Done. That easy.

There was a moment, as I was standing at the counter with a bloody gun dripping into a plastic bag, watching a man put on gloves to help me, that I saw the face of love. Either that, or it was the face of a hungry man in a hurry to get to a restaurant before it closed.

I stood in the cold rain wondering whether or not I'd kill the overzealous Homicide investigator before his partner did. There is a difference between a thorough investigation and the just plain stupidity that comes from inexperience and arrogance. This young man was cursed with a heavy dose of both and was bent on flexing his muscles to show the world that he was now a Homicide Investigator. Like on TV.

No one cared. Really. No one. Everyone on the scene had something they'd rather be doing than standing in the rain on Valentine's Night. Even the dead guy. He wasn't standing but I think it's safe to say that he would have opted to be somewhere else too. In a sense, we were all homicide investigators, doing different jobs but going the same direction, like cogs on a wheel. There was no need for anyone to get on a high horse. There are power trips, and then there are power expeditions, and this young man had his bags packed on the power train and was chugging like a locomotive over everyone on the scene. That left the rest of us, and his unwilling partner, to juggle the herculean tasks of processing one murder while not committing another.

I'd already processed the physical scene and had my evidence packed up in the truck, but I couldn't leave the location because another member of the murder investigation team was training and was taking an agonizingly long time to do her part. Not her fault. We were all there once. We couldn't help her. All we could do was be patient. The steak dinner that Cowboy Cop had planned for us had long since become a cold, empty plate anyway, but to save myself some jail time, I phoned Fergus from the safe darkness of my truck to vent.

Crime Scene Investigators are definitely square pegs in a round hole world and only another square peg can understand the frustrations of missing a steak dinner on Valentine's Day because you are standing in the rain over yet one more dead man while a megalomaniac rampages through your murder scene. He listened to me rant and rave about dead men and soon to be dead men, and as I was floundering and splashing in my pity party pond, Fergus tossed me a floating orange ring with a rescue rope.

He offered to come out and finish supervising the completion of the scene while I went back to the office to process my evidence.

The clouds parted and the angels sang the Hallelujah Chorus. God bless him. I missed out on my date night dinner but it didn't matter because Valentine's Day comes and goes, but Square Peg Friends who voluntarily wade into the Chaos Creek for you are better than any steak.

If asked, I'm sure Fergus would report that he did not respond out of pity but rather knew that if I were jailed for murdering the Overzealous Investigator, the unit would be short-staffed, thus resulting in more work for everyone else, so in the long run, he did it in his own self-interest. That's what Fergus would say.

My drug of choice was, and still is, caffeine. When I can't get coffee, a Dr Pepper will do in a pinch, and this, in time, morphed into its own vice. I suppose it started on a hot day at work, when I was feeling the siren call for caffeine but also needed the emotional security blanket of chocolate. Calories are null and void in the face of decay and maggots, hoarders and cockroaches. This gave rise to a new addiction — a Dr Pepper and a Butterfinger. It became so common to reward myself with this pair that upon arrival at a particularly nasty scene, the medical examiner's investigator would state, "This is a Dr Pepper and a Butterfinger call." No further description was needed.

Because the fire department in our city has a highly trained arson investigation team, there was little for me to do but stand in the smoking devastation and stare in horror. A gas line exploded, setting the house on fire. The young man next door heard her screams and rushed to help, but he couldn't get to the crippled old woman before her own oxygen tank exploded.

Like the rest of us who walked through the charred

remains, the young man will be scarred forever. With a heavy sigh, I photographed the creature curled in the ashes at my feet and cursed the unfairness of it all. Life is not supposed to end that way. She should have died peacefully, surrounded by grandchildren and great-grandchildren. Death should respect age and be more polite, creeping up with an inviting, outstretched hand, not blowing in like a hurricane to snatch her with violent cruelty. Death can be such a bastard.

I was shaken out of my pity party by the vibration of a cell phone. The Cowboy Cop was checking. I talked to him as I watched the sweat-soaked, sooty firemen continue to wet down the remains of what had once been a home, what had once been a life. An hour later, I turned my back on the injustice of life and death and drove to a convenience store, where the Cowboy Cop was waiting — with a Dr Pepper and a Butterfinger.

The beam of my flashlight highlighted the maggot as it crawled in and out of his ear. My first thought was "I need some effing caffeine." Pardon my French. That's CopSpeak, placing great emphasis on my need for caffeine at the very moment the maggot inchwormed out of his ear and back in again. While flies slow down at night, the maggots are busy little creatures and continue their bustling activity despite the hour.

There was a lamp on in the bedroom and the flies were beginning to rouse themselves and head for the light. There was, in fact, so much buzzing in the bedroom that I started to search for another body. Nope. No body. Just flies dancing around a single light bulb. My hair was tucked underneath a ball cap. I didn't want flies landing in it. There was a decomposing man in the hallway so I know where their little feet had been.

I flashlighted my way back to the body. He hadn't gone

anywhere. They never do. I avoided staring at the maggots as they marched from his mouth to his nose and back. It wasn't something I wanted to dwell on at the moment. Grandpa was wearing a Marine ball cap. Judging from the old photos on the wall, he wasn't wearing the hat to make a statement. Grandpa appeared to have been in the military. For some reason this saddened me. No veteran should die alone and be eaten by maggots. Even as my mind touched on that thought it flitted away to safer territory. Back to business. We needed to get Grandpa loaded up.

The body car team arrived. We moved furniture to allow easier access for the gurney. They laid out a heavy plastic stretcher. We borrowed some paper towels from the kitchen. Grandpa won't need them. Wrapping the paper towels around his wrists and ankles, they hauled him onto the waiting stretcher. His skin sloughed off underneath the paper towels. A layer of flesh stayed with the carpet. Disturbed, the maggots were furiously motoring around his face like commuters at rush hour. I snapped pictures and pretended I was somewhere else. As the body bag was zipped up, I stared at the photos on the wall. I really needed some freaking caffeine.

The doors slammed shut on the van and I eased behind the body car as it rolled out of the parking lot. They were headed to another dead man. I was headed to a 24 Hour convenience store. Maybe I should cut back on the amount of caffeine. Then again, maybe not. Not as long as I was still at work long after the end of my shift. Not as long as old men die alone. I tipped back my cup and let the caffeine slide into my veins as I looked out over the cloudy moonlit skyline. Semper Fi, Grandpa. Semper Fi.

CHAPTER 8

THE TROUBLE WITH FARMS

Like cocaine, farms have a way of taking over your life. Slowly but surely, all your time, money, and even your family, get sucked into the farm. It starts slowly, just like a drug addiction. Horses are marijuana, the gateway drug. They pave the way for property, barns, and fencing. But horses can lead to more dangerous vices — like goats. Goats are cocaine. Goats take over. I could buy a young goat for $40, graze him out for a year, and sell the same goat for $140. That's what got me into the goat business and it wasn't too long before I was looking for a farm name.

What's in a name? My farm name needed to be something that represented my little piece of property, my tiny chocolate chip in the cookie of this county. Over my back gate was a carved stone sign which read, "Failte."

It was a Gaelic welcome sign. The sign hung on an arched trellis which spread over the wooden gate. Fragrant jasmine cascaded from the top down either side. The Failte sign peeked from around the jasmine foliage. This gate was the perfect representation for my farm. Thus, Failte Gate Farm was born.

I had a full-time paycheck-making job but I enjoyed

ranching and it spoke to my soul in a way that straddling dead men did not, so I slowly began building up a herd of Spanish/Boer cross goats. While raising goats might speak to the soul, it also gives rise to whole level of cursing I didn't know was possible. When you have a farm, any time the phone rings be afraid, be very afraid.

"One of your goats is out! Another one has her head caught in the fence!"

I looked down at the dead guy at my feet. Which was the bigger emergency? Since clearly the dead guy wasn't going anywhere, I tried to coach my mother through goat extraction techniques. This is much like the flight tower trying to talk a hysterical passenger through ways to safely land an aircraft. It wasn't pretty. There was a lot of grunting and heavy breathing. Mom, not the goat. Finally, the goat was free and bounded off to join her companions. Now it was time to address the other problem, the loose goat.

I tend to pace when I'm on the phone. Deep in thought about life choices and goats, I paced as I talked with my mother. From time to time, I rounded a piece of furniture only to be startled by the dead guy on the floor. He should not have surprised me since there was only one dead guy and he wasn't exactly hiding behind the furniture playing peek-a-boo.

Back in the flight tower, I was talking my mother through the steps of coaxing goats with a bucket of grain. First she had to remove the dogs from the back yard. Check. She could do that. No problem. She returned to the goats. There was a big problem. All the goats were running loose in two separate pastures.

It is never wise to lure goats with oats when hungry horses are also in the same pasture. The problem was way too big for my mother to handle so I advised her to keep an eye on the goats while I called the Cowboy Cop.

He was less than enthusiastic about driving back over to my house to deal with goats, but agreed that Mother was in way over her head. As I called Mom to inform her that he was on his way, I paced. And almost stepped on the dead guy again.

Confident that Cowboy Cop was at the helm, I could now address Dead Guy. (He didn't talk much.) The phone rang. Cowboy Cop. He shook a feed bucket and the goats followed him. I thanked him profusely and went back to Dead Guy. It was okay. We had plenty of time, Dead Guy and I. And Dead Guy was patient. Dead Guy didn't have goats.

On the eighth day God created Border Collies. Or so Border Collie enthusiasts would have us believe. I trained sport dogs and working dogs for most of my adult life. Sometime in the 1990s a friend told me, "Sooner or later, you'll break down and get a Border Collie. Anyone who is serious about competition does."

The problem was that I wasn't serious enough about any kind of competition to buy a dog just to win. Then I discovered goats. Goats are like cocaine. They take over your life and turn it upside down. What started out as a way to weed-eat my fence lines had grown into a business. On paper the $100 profit on each goat sounded good, but it is a sad fact of life that raising goats could make Mother Teresa cuss like a sailor.

I needed help. On The Eighth Day God Created Border Collies. Those words are golden to anyone who has ever tried to work livestock by themselves. I needed help. I needed a Border Collie. I found Lily in a feedlot in North Texas. Her parents were working cattle dogs. I picked her out, pulled the ticks off her, and proudly drove home with my first Border Collie.

On my farm, if the small livestock wasn't locked up at

night, it was eaten by the Boogey Beast. Lily was really too young to be started on livestock yet but she naturally took to the job and unfortunately many times I had to ask a first grader to do college work. We were learning together. It wasn't about shows, or trials, or titles. It was about coyotes and bobcats. If my chickens and goats were not locked up before dark, the Boogey Beast would come to an All-You-Can-Eat-Buffet.

Torrential rains had returned. Dry pastures were flooded. Lily and her goats were about the same age. None of them had experienced heavy rains and flooding before. Spring rains had arrived. The heavens opened up and in a very short time the pen with the young females was under eight inches of water. Three inches of water filled their little barn. The goats were standing on a shelf. I had to move the females into another pen on the far side of the property — three paddocks away. It was getting dark and it was still raining.

At first I tried the practical approach. Open the door. Call the goats with some feed. That didn't work. They hollered back at me but had no intention of wading through floodwater to come to higher ground. Goats are very much like cats and oil. They don't mix well with water.

"Don't make me get the Border Collie!" I shouted.

Apparently they didn't believe me.

The Border Collie was only too happy to oblige. Lily stalked inside. The goats hustled out into the rain. Thus we began the laborious trek to the south side of the property, to higher ground. The young Border Collie was forced to push grumpy goats across high water. By then it was so dark that I could only see the goats that were white and the white tip of Lily's tail.

We were doing well until the little beasts squeezed through the wrong gate and ended up in the stallion paddock. The dog could have stopped them but I called her off because I didn't want her running goats over the stallion. The goats crowded into the stallion's stall. Stallion moved to accommodate them and then crowded in behind the goats. The stall was flooding. I tried to get the goats out of the stall by myself. It wasn't happening. There was no way were they going back out in that rain.

"Don't make me get the Border Collie!"

Again, they were not convinced. I held Stallion while I asked the Border Collie to move in. The moment she slithered along the wall like a shadow, the goats filed back out in the rain like obedient school children. Stallion stood in the corner, wondering what just happened. Did this count as a home invasion?

The small drainage creek in the pasture had become a raging current. Lily had to convince the goats to jump the water. By this time I hated goats and didn't care if the coyotes did eat them but the young Border Collie had more confidence. In short order, she got all the goats over the creek and headed to the south pen. Lightning flashed and thunder clapped. It was raining harder. I could barely see the dog.

By the time I got there, Lily had all the goats in a cluster beside the gate. She held them while I opened the latch. My next problem was making sure that none of the young male goats inside the pen ran out while the dog moved the young females into the pen. I called her over. She glared in the pen at the other goats. They fell over themselves to back away from the gate. Then Lily made a quick circle and picked up the females who were already sneaking off in the rain. I closed the gate. The dog stood in the rain and shook herself. I plopped on my knees and hugged her. We high-fived. Lily was quite pleased with herself.

In a perfect world, a dog her age would never have to do what she did, but that night I was so thankful for the generations of shepherds who bred a dog to go out in the rain, and get the job done.

A good friend of mine always says, "You can take the girl out of the country, but you can't take the country out of the girl." That's true, but sometimes, just sometimes, I'd like to look a bit more like *Sex and the City* and less like *The Hobbit.*

At work I dressed in a military uniform with military boots. At home I was either wearing cowboy boots or flip-flops. So one day after forcing the Cowboy Cop to watch two hours of *Sex and the City*, I decided to have a Girl Moment and get my nails done. *"I am Woman! Hear me roar!"*

Or at least let me step into a world with Jimmy Choo shoes and Louis Vuitton purses and feel like a girl. (Disclaimer: In reality I wouldn't know a Jimmy Choo shoe from a Payless shoe without the price tag. Ask me about Justin boots.)

Even if just for a few hours, I was determined to slip into a world of pink frills and polka dots on something other than a goat's belly. So I scrubbed my feet. I shaved my legs. And then I scrubbed my little Hobbit feet some more and washed my flip-flops. I grabbed a good book, climbed into my truck and headed for the local nail salon.

I walked in. Picked my color. Sat back in the chair with the Magic Fingers. Slipped my Hobbit Feet into the bubbling tub of warm water and relaxed. The Very Sweet Salon Girl took one look at my Hobbit Feet and asked,

"You want sea salt scrub? You want hot wax?"

I was perplexed. Did I want this? Heck, I didn't know.

"What's it do?"

"Dry feet. Make soft."

"How much?"

"Ten dolla"

The magic fingers of the chair pushed into my back and

prodded me to spend the extra money. The Sex and the City Girl on one shoulder whispered, "What's ten more dollars?"

The Hobbit Girl on my other shoulder whispered "The price of a bag of goat chow."

The Sex and the City Girl won. "Okay, do it."

I lost myself in a good book while The Nail Goddess transformed my little hobbit feet into something you could take out in public. By the time she finished with my hands, my toes were dry enough for her to paint on little flowers. I was in Sex and the City Heaven . . . until . . .

The Nail Goddess picked up one flip-flop and carefully slipped it on my foot, onto her work of art. A tiny warning bell sounded in my head. I know that bell. It is the chime of clock. Sure enough, as she knelt beside me, slipping the next shoe on Cinderella, the clock struck midnight, and The Sex and the City Cinderella was transformed back into Goaterella, The Little Hobbit. As the bell chimed, I saw a tiny piece of hay sticking out from underneath my shoe, and I knew. I knew what was on the sole of my flip-flop.

Oh. My. Gosh! Cocoa puffs — little round pellets of goat poop, were stuck to the bottom of my flip-flop. Although I had scrubbed my shoes, I had failed to take into account that I still had to walk through the yard to climb into my truck — a yard that goats walk through every single day.

It was well that I enjoyed my dusty rose toes because it would be another six to nine months before I had the courage to step into a nail salon, and then I chose a different salon.

More and more my happy place had become the farm and the Border Collie was the right hand that I needed. While the other dogs were willing, it was clear the Border Collie had been bred for the job and so she soon shouldered the bulk of the work. Since I knew nothing about training a herding dog, we were just scratching the surface of what Lily could be under the tutelage of someone who actually knew what they were doing. Thus I enlisted the aid of an old friend of mine who had become a professional herding dog trainer. She was the Sheep Goddess, the Wizard who led me down the yellow brick road to the next level of addiction.

Lily and I began taking herding lessons using Dorper Sheep, a South African breed of meat sheep known for shedding their wool. These sheep proved to be superior in many ways. They were much easier to handle than my meat goats, and pound for pound, they could go from birth to market much faster, so it just made sense to add some sheep. I soon bought five pregnant Dorper ewes from the Sheep Goddess and added them to my herd of meat goats. In very short order they out-performed the goats and although I continued to raise goats, I switched my primary focus to raising Dorper sheep.

If raising sheep and goats didn't do it, my relationship with the Cowboy Cop put me on the fast track to becoming a rancher. My first calving season was quite educational. Pulling a calf out of a straining cow is not exactly what I imagined it to be, but when you live on a farm, the best adventures always begin at home. The Cowboy Cop had become the Other Half, and we'd gotten serious enough to start living together while bouncing back and forth between both farms. After joining households with the Cowboy Cop, I had not only acquired additional dogs, horses, and a couple of donkeys, I was also responsible for cattle. Until this night the closest I had been to the actual insides of a cow was the meat aisle at Kroger's.

Raising horses and reading James Herriot's veterinary adventure books does not prepare you for actually sticking your hand inside the back end of a cow in labor. A definite necessity around a ranch is a neighbor who also raises cattle and since the Kindly Rancher Neighbor had a regular day job, it worked out perfectly for us because he could check on any problems when we were at work.

We had a pregnant cow about to pop. The neighbor looked in on her about 10:30 p.m. All was well. I got home from work and checked her about 12:30 p.m. All was definitely not well then. Something unidentifiable was hanging out of Cow-About-To-Pop. Since I lack a veterinary degree that gifts me with fancy words to describe her condition, let's just say, she appeared to be blowing a gigantic bubble from her butt.

Shouldn't there be feet in that bubble bag? I phoned the Other Half to voice my concerns but he was at that moment dealing with two prisoners who had chosen to fight so he advised me to call the neighbor. Kindly Rancher Neighbor had left his cell phone in another room and was sound asleep. I checked the cow again. Big Bubble Butt. No baby. She did not look happy.

Other Half phoned. He was okay and had two prisoners with multiple charges on them. I first became concerned when he started giving me instructions for how to pull a calf out of cow. This was not an experience on my bucket list. While I was staring at the cow, trying to imagine how this would play out, a strange man appeared in the darkness and scared the crap out of me. It wasn't the neighbor, but it was the next best thing.

Other Half had called his son and the young man had just arrived to help me. Most excellent! Unfortunately Son and I had herded cows, penned cows, doctored cows, and cussed cows, but neither of us had ever forcibly removed a calf from a cow's ass. Definitely uncharted territory.

Son looked at the back end of Cow and announced that he hated his father. This was not on his bucket list either. Despite her efforts to push out the calf, the Big Bubble was about the same size. Other Half called for an update. He informed us that we were on speaker phone and he was in the District Attorney's office so we couldn't cuss. This seriously limited our conversation.

Son announced this sport was out of our league. He mounted a 4-wheeler and rode over to Neighbor's house to wake him up. I stood with the cow. The rest of the herd had gathered around to watch. One cow mooed her encouragement, or perhaps it was sympathy. My Cow-Speak is a bit limited. Son returned. He didn't get a chance to wake up Neighbor because of a rather large, nasty Blue Heeler Dog on the front porch. That made perfect sense but didn't help us any.

Other Half phoned for an update. I cannot help but wonder what the other people in the District Attorney's office thought of a man trying to coach two idiots through labor and delivery of a stuck calf. Other Half gave us a grocery list of items to collect around the house and ordered us to call Neighbor's father for help since he was also a rancher. He did not tell us that Neighbor's father is a Grumpy Old Man who doesn't appreciate phone calls at 2 a.m. In hindsight, who does? After Son got off the phone, he informed me, yet again, that he hated his father. Grumpy Old Man had agreed to call Neighbor though. Maybe. Son wasn't sure. It was a short conversation.

Son and I collected ropes, towels, and soap. There was a knock on front door. I hit myself in the head with the door as I flung it open. Message received. Help had arrived.

We tromped out to the pasture to show Neighbor the problem. He looked at the cow for a moment and came to the same conclusion as Other Half, the calf must be pulled out with ropes. Although it was same news, Son and I were feeling better because even though situation was still bad, someone was now officially in charge. And it wasn't us.

The cow was already down, so Neighbor tied her back

legs together. Then he started poking and palpating the bubble. A tongue popped out. And maybe a foot. Neighbor started to feel around inside to sort legs. Shouldn't he take off his wedding ring? He could lose it inside the cow, right? He allowed as how this might be a very good idea. I was happy to be able to contribute something to this little adventure. With the wedding ring properly secured, Neighbor plunged a hand into Cow's butt and found a nose! And a tongue. A very, large Gene Simmons/KISS tongue. The tongue moved! The baby was still alive!

Neighbor then started talking us through the steps we need to take. In essence, we had to tie ropes around the front feet and pull the calf out. This was a problem. Big calf. Small opening.

Since Neighbor was unhappy with our choices of rope, (2 lariats and the rope from a boat anchor), he went home to get a more appropriate Calf Pulling Rope. I was given instructions to keep the skin pulled back so the calf could breathe. You have not lived until you've been assigned this task. It wasn't on my bucket list either. This was a job easier said than done. The feet kept pushing in front of the nose. I wasn't the one stuck in the cow but claustrophobia was closing in on me fast.

Just as I was checking the Gene Simmons tongue again, a ninja in black police tactical gear stepped out of the darkness. Other Half. He took his gun belt off and set it beside the fence just as the neighbor was taking off his coat. Pushing my sleeves up, I was still trying to keep my coat on, but it was hard to keep the cow shit and blood off my new Carhartt jacket. Neighbor and Other Half found the front feet and tied ropes around them. My job was to keep the nose up front so the calf could breathe. Son had a halter on the straining cow and was helping her balance as Other Half and Neighbor slowly pulled out a gigantic calf.

The calf slid out and to my astonishment, without saying

a word to each other, Other Half and Neighbor grabbed up his legs and started swinging him back and forth. Two grown men were swinging a 90 pound bull calf like boys on a playground. This begged for an explanation.

"To remove fluid from his lungs."

Well, that made sense. They set the calf down beside his momma and she started to lick him. Other Half and Neighbor were smeared with cow shit, blood, and goo. It was 3 a.m.

Hours later I watched the calf flicking his ears in the morning sun and thought about cowboys. Real cowboys. Being a real cowboy isn't about rodeo games. It isn't about the truck a man drives, the clothes he wears, or the brand of tobacco he chews. Being a real cowboy is about blood and cow shit. It's about coming over at 2 a.m. to help a neighbor pull a calf. It's about swinging calves in the moonlight.

Some days are like an angry goose. It's just best to retreat. It was shortly after 9 a.m. I had already killed two of my animals.

The Border Collie crawled in bed to announce that the sun was up and we had chores to do. I checked a yearling ewe lamb that had become partially paralyzed the day before. It appeared that she and one of the horses had collided and she'd come out on the short end. I'd given her some time to recover but she took a turn for the worse overnight. The consensus seemed to be a back injury but without very expensive tests we couldn't be sure. Although I was sorely tempted to whisk her to the veterinary university, I knew better. The farm couldn't afford it and I had other animals to consider. I could spend thousands of dollars on the lamb and still lose her. As heartbreaking as it was, I had to save that money for the care of the other animals.

I made the unhappy decision to put her down after chores and then went to feed the rest of the farm. I was mulling over the unfairness of farm life when all hell broke loose in the back yard.

The Cowboy Cop had a half-grown Blue Heeler pup which stayed at my house most of the time, and on this morning, he'd discovered a trespassing chicken. I had gotten bold enough to try chickens again and somehow one of my hens managed to get out of the chicken pen, cross a pasture, and climb into the back yard. With a Blue Heeler. It was ugly. I descended upon the Blue Heeler in a rage. Ranger had the good sense to release the bird and not suggest Anger Management Classes for me.

The only thing worse than a dead chicken is a disemboweled bird that is still walking around the barnyard. I come from a long line of women who can kill a chicken, and I'd heard stories about my grandmother wringing necks for the stewpot, but I'd never done it myself. This sounds easier than it is. Chickens are hardier than they appear.

First I had to catch the bird. Although one would expect that a bird with its guts hanging out would be easy to catch, such was not the case. When I finally got her, I grasped her neck firmly behind the head, hoisted her weighty body in the air with a swing, slung in a hard circle and then sat the bird back down. I was expecting a dead chicken. I was not expecting her to look at me and say, "What the *@#$ are you doing?"

Desperate, I swung the poor bird multiple times in an effort to put her out of her misery. By the end of it, the chicken was dead, I was a hysterical screaming mess, and the Blue Heeler pup swore off chicken killing for the rest of his life. After it was over, I sank into the cold mud and sobbed. Then I put my big girl panties on and went to get the rifle to shoot the lamb.

I spent an hour in the pasture digging the hole in the sucking mud. Each shovel of mud had to be scraped off with a boot. Once the hole was large enough for a year old ewe lamb, I walked way back to the barn and hoisted the crippled sheep into a garden cart. Careful not to tip her into the mud, with one hand pulling the cart and the other clutching a rifle, I began the long, slow journey to the back pasture.

At the gravesite I lowered the ewe gently into the ground, carefully placed the end of the barrel against her forehead, and pulled the trigger. Click.

She blinked at me. I yanked the rifle up and peeked. For some reason unknown to me, the Cowboy Cop had unloaded my gun. The sheep then witnessed the dichotomy of the human female rage as I exploded into both sobbing and cussing. Who unloads someone else's gun? The poor lamb had to lie in her muddy grave while I marched back to the house and returned with a 9 mm pistol. I apologized to the sheep, wished her a good journey, and pulled the trigger on a gun I knew was loaded.

My day began with dead chickens. Well, actually it was only one dead chicken, with visions of many more to come. A canal ran along the entire south side of my property. This canal was a Predator Superhighway and the main reason why all small livestock had to be locked up when the sun went down and the Zombie Wars began.

My bird pen was also on the south side of the property, right along the canal. It was about a 1/4 of an acre, covered in bird netting on the top, field fencing on the sides, and a short sheet of tin along the ground. The chicken coop was a metal/wood building enclosed on three sides. The fourth side had field fencing covered with bird netting. There was a wooden door and a piece of heavy welded wire cattle panel across the wooden door, like burglar bars. With this arrangement the chickens could put themselves up at night when I had to leave the house before dark. Anyone caught outside the henhouse after dark was in danger. Or dead.

This set-up had worked — until that night. My first clue was the pile of feathers beside the chicken coop door. The Boogey Beast had managed to get inside the main pen and slip up to the chicken coop where it then grabbed a chicken that was sleeping against the wire. Although the Beast wasn't able to pull the whole bird through the coop wire, the hen was killed and eaten as far up as the Beast could pull her through.

I wish I had a $100 bill for every dead chicken I've had to pick up over the years. Needless to say, there were no eggs that day and none of the birds wanted to walk past the scene of the attack to get out of the coop that morning. I'm sure it was a bit traumatic to watch your girlfriend get eaten. It was time to seriously consider the idea of getting a Livestock Guardian Dog.

The Sheep Goddess had four of these Big White Dogs to protect her farm. I'd seen them chase off a coyote and was immensely impressed with the intimidation power these dogs provided. I just wasn't quite sure my farm needed another dog. Still, it started the idea percolating in my head.

The Other Half set up a game camera in the coop and it was determined that, in this case, our Boogey Beast was a raccoon or perhaps a family of raccoons. Despite my best attempts to fortify and re-fortify the coop, every morning I still rose to find the Beast had visited during the night. The coop looked like chickens exploded, leaving scattered pieces of birds everywhere and shell-shocked survivors. I eventually moved the remaining birds to Other Half's farm. Dora the Explorer was one of the survivors.

At that time the Facebook game Farmville was all the rage. Because I had a real farm, there wasn't much time for computer games so I was dumbfounded when a friend said, "I just can't wait to get home at night so I can work on my Virtual Farm!"

What the hell is a Virtual Farm? She went to great lengths to explain that it was just like having a real farm, only on the computer.

"Are there virtual coyotes on the virtual farm?"

"Of course not," she said, "It's a VIRTUAL farm!"

This begged more questions. Apparently there were also no virtual raccoons. No virtual vet bills. Exactly how does one farm without virtual predators and virtual vet bills?

I bet there are also no virtual dead chickens on a virtual farm.

CHAPTER 9

A WARRIOR ARRIVES

If you pick up enough dead birds, eventually you'll get a Livestock Guardian Dog. I'm not sure exactly what the number is, but I'd finally reached it. If I had stopped to count all the animals I'd lost to the Boogey Beast over the years, a Livestock Guardian Dog would have paid for itself many times over. So when my sheep starting lambing it finally tipped the scale. One coyote raid could wipe me out completely. A Livestock Guardian Dog lives with the stock as part of the flock and protects them. I needed one of those dogs.

I bought a 12 week old white fuzzball over the telephone and drove across Texas to get her. The parents were working Livestock Guardian Dogs from a large sheep ranch. We were expecting to see a mother and perhaps a few cute pups, what we did not expect was the rancher to slip on heavy leather welding gloves to catch a feral Mowgli-child ball of fluff and hand her to me. Like a possum, the puppy showed me every tooth in her mouth before I hastily stuffed her into a dog crate. With the wild thing secure in the back, I drove the five hours home wondering what I'd done.

Since she was wild and had the small possibility of

drawing blood, I named her Briar. At every rest stop, each time I peeked into the crate, the pup snarled at me. Clearly bathroom breaks were not an option. Just drive fast.

It was dark when I hauled the dog crate into a sheep stall and opened the door. Dragging her belly across the wood shavings, the puppy crept across the stall. Heavy with the emotional exhaustion of a kidnapping/alien abduction the pup collapsed on a bed of hay, her nose touching the hoof of a lamb. The lamb pulled his foot back as if the dog were a nasty thing he'd stepped in. Using wire panels, I set up a temporary pen around the puppy so that she could be with the sheep and yet still be protected from them.

Back then the advice given out by many ranchers for training Livestock Guardian Dogs was to put the pups with the stock and pretty much abandon them, the idea being that the puppy would bond to the sheep and grow to protect them. In reality, this antiquated, hands-off approach leads to gigantic dogs that are unmanageable at best, and at worst, dangerous. I didn't know anything about training Livestock Guardian Dogs. I was winging it.

Although the ranch Briar came from was large enough to have Big White Dogs that couldn't be touched, mine was not. I needed to be able to handle this puppy, so my first order of business was taming her. She had raw hot spots under her matted coat so grooming was our first hurdle. For this adventure I enlisted the aid of Other Half's patrol dog, Xena.

Xena's kind and nurturing nature made her an obvious ambassador for bridging the gap between the wild puppy and our farm. Briar was too little and too wild to go with the sheep when they went out to pasture, so during the day she was locked in the barn where she could see them. Not only was the pup scared, she was also lonely.

Armed with a comb, a pair of scissors, and a gentle German Shepherd, I readied myself for a fight with the feral pup. Her body was a mass of untamed white, fluffy curls with a gray mask across her eyes which gave her an odd 'Caped Crusader' look that fit right in with her new role as my champion warrior in our ongoing battle with the Boogey Beast. But how exactly does one tame a warrior?

Her dark eyes darted around for an escape route as I stepped into the stall. Xena politely folded herself around my legs as she sought out the newest addition to the family. The stately German Shepherd stood over the masked ball of ragged fluff and gave her a thorough sniffing. Clearly in the eyes of a true solider, this new warrior pup didn't measure up as much of a fighter but was instead, in desperate need of a friend. The pup responded to Xena's olive branch with clear relief. Finally here was someone who spoke her language, someone who liked her. Within days the shepherd, who was one part Rin-Tin-Tin and one part Mary Poppins, helped me tame the pup to the point where I could catch her and she'd stay quiet for an uneasy grooming.

Although Xena was her friend, the sheep still barely tolerated the puppy who dearly wanted to be a part of the flock. The ewes didn't trust her and the lambs were much like children on a playground. Nobody wanted to hang out with the new kid on the block.

Each day I sat on a bucket in the pasture with my camera and watched as Briar lurked at the edge of the flock, wanting to belong. From time to time she'd wander up and lie down beside me. I'd ruffle her fluffy curls, smile into her masked face and assure her that one day she would grow to be a strong and mighty warrior and the ewes who were mean to her today would huddle behind her then. And she would make them feel safe. I also assured Briar the ram lambs that were mean to her today would end up in a freezer by next winter.

Such bedtime stories are of little consolation when you

are lonely, but soon a day would come when Briar could stand up on the playground and prove her worth.

I first spotted the little bastard in my camera lens as I sat on my bucket scanning the pasture for something of interest. He had that carefree gait of a gunslinger for hire as he moved behind the flock, and I might have missed him altogether if the pup at my side had not raised her head and growled. He had our attention as he continued on his path, confident that by reputation alone, no one would dare to interfere. He was wrong.

Briar eased herself up with a stalk which accelerated as she acquired target and flung forth like a loosed arrow. He stayed the course, placing faith in both his path and his name of ill repute. One of the ram lambs noticed him. Clearly this was more interesting than the weed he'd been nibbling, so the lamb moved toward the intruder. A second lamb noticed and was also moved to abandon his halfhearted attempts at foraging in favor of this new excitement. They approached the intruder with great interest.

In answer to their audacity, he darted at the first lamb in a mock attack. The second lamb stomped on him from the rear. Red Wooster squawked in rage and flew a few feet away before continuing his journey in another direction with a new bounce in his step. A third lamb galloped past and sent Wooster careening in yet another direction. He cackled his rage and hurled insults at their insolence. Didn't they know who he was? The entire neighborhood was afraid of him! Wooster's rage stopped him and for a moment the rooster stood in the pasture attempting to muster up his dignity and gather what was left of his somewhat dented reputation. He narrowed his beady little eyes and readied himself as the next lamb galloped forward.

He never saw the dog coming. Young David of the Playground struck the Goliath of the Neighborhood. For a moment it was fur and feathers. Then Goliath ran. Red Wooster ran as fast as his little drumsticks could carry him. The pup and the lambs played pinball across the pasture with the rooster and by the time the bird made it to the fence, Briar had become part of the gang.

Trying to juggle a farm job and a paycheck job was a constant struggle. Some days I was better at it than others. My success was directly proportional to the amount of sleep I got the night before. The problem with life on a farm is that regardless of what time I dragged in from work, the farm still woke up at 7 a.m.

Border Collie crawled across the bed to inform me that the sun was up and so was she. The goats started screaming, which invariably set off the sheep. This isn't a problem if you got to bed at midnight, but if you came in from work at 4 a.m., it's a problem.

An end-of-the-shift murder call had me getting in late that morning, and thus I'd only had about 4 hours of sleep when the farm woke. They were all bright-eyed and bushy-tailed. I was not. I was not even close. I staggered to the refrigerator for a bottle of Starbuck's Mocha Frappuccino. If they make frappuccinos illegal, I'm afraid you'd find me strung out in a crack motel somewhere, except they'd call them "frapp-motels," and dealers would smell of coffee and use code words like "grande" and "vente." But I digress.

I popped open a frapp and wobbled to the patio door to slide into rubber boots. It's hard to put on rubber boots while you're mainlining caffeine and as luck would have it, the cap of my frapp fell off and rolled under the couch. I try to keep the house swept but nevertheless, dog hair can accumulate under the couch. By the time I move the couch to sweep, you could make a poodle out of the hair trapped under there. The lid leaned and wobbled a bit as it disappeared into the cavern beneath the couch. I got down on my hands and knees and groped about in the darkness until my fingers touched it. The victory was short-lived. The lid had a layer of dog hair stuck to it. How many germs are in dog hair?

The question didn't concern me for too long. Someone who steps in blood for a living can't be too picky about a little dog hair. With that in mind, I wiped it off, slammed the lid back on my frapp, and tripped outside to tackle the day. I locked the main pack of dogs in a paddock to keep them out of the mud then staggered to the barn to release Briar and the sheep. As the sheep filed behind us Briar bounced up and down beside me. By then she was as solid as a cinder block with legs. She was built like an "excrement domicile."

It made my head hurt just watching Briar dance. Once in the pasture, I fed both the puppy and the sheep. She wagged her little tail and occasionally paused in her heifer-like snarfing to smile at me. I sat in a lawn chair and took a long slow sip of frappuccino. It should be against the law to be that happy in the morning.

Briar finished her breakfast and puttered off. The sheep hoovered down their food while I kept a watchful eye on Hulk, the biggest ram lamb, lest he choke again. Several days earlier Hulk was bolting food down so fast that the little booger started to choke and I was forced to do the Heimlich maneuver on a fat lamb. Although I'm a trained First Responder, I don't think the police department had lambs in mind when they taught the class. It must have worked however, because the little greedy pig lived. He can thank the Houston Police Department's Basic First Aid class for that.

I stood in the pasture, letting the caffeine slowly drip into my veins, wishing I was still in bed, when a black and white blur bounced past. It took a little effort to focus on the Bounce. The smallest lamb, Tiny Tim, was spring-bokking his way across the pasture. Like a little antelope, he leaped toward Briar. She was deep in thought with her nose crammed in a bush when he stopped in front of her. For a moment they stared at each other, then like a sewing machine, Tiny Tim started bouncing up and down in front of the dog. Briar's eyes lit up and the chase was on. The cinder block managed to get up considerable speed but Tim turned on the juice and kept just out of reach.

Tim was delighted. I was not. I didn't want Briar discovering that she was a meat-eater and sheep could be on the menu. Briar might begin to see lamb chops instead of her little snuggle-buddy. One could almost hear the *National Geographic* theme song playing in the pasture as Briar chased Tim.

It was time to end this. As the pair raced past me, I chunked a bucket at Briar's head. Bull's eye! She staggered a bit but then spied my leather gloves as they fell out of the bucket. Pennies from heaven! Briar loves chewing on gloves.

She abandoned Tiny Tim and snatched up a glove. With a jaunty air, she danced around to show me that although it was raining buckets, it was also raining leather gloves, and this was a Most Delightful Thing. Like Winnie-the-Pooh, Briar's world is pretty simple and it's easy to make her happy. I took another sip of frappuccino. Briar was probably right. When Life throws a bucket at you, don't get discouraged, your favorite leather gloves just might fall out of it.

The lifespan of a chicken on my farm was from birth until the first time it crossed paths with a coyote, a raccoon, a hawk, or a Blue Heeler. After the Great Boogey Beast War, we lost our hens to an enterprising raccoon.

That does not mean, however, that there were no chickens around. My mother had a small house on the east side of my farm and she raised a little flock of New Hampshire Reds. They were loose during the day and she rounded them up each evening to lock them in Fort Knox on her back porch. The birds had absolutely no concept of what was off limits to them. On that day Blue Heeler and Briar were in the back yard because the sheep were in lockdown to keep them off the pasture during a period of heavy rains. Briar was enjoying some off-duty yard time. This proved to be lucky for the chicken. Or unlucky for the chicken. It sort of depends upon how you view torture.

I came home to find chicken feathers all over the back porch. In my business, we call that "a clue," so I followed the trail of chicken feathers through the doggy door and into the laundry room. This was not the high point of my day.

Fortunately I didn't find a dead chicken lying beside the laundry basket. Thunderstorms were rolling through and it was raining harder than a cow pissin' on a flat rock so I didn't give the back yard more than a quick peek. There were no floating chicken bodies as far as I could see. I needed to get ready to leave for work. As I busied myself with getting ready, a stubborn little voice in my head nagged. These chickens were my mother's pets. I finally caved and called her. She "might" be missing a chicken. Nowhere will you find a more responsible Keeper of The Flock than my mother. So despite the fact that it was raining, my mother, in her muumuu, dutifully trucked out in the rain to hunt for the missing chicken. She splashed her way to my back porch and like Columbo, examined the crime scene. I've seen paid Homicide Detectives put less thought into a murder scene.

Alas, she couldn't find a body either. So she headed back home and I headed for the shower — until something caught my eye. When passing through the kitchen, I glanced out the window in time to see my Livestock Guardian Dog bounce in the corner of the Kitchen Garden. (I use that term loosely. At one time it was a Kitchen Garden. By then it was a fenced area containing the dead bodies of tomato plants, and some weeds.)

There was no mistaking the fact that Briar had something in the corner. My mother saw it too, and she headed through the opened garden gate to examine Briar's treasure. Sure enough, Briar had a live chicken. She'd been hugging and loving, and licking, and generally making that chicken's life a living hell. Briar was thrilled with the chicken and treated it much like an all-day sucker.

This might have explained why I was home for an hour and heard Briar and Blue Heeler get into two minor dog fights. My guess is Blue Heeler wanted to liberate Briar's chicken. (Mercy killing, perhaps?) There is no telling how long the poor bird had to endure Briar's love. She was Bugs Bunny's Abominable Snowman who grabbed up Daffy Duck in a bear hug and began to stroke him roughly while chanting, "I will name him George, and I will hug him and pet him and squeeze him . . . ."

"George" survived her ordeal but was more cautious about walking through my back yard after that.

Webster defines stupidity as the state of being foolish or unintelligent. Their listed example is moving a Belgian Malinois onto a sheep farm. Not really, but it could be. In our defense, the arrival of Oli wasn't planned. Xena was having a harder time leaping into the patrol truck and it was soon obvious that retirement was the only option. Oli was her replacement as the Cowboy Cop's new patrol dog.

Oli was the opposite of Xena in every way. While Xena was a stately, classic example of a German Shepherd, Oli was a tiny, tawny psychotic, always in motion, Belgian

Malinois. Xena looked like a cop. Oli looked like a crackhead. Xena was gifted with a heavy dose of common sense and could actually be trusted loose on a farm. Oli was a Predator Deluxe who woke up in the morning and said to herself, "What small creature can I kill today?"

We didn't quite understand the height of her prey drive until the morning she pulled log after log of stacked firewood away from a fence in order to gain access into the isolation pen with new sheep. If you insert a Malinois into a pen of sheep, you have the recipe for chaos.

I'm not sure if he was alerting us to murder, or cheering Oli's plays like a spectator at a football game, but Blue Heeler's frantic barking brought us outside before she could kill the whole lot of them. As it was we only had two victims with major injuries. Roanie, a brown speckled ewe, was standing in the center of the pen with her back to a pecan tree. She was amazingly calm despite grievous injuries. Jamaica, a large spotted ewe with long shaggy dreadlocks, was found backed into a corner hiding behind one of the horses.

A farm knows when you have some free time and will find a way to eat it up. Other Half and I were both on vacation and earlier I actually had the gall to wonder out loud what our plans for that day would be. As it was Oli had our day already mapped out. Large chunks of flesh had been ripped from their hindquarters and both sheep had right hind legs which dangled at their sides. Although we were certain they'd die of shock, we treated the sheep as if they'd survive. On a farm it ain't over 'til they're in the ground.

First we gathered vet supplies. Then we called Dear Friend Kaye who was the vet's wife. Sewing up sheep was definitely a three person job. That's another thing about farms — they will not only suck up your free time but that of your friends as well.

Good friends know this and so with a sense of humor and a strong stomach, she joined us for that day's farm adventure. Other Half had stitched up cows, horses, and dogs, but he hadn't stitched up sheep before and so there was a great deal of discussion (argument) about whether or not to use sutures or the new staple gun that he was just dying to try out. I voted for tried and true sutures. He wanted to play with his new staple gun. We called Vet for advice. Other Half was delighted to hear a vote for his new gun.

We compromised. He used sutures on part and stapled part. Vet's Wife and I held the sheep while he stitched and tried to repair the hamburger that used to be a hind leg. It was slow work. Soon we were smeared with blood, betadine, and sheep poop.

Most farmers will tell you that sheep are born looking for a place to die. Turning a police dog in with them tends to speed up the process though. By the time Vet-With-An-Actual-Diploma arrived, Cow-Man-with-Vet-Skills and two Vet Wanna-Be-Assistants had stitched up the patients. Vet admired the stitch job while Other Half preened.

Thus began the uphill journey for Jamaica and Roanie.

"If your time hasn't come,
not even a doctor can kill you."
Meyer A. Perlstein

We stitched up the damage and shot them up daily with penicillin and banamine. Jamaica's injuries were not as severe as Roanie's but in both cases you could see daylight through their back legs. Oli had grabbed each sheep by the leg and shook. Since a police dog ain't a poodle, the result wasn't pretty. Jamaica was unlucky enough to have ear tag #13. Dear-Friend-Who-Is-Vet's-Wife-And- Who-Was-Helping-Me-Keep-#13-Alive gave all sheep and goat breeders this advice: "Ear tags should be like elevator floors. You should just skip #13."

Jamaica was beginning to remind me of the poster of the one-eyed, three-legged, neutered dog named "Lucky." In the short time I'd had her, the dog mauled her, she'd endured stitching, stapling, and daily penicillin injections, and to top it off, the poor thing had a miscarriage. We finally cut the darned ear tag off the ewe. It was apparently not enough.

That Saturday morning she seemed a bit off color. It was nothing you could put your finger on, just a case of what vets refer to as NDR (Not Doing Right) and after everything she'd been through, who could blame her? By Saturday night her condition was unmistakable — if you'd ever seen it before. We hadn't. She stood stiff as a board with white foam around her mouth. Jamaica was the Hollywood version of a rabid sawhorse. As is so often the case, we couldn't get a vet out on the weekend. Because of the foaming we assumed it was an intestinal problem and believed the sawhorse-like position was caused by pain. Thus we treated the symptoms. That didn't work.

Sunday morning there was still no vet available. We tried the next best thing, the Internet. We were unable to google our way to a diagnosis. Since I was on several yahoo sheep groups, I put the question to them and was quickly rewarded with multiple cries of "Tetanus!

Do what? For real? We started her on the antitoxin and fluids immediately. By Sunday night she was paralyzed from the neck down. I made the decision to shoot her. Before I got out there with a rifle however, I received multiple emails telling me of ranchers who had gone through this and had their sheep recover, so I called Dear Friend Kaye for moral advice. I wanted to give this ewe every chance to live, but didn't want her to suffer. I have shot sheep who were in better shape than Jamaica was at that moment. Dear Friend Kaye and her Husband-The-Dog-Vet had a bottle baby goat and were thinking about getting sheep. He wanted some experience with sheep and so they suggested bringing Jamaica to their garage to treat her in a more "sterile" environment" than the horse stall where she had obviously contracted the tetanus. We discussed a course of treatment with my large animal vet and devised a game plan. The future still looked dismal and I hated to prolong her suffering but this ewe had shown such a remarkable desire to live. As long as she wanted to live, we agreed to help her.

The experience gave me a greater respect for tetanus. It's an ugly disease. While I don't know what shots she had prior to coming to my place, we gave her the antitoxin and she still got tetanus. From what I understand this is very common. My advice would be to know the early signs of the disease. On Saturday night Jamaica was a textbook example of tetanus but I didn't recognize it.

Had we caught it early and started her on massive doses of antitoxin then things may have been different. I didn't have enough respect for the disease. For me, tetanus was simply a shot you got if you cut yourself. I never truly understood how ugly that death is for the victim. Jamaica was like a cadaver in rigor mortis. She was stiff, and yet, she was still breathing, conscious, and still swallowing her green smoothies.

The farmer inside me said, "Put her down."

The vet inside me said "Let's try to save her."

Ultimately while Jamaica won many battles she lost the war. We had to put her down. The tetanus was simply too much and her immune system finally gave out. We learned a great deal from this experience. My vet shared that in cases like this, "It's 30% medicine and 70% luck."

I regret that I didn't recognize the signs of tetanus hours earlier and start the antitoxin then but as one sheep rancher told me, "Most folks lose the first ones. You learn. And then you're able to see the signs earlier."

That still left Roanie.

A sheep is not happy alone and with the death of Jamaica, Roanie was a sheep alone. Her injuries were far worse than Jamaica's and so I fully expected her to develop tetanus too, but on the vet's advice, we tossed her into the pasture with the rest of the flock. She was still on three legs but her emotional health was vital to her recovery. In hindsight, perhaps we stumbled on the key by happy accident. An ole time sheep rancher later told me that tetanus is a disease of dark places and so Roanie was not as likely to come into contact with tetanus while lying in the pasture as she was while lying in a dark horse stall. Although I'm not sure if there is any truth to this, I will say that turning Roanie loose was the beginning of a long and happy friendship.

The ewe hobbled out into the pasture where she was cautiously greeted by the giant white puppy. Briar sniffed the badly mangled back leg. She licked the ewe's ear. The injured ewe leaned over and into the dog. And they just stood there, the sheep leaning on the dog. The dog supporting the sheep.

"Are you getting this?" my mother whispered as I clicked away with my camera.

"Yes!" I hissed back, afraid to catch their attention and lose the moment.

It was, and still remains, one of the most beautiful interactions I'd ever witnessed between different species. The dog understood the sheep was hurt. The sheep leaned on the dog for support.

That was the day that Briar truly became a Livestock Guardian Dog. For the first time, she was faced with a sheep who was completely helpless and the pup stepped up to the plate. Briar became Roanie's constant companion, and despite the fact that this sheep had every right to fear dogs, Roanie became Briar's friend.

CHAPTER 10

INAPPROPRIATE LAUGHTER

The mind of a Crime Scene Investigator will go in many directions, but all the roads will lead to death. When she was a pup, one of Briar's favorite games was to pull the leather strap on my rubber boots as I walked in the pasture. Sometimes she missed and sank her puppy pearly whites into my leg. This resulted in some interesting bruise patterns. One morning I looked at my leg and thought, "I hope I don't die while I still have these fresh bruise patterns. The medical examiner will really wonder about this."

Normal people don't think like that. Normal people think "the dog is tearing my jeans." Normal people think "I'll be glad when she outgrows this stage."

This got me to pondering the kind of weird crap that CSIs think. Here are just a few thoughts that ramble through our heads:

* Your friend is late for work. You hunt him down like wounded prey because you don't want to find out he's dead and the maggots got him because you didn't search for him. On the Crime Scene Continuum being dead is not as bad as the maggots getting you.

* You are accidentally kicked in the head by a horse. Glancing blow. You survive the kick but immediately phone the Other Half to inform him because you don't want to drop dead in the pasture later and have the fire ants eat you before he finds your body.

* You always adjust the water temperature to "just right" before you step into the shower. You do this because if you have a seizure or a heart attack, or if you fall and are knocked unconscious, you don't want your body to cook in the tub.

Yes, that is a thing. It happens more often than you think. It is especially a problem in apartment complexes where the hot water never runs out. All I can say about this is that boiled human does indeed smell just like boiled chicken. It is why you will never find a boiling chicken in my house. We all have our crosses to bear. That is one of mine. Always test the bath water and make sure the dogs are fed.

Like many of the rest of us, dead people have dogs. Few things can complicate a death scene more than a dog that's been waiting for days for somebody to come to the door. By the time the mail and newspapers finally pile up enough to get some interest, Peanut has long since run out of Purina and started in on the old lady's fingers.

Tiny dogs like Chihuahuas will eat you pretty quickly, but Pitbulls and Rottweilers normally wait until you decay to the point where you aren't good company for anyone anyway. It probably starts off the same way it does when the dog shreds your couch. Anxiety and boredom. The anxious dog is licking your rotting arm, when oops — your hand falls off. He might as well take this with him so he drags it through the house and hops on your bed to chew it because it tastes good and it reminds him of you. The crime scene investigator then tries days later to piece together the trails of paw prints through body fluids that may or may not lead to missing body parts.

Even outdoor scenes can be complicated by dogs. It wasn't unusual for Tramp the Ghetto Dog to come bee-bopping through the scene. Having no respect for the yellow tape, to the envy of our audience in flip-flops, Tramp would scoot under the line and slink right up to the body for a sniff and a look-see. If you weren't careful, he'd hike a leg on your dead guy.

Many times the first clue that we even had a dead guy was when Fluffy brought home a head. Dogs just love skulls. Skulls are like soccer balls. They roll and bounce and are quite chewable. That kind of toy does tend to bust up a family barbecue though.

My most memorable pup was a Chihuahua. Although everyone in the room was wearing boots and Princess was an ankle-biter at best, she singlehandedly stopped a crime scene investigation because of her steadfast determination to guard her dead owner.

His body was slumped against the couch. There was just enough room between his back and the couch to fit a frightened Chihuahua. Princess had positioned herself behind the body like a moray eel in a coral reef and she had the same impressive array of teeth. We tried coaxing her out. Even on a good day, Chihuahuas don't coax. Chihuahuas with dead owners are more than highly suspicious. No one wanted to get bitten but no one wanted to write the report about how seven public officials let a four pound Chihuahua hold up a death investigation, so we took a vote. The patrol officer lost.

He grabbed a towel from the bathroom. We sacrificed the sanctity of a crime scene for our mission because rabid Chihuahuas trump scene integrity. While someone stood on the opposite side of the body to prevent Princess from scooting out that direction, our intrepid officer risked life, limb, and certainly his fingers, to scoop up Princess with the towel.

Ironically, as soon as she was captured, the tiny beast mutated into a very sweet, very scared, little brown dog. Everyone wanted to take her home. (Except me. I didn't need any more dogs.) We finished our investigation as Princess charmed the patrol officers and the body car attendants. They held her where she could see her owner and supervise our progress.

After the job was done, no one had arrived to take custody of Princess, so quite a few folks left their contact information to adopt the scrappy little dog.   Princess eventually ended up in the hands of family members but not until she had terrorized and charmed the city's finest. So tip your next beer to Princess, one helluva little brown dog.

On television the CSIs are always so cool. The camera pans as they smoothly remove their sunglasses and squint down at their evidence. They are so cool. They are so fake.

In reality CSIs are much different. We probably have our cool moments but for the most part, this particular night was a pretty good representation of exactly how cool we are not. It was hot. I was sweating. I wasn't glowing. I wasn't perspiring. I was sweating. I was coughing. My nose was running. It's not cool if you drip snot on a body. I don't think I've ever seen a television CSI with a head cold.

I had a new supervisor. The scene was complicated so he came along to help. It was the first time we'd ever worked together. We bonded over a tape measure. A murder scene is diagrammed in order to present a two-dimensional version of the scene for the jury. I used a fancy laser for many of the measurements, but curtains, mirrors and furniture can get in the way, so many times I had to resort to the tried and true — the tape measure. The Home Depot special! Bright yellow! In real life the CSI looks less like "tank tops and sunglasses" and more like Tim "Tool Time" Taylor from the television show, *Home Improvement*. My tape measure was getting a little old. The end was a bit torn around the two inch mark. It wouldn't roll all the way up, so for more than a year, I had just worked around that little quirk. Why buy a new $30 tape measure just because the last two inches won't roll up? I learned why that night.

My new sergeant was holding one end of the tape measure while I stood on the far side of a room with the opposite end. We took our measurement and I informed him that he could "let 'er go!" So he did. That sucker zoomed back at me like a freight train and disappeared completely into the yellow case. No problem. I could just pull it back out. Nope. Like a turtle sucked up in its shell, the tape measure wasn't coming out. They don't have this problem on television. On television there are also not ten people in an apartment waiting on the CSI to get finished. So I yanked on that puppy and the end popped off. What the ****!

I stood there holding the last two inches of a tape measure while the rest of it hid like a turtle in a bright yellow case. Let the cussing begin. Fortunately my new sergeant was old-school and had no problem with supervising sailors. He looked at it. Then he cussed. They just don't show this stuff on television. Gil Grissom has never, to the best of my knowledge, gotten into a verbal altercation with a tape measure. Why don't they show that? That's real.

The next bright idea was to take the case apart so we could pull the end of the tape out. Sounded good in theory. We trotted to the truck in search of a screwdriver. Once we closed the door on the home and headed for the truck, throngs of on-lookers and media were watching our every move. It was annoying but there was nothing to be done about it. Frankly, if they want to stand out for six hours in flip-flops and watch me walk back and forth to the truck, then so be it. These people clearly need more to do in their lives. So we walked to the truck. And we searched for a screwdriver.

A Ford Expedition can be completely filled with equipment and you still will not be able to find a screwdriver the right size. (But we entertained multitudes of people with our search.) When we discovered that my pocket knife would work, we were back in business. Maybe. What happens when you open the case on a tape measure? We didn't know. The crowd found it vastly amusing.

When the last screw is removed and you begin to lift up the case, the tape will unwind like a giant metal snake - loudly. You will try to clamp the case back down, but alas, the yellow snake will continue to unwind. It is hard to look professional while cussing a 30 foot long metal snake. Trying to get it back together is like trying to stuff the genie back in the bottle — fruitless, but again, it entertained the crowd. I guess you might as well get some kind of show when you stand around in flip-flops for hours. But it didn't stop there. We were nothing if not determined, and since we couldn't find another tape measure in the truck, we were desperate. Desperate times call for desperate measures. Mindful of our audience, we trapped the bulk of the tape in the case and stomped back to the apartment. Inside, we painstakingly rolled that sucker back into the case. Instead of screwing the case shut, my sergeant held the case clamped tight in his bear-paw hands and we carefully finished the measurements we needed. After that, he set the tape measure on a table in the living room, where it waited like a cobra in basket. And that's where the medical examiner found it.

We were actually in another room when we heard it —

the familiar racket of a yellow metal snake unwinding and the short bark of a very surprised man in glasses. It was funnier when he did it than when we did it. I noted that he managed to refrain from cussing up a blue streak though. Perhaps he's higher up the Evolutionary Ladder than we are or maybe he just hasn't learned all the good words yet. Time on the streets will teach you all sorts of new languages. It's actually kind of a pity that it happened inside the apartment. The Flip-Flop Crowd would have loved it.

I got so used to the Flip-Flop Crowd hovering behind the crime scene tape and feeding on gore that occasionally I was surprised by the zebra standing among horses.

The body lay sprawled in the parking lot between the taco stand and a row of flea market tables. With apartment complexes on three sides of the scene, the crowd pressed closely at the yellow tape. They had just come home from work and this was reality television at its finest.

The camera crews got their film footage and their sound bite so they had just packed up their gear and rolled away. I was hot. I was tired. I was hungry. It was already getting dark. As I walked near the edge of the parking lot, a plaintive voice called over the tape.

"Miss Officer! Miss Officer! Hey! Come 'ere!"

Most of the time I ignored spectators, but something about this guy reminded me of a cat on the front porch, yelling for attention, so I took a step in his direction.

"Yes?"

"Hey, Miss Officer! How much longer you gonna be?"

This puzzled me. What did he care? "I dunno. I'm still waiting on the Medical Examiner's Office to come pick up the body."

He frowned. "So how long's that gonna take?"

A crowd of men gathered around him. Clearly he was

their spokesman.

"I dunno. They're working on a drowning now. They'll get here when they get here."

He translated and there was much frowning and groaning. This had me more intrigued than the dead guy going into rigor on the pavement.

So I asked, "What's the deal?"

He enlightened me. "We just got off work. We want to know how long before you move the dead guy so the taco stand can open back up."

A good street taco is probably worth the wait. Over time death sands away at your social skills leaving a morbid sense of humor that can make you stand out like a turd in a punchbowl.

"Normal is nothing more than a cycle on a washing machine."
Whoopi Goldberg

~

Unlike my Other Half, I don't care much for gun stores. It isn't the guns, it's the machismo and air of superiority that surrounds them. I just don't like the condescending attitude of men who make assumptions that because I'm a woman I know nothing about guns and "the real world" outside the mall and the kitchen.

I've been in a lot of guns stores in my life and initially they all treat me the same. Since I'm fairly certain that I've done things in my lifetime that these manly-men would never dream of doing, I take offense at their condescension. I also don't like the faces of dead animals staring down at me but that's another issue entirely. My Other Half just loves gun stores and for some reason that defies logic, he insists upon bringing me. From time to time he regrets it.

There I was at yet another gun store, staring at the faces of more dead animals, impatiently waiting on him, when I temporarily tuned in to the male conversation. The men, dressed in their starched jeans and shooting shirts, were sharing with Other Half the sad tale of a man who had recently been hit by a train. My ears perked up just to see if I was familiar with this case.

They explained that a man and woman had been fishing from a railroad trestle. This is a leisure activity fraught with danger and such was the case. A train came and the woman ran to safety. Witnesses report that the man had plenty of time to run but insisted upon reeling in his fishing line first.

The men telling the story shared the grave news that because the young man refused to drop his fishing pole, he was hit by the train. I am not a hard-hearted person but that struck me as Darwinism at work, so I barked in laughter. Apparently laughter in such a situation is inappropriate. Who knew?

One of the men leveled a look at me that said it all. He clearly couldn't wrap his mind around the fact that I found humor in this story. There it was. The glaring spotlight illuminating my social skills. No death should be funny, but then I thought about it some more, and the more I thought about it, the funnier it got. I was like a kid giggling in church.

Stifling snickers, I looked around at the faces of exotic animals mounted on the wall. While the mighty, manly hunter may have thought I was the cold and heartless one for laughing at such a tale, the wolf mounted in the corner, staring at me with glass eyes, might have had an altogether different take on it. So which is worse, being thought of as a mindless piece of fluff flittering between the kitchen and the mall, or being thought of as a cold, heartless creature who laughs inappropriately? I decided that on that day, I was gonna stand with all the dead animals mounted on the wall and choose to be cold and heartless. So I laughed.

"My darling girl, when are you going to realize that being normal is not necessarily a virtue? It rather denotes a lack of courage!"
Alice Hoffman

~

The carpet was so plush that I had the overwhelming desire to take off my boots and wriggle my toes in it. Even the air in a high rise luxury building just smelled better, or maybe that was the eucalyptus. As we walked down the hallway brass placards marked each room. Perfectly manicured plants sat in the corners like obedient dogs.

The elevator dinged and we stepped inside. The mirrored walls gleamed with an absence of smeared fingerprints. I stared at my reflection. What a contrast. People who live in luxury apartments have hair that "cascades" down their back. My hair had escaped the clip and, plastered with sweat, was hanging down in droopy tendrils. It wasn't flattering.

The elevator dinged again and we stopped. The door slid open to reveal two elderly women. Even at this hour their creases were pressed, their make-up was flawless. Aristocratic eyes swept across us. I tossed a stray strand of hair out of my eye and smiled back at them in silence. This was awkward.

Upper class eyebrows crawled up their foreheads but no one said a word as the elevator door closed again, leaving them outside. They opted not to ride with us. The medical examiner and I turned to each other and shared a blue collar grin. The three of us continued our journey. When the elevator dinged again, we had reached our destination, and as the door opened, we rolled the gurney with our body into the hallway. The plush carpet crushed under my boot and the smell of eucalyptus faded as we rolled away.

Comedian Bill Engvall has become famous for a running joke about giving signs to stupid people so the rest of us would recognize them immediately. If they carried signs proclaiming they were stupid, we wouldn't waste much time wondering about them. Makes sense. We need these signs on crime scenes. Imagine.

A local fast food restaurant is the scene of gun battle during rush hour traffic. For over seven hours police and crime scene investigators have been crawling all over this restaurant, the parking lot, and the streets around it. At the seventh hour, with three crime scene trucks and two patrol cars still inside the parking lot, with uniformed officers still milling around, the yellow crime scene tape finally comes down enough to allow employees back into the restaurant.

I am sitting in my truck, waiting for the other CSIs to finish packing up when I notice that I'm blocking a vehicle that's trying to get through the parking lot. What the hell is he doing? Curiosity gets the best of me. I ease aside to allow the car to slowly bull his way into a cold crime scene. In addition to three CSIs in the parking lot, there are also at least five uniformed police officers, and three more homicide investigators standing nearby. Like faded flowers, crime scene tape still loosely droops in parts of the perimeter. Despite all this, with the patient determination of a cow pushing its way to the feed trough, this car slowly eases its way through the parking lot — and into the drive-thru!

Where he waits. And waits. While employees inside the building wade through broken glass and spilled drinks in an effort just to find their car keys so they can go home after seven hours of waiting outside, he waits in the drive-thru for a voice on the speaker to take his order. And waits.

When he finally gives up and leaves, I fight the urge to pull him over, walk through the red and blue flashing lights, and hand him his sign.

His bloody index finger was still curled in the trigger guard of the pistol. A New Orleans Saints ball cap was on the sidewalk, its brim resting at a jaunty angle. A bag of marijuana peeked from underneath it. It was safe to come out. The shooting was over. His surprised eyes said he didn't expect this drug deal to go that wrong.

The cold January wind blew the papers on my clipboard as I stepped out the door. Family members were already wailing on the other side of the crime scene tape. They found out on Facebook. Death is the occupational hazard for ripping off drug dealers. Mr. January just discovered that. His placement in the doorway was too perfect. The gun in his hand. The finger on the trigger. Mr. January was the classic candidate for a CSI calendar. The homicide investigator and I discussed it at length. Yes, he would make a perfect Mr. January.

We'd played with the idea of creating a calendar just for Homicide and the Crime Scene Unit. It would highlight twelve of our most creative and memorable photographs. Pictures that make a statement.

My submissions would be:

1) Photo of a large printed sign inside a manufacturing plant reading:
Safety! So easy even a caveman can do it!
Underneath this sign was a severed arm from an industrial accident.

2) Picturesque landscape photo of the city skyline with the afternoon sun glinting off the mirrored

skyscrapers: The sun is behind the buildings, backlighting the skyline, providing an artistic illumination. The city's namesake bayou meanders out of the metropolis and toward the viewer. Welcome to the Bayou City! It is a Chamber Of Commerce photograph until one looks closely and notices the human body floating in the bayou.

So along with Mr. January, those would be may submissions to the Crime Scene Calendar for that year. Sadly, although we had a plethora of photographs vying for this top honor, people with higher rank and better task kept us from actually printing the calendar.

Not only does death investigation give you a unique sense of humor but because you now know 101 ways to die, you are particularly sensitive to the careless behavior of others. Few things upset my metabolism more than being shot at. I'm a cop, so it's certainly not outside the realm of the imagination but I never expect to have bullets whizzing by me in my own pasture. It was a bad day. Or it was a good day. Kinda depends upon how you look at things.

I turned the barn water on for the first time after a hard freeze and was greeted by a geyser. Never a good thing. Pipes were busted in the stallion's stall. Since Other Half was working that day, repairing the pipe was a one-woman job. After two trips to Home Depot I got the pipes fixed. By myself. That should count for something like an Academy Award. Or at least some chocolate. I was so busy congratulating myself on a job well done that I failed to hear the ominous soundtrack music playing in the background. I did, however, hear the gunfire when the bullets ripped through the tin of my barn.

The two C's of a gunfight are cover and concealment. Cover is an object that keeps you hidden and provides protection from fired bullets. Concealment keeps you hidden but provides no protection whatsoever from a bullet with your name on it. A tin barn is concealment, not cover. There was absolutely nothing to slow down the bullets whizzing through the tin walls. Since I had no reason to believe that anyone was actually trying to kill me, the next guess was that someone was hunting along the drainage canal.

There's normal. And there's crazy. My compass tends to point a little toward crazy. Especially when getting shot at. When normal people are shot at, they don't run toward the gunfire. Crazy people get pissed off though. Really pissed off. So I raced outside the barn screaming "Stop! Stop! You're shooting at me!" (And lots of cuss words that cannot be printed on a family-friendly program)

Gunfire answered me. It was coming from the forest across the canal. Bullets were hitting tin, splintering wood, and whizzing past both sides of me.

"Stop shooting! Hey *#@!! STOP SHOOTING!"

There was a lull in the gunfire. Did the shooter finally hear me? Nope, he was re-loading. Bullets started whizzing again just feet away. They say, "You never hear the one that gets you." Those are not comforting words when you're listening to them ping around you. My only hope was to stop the shooter.

As I ran out of the pasture, I phoned Other Half and screamed for him to get on the police radio and have the county deputies get out to the street across the canal from our pasture. Then I leaped into my truck and slammed it into gear so fast I dropped the transmission in the driveway before peeling off in a cloud of dust. A 4-Wheeler passed me heading the opposite direction. My phone rang. Mom. Her house wasn't getting hit but she could hear the gunfire. The Constable next door to her was on his way to stop the shooting. He was crossing the canal on his 4-wheeler. Fortunately he got there before me.

By the time I slammed my truck into park, dropping the rest of my transmission in his yard, the Shooter had already put up his gun. My Constable Neighbor was sitting calmly on his 4-Wheeler waiting for the Sheriff's office to arrive. A dozen people were standing on the Shooter's porch, watching the show. This was definitely more interesting than their Super Bowl party.

I descended upon the Shooter in a rage. I was not dropping the F-Bomb, I was slinging F-Bombs like missiles. The Shooter objected to my language in front of his children.

"Oh really? Oh really! Well I object to being shot at!

He suggested that I might want to get off his property. This unleashed more exploding f*bombs so he backed down. The Shooter informed me that the bullets hitting my barn could not possibly be his. Yes, he'd been shooting, but he was a long way from my house, and he'd been shooting at a box. A box. A cardboard box.

This Rocket Scientist had been shooting a 9mm handgun at a cardboard box on the ground. There was nothing behind that box — but my &#@* FARM!

I unleashed more screaming. My Constable Neighbor sat on his 4-Wheeler, afraid to move. He'd never seen me like this and was a tad afraid. Then again, my neighbor had never had bullets whizz past his waist on a sunny Sunday afternoon. It tends to push one into a rage.

In the midst of this tirade Other Half continued to ring me. I finally paused to answer the phone. He was his own brand of hysterical when he discovered that I'd confronted the shooter before the deputies had arrived. In my defense, the shooting HAD. TO. STOP. I didn't have time to wait for deputies. I had horses, cows, sheep, and dogs, which were getting shot at. He advised me to call the county dispatcher right then. So I did.

I answered her questions. Yes, the scene was under

control. I wasn't really under control, but the shooting had stopped. I confirmed the address for her. Yes, I could see the deputies flying towards me now. No, no one was hurt. Not yet. I resisted the urge to beat the shooter over the head with his *#@!ing cardboard box. A very narrow thread was keeping me from falling over the edge of sanity.

I was quite prepared to have Other Half bail me out of jail for assault. It crossed my mind. It did. I weighed it. Understood it. And accepted it. If the rocket scientist had been anything but sorry, I was quite prepared to assault him with his cardboard box and take my punishment.

Three patrol cars zoomed up. The shooter was visibly relieved. Finally someone could rescue him from The Crazy Woman. I assured deputies that the scene was under control (translated: I have momentarily suppressed my overwhelming desire to choke the crap out of this Rocket Scientist.)

We walked out to his cardboard box. They were vastly amused to hear that he didn't realize how far 9 mm bullets would travel. Perhaps it is amusing if bullets are not whizzing around you. They pointed out that his cardboard box was woefully ill-equipped to stop 9 mm bullets. He apologized. He was very sorry. He was sorry that a little target practice on Super Bowl Sunday had unleashed some psycho woman like a mummy's curse from a tomb and he dearly wished she would crawl back under her rock.

The deputies assured our Rocket Scientist that if Psycho Woman wished to press charges, he would be arrested for Deadly Conduct, which is A Very Bad Thing. I considered doing this but nothing good would actually be accomplished that hadn't already been accomplished. Rocket Scientist now realized that a crazy woman lived on the other side of the canal. I think he was more afraid of the crazy lady than jail. Satisfied, I went home and checked my livestock. They were okay. I didn't have to spend the night in the county jail for killing the Rocket Scientist with his cardboard box. But who knows? That may have been a public service. Firearms are not toys. If you want to have one, be responsible. Learn to use it. Otherwise you are as dangerous as a chimpanzee with a machine gun.

CHAPTER 11

TYIN' THE KNOT WITH
LEPRECHAUNS & BORDER COLLIES

The Cowboy Cop and I were married in a simple outdoor ceremony on a lovely, sunny morning. Rather than have a big wingding, we opted instead to invite friends and family to meet us at the Houston Livestock Show & Rodeo for celebrations. On that day we officially blended farms and families. It was a day typical of us, representative of who we were - a horse show, a sheepdog trial, and cow shit on your boots.

~

In every way the sheep were outperforming the goats. Not only did the lambs gain weight faster, but sheep were easier to handle in a group. This is because sheep aren't exactly free thinkers. They aren't the brightest crayons in the box. The goats however, ah, the goats. They take thinking to whole new level. I'm not talking about Albert Einstein-Thomas Edison Do Something To Bring Goodness to the World kind of thinking. I'm talking career criminal kind of thinking. I'm talking about people who put every waking moment into finding ways to make their lives better and screw everyone else. It's who they are. They can't help themselves. Even as they made my life more difficult, I had a grudging admiration for them.

The little beasts had figured out how to screw up my Border Collie. The goats had learned that when the dog went out to bring them in, all they had to do was stand still while the sheep flowed around them. Like boulders in a fast-moving river, the goats stood and watched as the sheep jostled past. They pretended that the dog had actually come to gather the sheep and they were merely spectators to this daily ritual. The sheep go out. The sheep go in. The sheep go out. The sheep go in. The dog moves the sheep into a nice neat ball and rolls it toward me. As they sweep past the goats, the goats just stand there like spectators to a police chase.

"We just standing here in our flip-flops, watching the show."

I used to have the dog bring in both flocks together. What a train wreck! Sheep flock. Goats scatter and run like hell. The dog gathers sheep. The dog heads off and drives goats. She couldn't do both at the same time. It was screwing up my dog so we abandoned that. It all came to a head one day when I was running late for work.

I marched out to the pasture. The sheep immediately came running. Goats stood and watched the sheep. The goats snickered as Lily attempted to blend them into the flock. I stamped my wooden crook into the ground and cussed. The goats were not impressed. While the Border Collie and I were farting with goats, the sheep ran through a hole the goats had made in the fence. I cussed some more. Border Collie was confused. Goats? Sheep? Which ones did I want?

Clearly we had to deal with the sheep before we could deal with the goats. While the Border Collie could slide through the hole in the fence, I had no such desire to get down on my knees and crawl through the damned hole so I took Lily through the barn with me as the goats climbed through the same hole the sheep had used. We popped out of the barn in time to see the last of the goats sliding their scrawny little asses through the fence. The sheep and goats were then together again.

I sent Lily after the sheep. The goats processed this pretty quickly and started to sneak back through hole. In an amazing leap of logic for a sheep, the entire flock also jumped to the conclusion that, like the goats, they could run for the hole too. I screamed. The Border Collie went to head them off, but hesitated. The first of the goats made it to the hole.

"Lily!!! Get 'em! Get 'em! Get 'em!" (911 call to a Border Collie)

The Border Collie saluted and raced off. By the time she made it to the hole, all the goats and two sheep had squeezed through and were standing on the other side jeering and making faces. She ended their end zone dance by rounding them up and bringing them to me. This required pushing them through a small ditch filled with water. They balked. She pushed. The dominant ewe decided to make a break and run for the hole in the fence again.

Lily grabbed the ewe by the back hoof and held on. For a moment the action stopped. Everyone was in shock. I screamed at the dog. She let go of the Newly Educated Ewe. With her sanity restored, the ewe ran back to the flock as they rushed into the shed to hide.

I didn't want teeth on my sheep but it was easy to understand the dog's frustration. No harm, no foul. The sheep were hiding in the shed behind a dead lawnmower, some old wire, and various dusty barn junk items that hadn't seen the light of day in years. They wouldn't come out, so I had to send in the Border Collie. She crept in slowly. One by one, the dog moved the ewes out of the corner and around the junk. A roll of field fencing was lying on its side in the corner. It was just the end of a roll, not enough to do much with, just a small tunnel of woven wire. The last ewe, in a move that only a sheep could understand, lowered her head and crawled into that roll of field fencing.

The Border Collie looked over her shoulder at me as if to say, "Did you see that?"

I did, and was as amazed as the dog. Okay. Well then. The dog and I watched the ewe wriggle into her new Field Fencing Suit. The sheep stuck her head through the other side, stuck her legs through the wire on the bottom, stood up, and waddled to join the flock wearing her new wire suit!

The rest of the flock appeared not to notice the new fashion accessory. The ewe joined the others and Border Collie moved them all into the barn where their dinner was waiting. While they jostled at the feeder, I managed to extract the ewe from her new wire suit. I then went to the pasture to gather the two sheep who slid through the fence with the goats

It was time to get the goats in. I smacked my crook on the ground and the dog saluted. We headed to the pasture. The goats saw us coming. Instead of running, they obediently got into a nice single-file line and marched into their little goat prison. Goats do that kind of thing just to screw with me. As I closed the gate and headed for the house, I saw one of the goats checking out the discarded roll of field fencing and I wondered. What goes through the mind of a goat? Clearly a lot more than goes through the mind of some sheep.

The wooden staff clattered harmlessly across the ground after Other Half flung it at Blue Heeler. The dog scampered a few feet to the right and raised his eyebrow as if to announce, "Well then, just pen her your own damned self!"

I sat on the tailgate of the truck with the Border Collie and watched the train wreck in the pasture. They couldn't be called a team. Other Half's screaming flustered the little space cadet who wanted to work cows but refused to listen to direction. It was a match made in hell. Despite barbed wire and electrical fencing, the yellow heifer was doing the end zone dance on the other side of the fence again. She was out and there was no choice but to let the dog try to retrieve her. And try not to scream at him.

This was apparently too tall an order for both the man and the dog. The dog refused to slow down and instead pushed the cow so fast that she didn't even see the gap Other Half had cut in the fence as an entrance back into the pasture. The heifer and the dog just blasted past the opening. There was more cussing. The dog answered this with a solemn, "Then just pen her your own damned self then." And he trotted off. Again.

From the back of the truck I offered advice that neither one wanted but with an impatient nod, the man agreed that he wouldn't scream at the dog. They got back to work again. Moments later the dog chased the heifer completely out of that pasture and into another one. Other Half threw up his hands and stomped away leaving the cow and the dog wondering what to make of that.

The Border Collie had been watching all this with great interest. Born and bred to be a cowdog, Lily had been cheated out of her birthright because I was too afraid she'd get hurt. Cows kill dogs. There's no glossing over that fact. Not only was this Border Collie essential to me as a sheepdog, but she slept on my bed at night. Losing her to a cow was out of the question but as she stood on the tailgate and whined to be put in the game, a thought occurred to me. Was this dog so different from us?

I was cop. Other Half was a cop. When the gunfire starts

we run toward the action. How is that any different from a dog bred to run toward danger? I mulled this over some as Other Half tossed cattle cubes into a feeder in the roping arena and the yellow heifer climbed back through fences to eat with the rest of the cows. Blue Dog bounded up with a smile at me and a nervous glance at Other Half. The dog at my side, the Border Collie, was staring at the cattle with narrow-eyed intensity. Blue Heeler wasn't really bred to be a cowdog, but this Border Collie was the result of generations of breeding stock dogs and her genes screamed to work.

After Other Half and Blue Heeler tried once again to sort the cattle in the pen and the dog muddled after the wrong cows again, I made the decision. Let her go. Let her be who she is. We jumped off the tail gate and she stepped into the arena. It took her less than three minutes to sort the calves. Thus was the birth of a Cow Dog.

By the light of the smuggler's moon I listened. Yep. There it was. The sound of trouble. I padded back into the house, locked up the rest of the dogs, and flicked a finger to confirm to Lily, that yes, once again, she was the "chosen one." The little dog raced to the front door and waited while I put on my boots.

I stood on the porch and listened again. The water well was still running. Since I'd done a livestock check earlier, I knew no water spigots had been left on by humans. That meant a cow had rubbed her head on a spigot and turned on the water. It was now 1:30 a.m. It's possible that the water could have been running as early as 8:30 p.m.

And it was. By the light of the full moon I could see the damned calves had flooded the barnyard again. Clearly it was time to lock them in the back pasture, but first, they must be sorted.

Other Half bought a few more little heifers to add to the

gene pool. They were considerably younger than the other calves and they weren't getting their fair share of groceries. Because of that they'd been separated from the big calves.

But Other Half had just decided to turn everyone together in the front pasture to enjoy the lush grass that was growing so fast that even the sheep couldn't keep ahead of it. Scratch that little experiment. Cows cannot be trusted with water spigots. I turned off the water and glanced at the Border Collie. Her eyes bore into me, blazing as bright as the full moon over our heads.

No rancher wants to sort cattle at 1:30 in the morning. No Border Collie doesn't want to sort cattle at 1:30 in the morning. So with a sigh, I turned toward the pasture. She gave a happy bark and off we went. I trudged through the high grass while she bounced along. No one should be that happy in the middle of the night without loads and loads of caffeine. Despite my bad humor, her happy bounce tugged a smile out of me.

Ready. These dogs are always ready. With a quick salute, she raced out and brought the calves up. The youngest calves had never been worked by a dog but this actually made it easier to sort them from the rest of the crew who wanted no part of the little black & white face with crazed eyes which glowed in the moonlight. The younger calves were a bit bewildered by their nighttime visitor who momentarily stared at them like a serial killer but then moved on to other victims. She selected the big calves and pushed these troublemakers into the arena where they could be released into the back pastures.

It took me longer to walk out there than it took the Border Collie to separate the cattle and push the offenders back into jail. By the light of the smuggler's moon we walked back to the house. She had that jaunty little trot with her gay tail waving in the air like a flag raised to the world.

I couldn't help but smile as the moonlight shone off her bright eyes. She searched my face, hoping for more chores ahead. I listened in the silence. The water well was quiet once more. It was a good night to be a farm collie. It was a good night to have a farm collie.

In June of that summer my dog, Kona, died of renal failure. His death marked the end of an era, and thus closed the final chapter on the book of my work with cadaver dogs. The only way to survive in a career that is so focused on death is to have a healthy life outside the office, so after Kona's death, I didn't get another Cadaver Dog, but I did end up with another dog.

Lily proved herself to be such an asset on the farm that more and more Other Half reached for her to work cattle. It was apparent that he needed his own cow dog. Trace came from a line of dogs bred to work cattle in dog trials and brought a level of intensity we didn't even know was possible. So great was his desire to gather livestock that we had to place a layer of concrete blocks under the yard fence to keep him from slithering his skinny little ass into the pasture to work the stock.

Some days you tackle the farm, and some days the farm tackles you. Perhaps I was just grumpy. You shouldn't work livestock when you're grumpy but some things can't wait. Or they can, but you're too grumpy to realize that.

I had some yearling rams that needed to be moved. Common sense would tell you to wait until Other Half or Dear Friend Kaye could help but I was grumpy so as far as I was concerned, it needed to be done right at that moment. Right now. Before coffee.

I locked up everyone but Lily, #1 Border Collie, and started to separate sheep. This produced a din of barking from the non-participants. Barking before coffee is a Bad

Thing. I snarled at the Main Barker. Ice, Kona's sister, was offended that I would speak to her in such a manner. She temporarily shut up long enough to file a complaint with Human Resources Department.

The barking resumed once more the moment I started working sheep again. I threatened her with the pound, she threatened to call the Humane Society on me. Lily and I soon had the two young rams separated and were moving them through the barn, into the back yard, and toward an opened gate which led to more paddocks. All was well until the rams decided that the opened gate was too close to the dog kennel. The kennel was not really that close but if the rams saw it as a problem, it was a problem. It was easier to move the dogs than it was to convince the rams to move past the barking dogs.

While Lily watched the rams, I grabbed the dogs and threw them in the house. Problem solved. I thought. The rams did not. The rams announced that the kennel which used to contain the dogs was also too scary to walk past. Butchering these rams was looking better and better. They definitely needed to be removed from the gene pool. I was short on caffeine and short on patience but Lily's patience was rewarded and in time they were through the back yard, through two small paddocks, and into their new Bachelor Pad Prison. Safely in their new prison, the marble that was their brain had stopped rolling around and settled back into its hole, so the rams discovered the rye grass and wandered off.

They needed fresh water and the hose which fed their tank had a giant hole in it. (Probably because someone drove her truck across it.) More water sprayed from the geyser than came out the end of the green hose. It needed to be replaced so I trudged to the barn in search of another one. I found a stiff and dusty yellow hose that I dragged through the barn, across the yard, through some dog poop, and into the paddock.

I attached this ancient yellow hose to the spigot, turned it on, and the yellow hose also produced a geyser. Did I drive over every hose on the property? Since this geyser was not as large as the first one, I approved the hose just for that day. (Which meant that I wouldn't get around to replacing it for months.) With the geyser issue decided, I pulled the hose toward the trough. It was six feet too short.

The dog was slightly confused at this round of cussing because it did not involve sheep. I stalked back into house for a cup of coffee.

With coffee safely in hand, I was then able to more calmly re-examine the length of hose. It did not grow any longer while I was in the house. Perhaps I should have fertilized it.

There is more than one way to skin a cat, and caffeine allowed me to see through the fog and find that way. If I pulled the hose underneath the horse trailer instead of going around the horse trailer, it 'might' be able to reach to the trough. But how was I gonna run the hose underneath the trailer without getting down on my knees and reaching under there? I could stand on one side and ask the dog to fetch the other end of the hose to me. How many additional holes did I want in the yellow hose? Scratch that.

Instead, I pulled the hose underneath the tongue of the trailer. Finally! Things were working in our direction. The hose was still one foot too short of the trough but I could hold it in the air to make up that extra foot. We were on a roll.

My attention was drawn to the Border Collie when her ears said, "Hmmm . . . look at that."

"Huh?" I turned around.

The rams who had been grazing in peaceful bliss were perfectly upright, making the There's-A-Predator-Stare. Where was the predator? Then I saw him.

Apparently when I went into the house for coffee, Trace had slithered his tiny little ass out behind me. A four month old puppy in a paddock with two yearling rams is a recipe for disaster. I called to him. Deep in stalk mode, he glanced out the corner of his eye and said, "Shush Mom! I'm getting my groove on!"

I watched my toddler neatly gather two rams and start walking them towards me. He walked. They walked. No running. No barking. Just smooth, deliberate stalking. And it was working for him. He had on his Super Suit and was in full Superhero mode. Still no running. No barking. Just slowly creeping the sheep in my direction. I put Lily on a stay and walked out of the shed.

The rams decided that on second thought, perhaps they didn't want to go into the shed and turned to move away from me. Trace cut them off and headed them back in my direction again. This time they moved into the shed. I let them pass, and as he slithered by, I snatched him up and whisked him back into the house where we could pack his Super Suit away for another year when he was ready to be a real stockdog.

In time the little superhero grew to become a pretty handy cow dog. He was full of quirks and never failed to keep you on your toes.

I share this tale not to frighten, but to serve as a Public Service Announcement.

While in the shower enjoying the well-earned ecstasy of hot water cascading down my spine after a bone-chilling morning doing barn chores - the shower curtain is ripped open! (Cue music from the movie, "Psycho.")

It isn't Norman Bates, but it is a psycho. A red and white furry face appears. Trace, the red Border Collie, has his green Kong dumbbell. He smiles at me and drops his toy in the shower. It rolls to my feet and rudely bumps my toes.

He stares at me like Obi Wan Kenobi.

I wait for the adrenaline still coursing through my body to settle while he grins impatiently, then I reached down and toss the damned thing out of the tub. And a monster is born.

I don't even have enough time to reach for a bar of soap before he reappears with another cold blast of air. He tosses the cold green toy at me and disappears behind the curtain. It rolls to my feet again. What have I done?

The cold hard reality of my error is bumping against my toe. Just in case I am uncertain, the shower curtain is ripped back again and his laughing psychotic little eyes order me as deliberately as a Jedi Master to a Star Wars Storm Trooper.

"Throw it," he whispers.

Helpless, with the cloudy mind of the feeble, I bend over, and toss the toy out of the tub.

Yes! The subject has been trained!

I take a side note here to point out that the subject being trained was not the dog. Life with a clever dog involves lots of patience and persistence on both sides. Be keenly aware that if you live with a Border Collie, they will spend as much time shaping your behavior as you spend shaping theirs. It is a fact of life. Don't fight The Force.

And here is the really sick part:

I stand in the shower, well aware that I've created a monster, or more precisely, have just been trained by a monster and have thus cemented this behavior firmly into his repertoire of annoying yet charming job skills. After all, who doesn't want to play fetch while taking a hot shower?

Even as I toss the toy again I consider how I will explain this to the other member of my household. The toy reappears at my feet. I let it lie there as I shave my legs and ponder the implications of my error. Obi Wan Kenobi runs out of patience and climbs into the tub to retrieve the toy.

He then flings it up in the air and out the tub. I listen as he plays fetch with himself outside the shower curtain before it is ripped back again and the toy once again rolls to my feet.

The little red leprechaun stares at me with laughing eyes. I know what he's doing. He's counting. How many times must he roll the toy to my toes before I toss it? At what angle must it hit my big toe before he is rewarded? He is playing with the variables in his head. I continue shaving my legs. He wriggles into the tub, grabs it again, and flings it out. There is more bumping around as he sets himself up for his next try. He is a golf pro. He studies the slope of the tub and the position of my feet as I shave the other leg, and slowly, ever so slowly, he opens his mouth and takes the shot. It bumps my foot and I toss the toy out of the tub.

SCORE!

He is now both a mathematician and a pool shark, counting tries and converting perceived angles in his head. I waste hot water and play fetch with him while I wash my hair. Even as I create, shape, mold, and fire the monster in the kiln of a hot shower, I am charmed. What a delightful little creature! What a terrifying little psycho!

What a mess we made on the bathroom floor!

So the lesson here is this: If you don't want to be the trainee as often as you are the trainer, don't get a Border Collie. But if you are charmed by a leprechaun-pool-shark-mathematician-clown-into-world-domination, run, don't walk, to your nearest Border Collie rescue organization. And if you do, buy lots of Kong toys and bath towels.

The key to a good horror flick is suspense. When armed with popcorn and a supersize coke, suspense isn't a bad thing. When you're naked in the shower, suspense is highly overrated.

An arctic cold front was rolling across the country, and

we were trying to juggle a farm and too darned many dogs. On that particular morning, in preparation for nasty weather and lots of time spent in dog crates, I had shuffled the indoor dogs outside and vice versa. Thus I found myself, once again, taking a shower with young Norman Bates, Trace, the Border Collie. Since the first time was such an adventure, I removed all dog toys from the bathroom before stepping in the tub.

But the problem with clever dogs is that PetsMart doesn't have to carry it for an object to become a dog toy. And so it was that I took a quick scan of the bathroom before stepping in the shower. Let the suspense begin:

Pull curtain back to peek at Norman Bates. He is staring at me with yellow wolf eyes. Close curtain and pick up soap. Begin to mull over his expression. What was he thinking? Did I puppy-proof the bathroom properly? Mentally run through a diagram of the bathroom in my head. What can he turn into a toy?

Peek through curtain again. His yellow wolf eyes are still staring at me. This time he's smirking. Close curtain. I'm certain the little creep was smirking at me. What's he up to? Peek through curtain again. He is lying on the bath rug. He raises a Spock eyebrow, daring me to question his innocence. I close the curtain. My cell phone by the sink rings. Because I'm soaking wet, I stay where I am and continue washing my toes. The shower curtain is ripped open.

A cold blast of air rushes into the tub. His dancing eyes smile, "Your phone's ringing!"

He stays there, with the shower curtain draped over his head, staring at me intently, letting in the cold air. I assure him I will return the call later. He backs out. The phone continues to ring. Norman Bates slashes the curtain open again.

"Your phone is ringing! Want me to get it?"

I see the direction his mind is working and assure him that, "No, I'll return the call."

He disappears again. The phone stops ringing. I go back to my soap but the ominous music soundtrack in my head begins. Something is going on. I peek out the curtain. He is staring at me. Staring at me. Staring. Staring. Staring. Playing his Jedi mind games. Staring at the phone. Staring at me. I refuse to be trained by a dog. After all, I'm the trainer here.

I tell myself that I won't be long and go back to my shower. Still, the music dances in my head like his dancing eyes. I reassure myself that there is nothing in the bathroom he can hurt, but the mental picture of an expensive iPhone being thrown into the shower pops in my head.

He wouldn't.

I peek through the curtain again. He would. His front feet are already on the toilet and he's staring at the phone like the RCA puppy listening to his master's voice in a phonograph. It rings again. He grins at me from the toilet seat. His smile says, "Your phone is ringing again! Must be important! Want me to bring it to you? Huh? Huh?"

The music in my head has reached a climax. The chance that an iPhone will come flipping into the shower like a hockey puck is about to become a reality. I bounce out of the tub with a bark and answer it. It's Other Half. I'm wet, so I put him on speaker phone. The glazed yellow eyes at my dripping feet point out my error.

"Dad? Dad? Dad's in the box?"

Hmmm.... yes, to a Border Collie, Dad is indeed in the box. And that is a bad thing. I hop back in the shower. I peek around the curtain. He continues to stare at the phone like a puzzle.

How is it he has never noticed cell phones before? Judging from his expression, Kong is about to add an iPhone to their inventory. I doubt Otterboxes cover that. I'm sure AT&T Insurance wants to hear this excuse.

"Yes, my dog tried to get my husband out of the Otterbox. No, he's not a Labrador, he's a Border Collie. Yes, you're right. It wouldn't be a bad idea to upgrade my insurance."

I was arriving on a scene at work when my phone rang. Dear Friend Kaye Married to Vet who lives on the next farm over called to announce that her husband came home from work to find that one of her goats had been eaten - not just killed, but eaten - entirely. There was little left but a hide and some bones. Been there, done that. Ken the Goat got the t-shirt.

Welcome to the Predator Superhighway, the canal running beside my farm. In the past the predators treated my farm like a cafeteria. And what wasn't to love? Goats, sheep, chickens, turkeys, geese - you name it, and it was on the menu.

That was until I brought home Briar, the little warrior who grew to become a Big White Dawg. The moment Briar started work, the killing stopped. The cafeteria was closed. So the predators simply went around the dog, crossed my back pasture and went to my neighbors. Dear Friend Kaye raised goats, chickens and turkeys. The neighbor between us raised Barbado sheep - for one season. The coyotes put him out of business.

I had lambs on the ground and I still had goats. Briar could not be everywhere. So as I stood over another dead guy, I hustled to call the Other Half and inform him that when he came home from work, I wished for him to move the goats into the pen with the adult sheep so that Briar could guard them all. And by the way, I was on a dead guy and I'd be late.

Then I called my mother and asked her to check on my

goats before Other Half got there. Dead men are patient and the one at my feet didn't complain as I circled the wagons at my farm, preparing for the onslaught of coyote attacks that would begin. Once I was satisfied that I'd done all I could do, I addressed my dead man. He and I discussed his evening, which had not gone well, and I got to know him better.

When Other Half got home, I was still processing evidence at work. So while I photographed, boxed, taped, and tagged, I listened to him on the phone as he tried to move goats around at midnight.

First he had to get Lily out of the kennel without letting Trace out. No small feat. Trace is really quick. That done, he and Lily headed to the pasture. It was dark but the goats saw the dog coming and slithered into a pasture with the horses to avoid her. There was much cussing. He yelled into the phone that he wanted to leave them all outside. "Let the wolves get 'em! I'll pay you $100 for each one they eat!"

I ignored that and continue to put red evidence tape on my boxes. Other Half opted to put Lily back up because having her work in the dark while a horse was bouncing around bucking and charging goats was unsafe for the dog. With the dog safe, he started again. The horse was still chasing goats. There was more cussing and he asked me how much the horse was worth again. Seven thousand dollars was more than he wanted to pay me for the satisfaction of shooting my horse.

I continued to package up evidence as he quit talking and the line went silent except for the bleating of sheep, the barking of penned dogs, and the occasional cuss word. After all was said and done, it took him over half an hour to move the goats into the pen with the sheep. I continued to tape up my boxes in silence. It wasn't a good time to point out that if he had just put the over-active horse in a stall, fed everyone some hay, and got Lily, he could have moved the goats in less than 5 minutes. As he flipped the light off and walked out of the barn, he announced, "We need to sell all these animals! Every one of them! No more sheep! No more goats! Ponies too! And just have cattle! Cattle aren't this much trouble!"

I bit my tongue. Just that morning a half-grown bull calf had crashed through the pipe cattle panels when we were trying to load him into a stock trailer. Instead of reminding him of this, I kept putting red evidence tape on packages and just let him roar. It was a fight best left for another day. Half the battle in the struggle to keep peace at home can be accomplished by knowing when to keep your mouth shut. That, and being an hour away from the storm helps.

As a rule, sheep don't try to kill you. The same cannot be said for cattle. Other Half is a cow man and like most of his kind, he has an ingrained prejudice against sheep and sheep people. Cow people tend to hold themselves above sheep people. I haven't quite figured this out since my sheep have never tried to kill me and yet, cattle seem to do so on a semi-regular basis. For all his griping about sheep, I do enjoy rubbing his nose in it when cattle don't cooperate.

The job that night was to separate a cow from the herd, clean out the nasty afterbirth hanging from her butt, and then give her a dose of antibiotics. This was a first time mother who hadn't passed the placenta after giving birth. The stringy mess hanging out of her back end was beginning to rot but was showing no signs of coming out on its own.

Since we didn't have a squeeze chute or a head gate at that place, I asked the Cowboy Cop exactly how he planned to control the cow while we cleaned her up. His plan was to rope her and have Son put the bull tongs in her nose, whereupon she would hold still while he worked.

Say again? Bull tongs are rounded tongs on a chain with a rope for a handle. The curved tongs are placed in the sensitive nose of a cow and by all appearance, are extremely painful, thus the animals often opt to go motionless to avoid the pain. Or they go bat-shit crazy. In my experience, it's a toss-up.

I don't like bull tongs. I shot his plan full of holes. The way I saw it unfolding was that he'd rope the cow and she'd go ape-shit and he'd be flipped around like a monkey on a string and the cow would end up kicking the shit out of him. It seemed to be a quite logical conclusion to me, but I'm a sheep person.

Men often feel that because they are on the top of the food chain, simpler thinking creatures must bow to their will. In my experience the chances of this happening is directly proportional to how big the animal is and how much cooperation you gain. It wasn't happening that day.

My plan was much simpler and involved less chance of physical harm. Since we had no stocks or squeeze chute at this property, perhaps we could improvise one by undoing the pipe panel corral and scooching it toward the roped cow, thus pinning her against the board corral fence where we could safely work.

And there it was. The dividing line between men and women. The point where the man decides that he knows it all and dismisses the woman.

And so he did. He did it his way. He roped the Big Black Cow. She bawled and the rodeo commenced. I stood on the fence and watched this unfold like the pages of a novel I'd read before. It was midnight. How long would the wait at the Emergency Room be at that hour? She finally slowed down a bit and in time, the two men got bull tongs on the enraged and frightened cow. While she was snubbed to the fence everyone re-grouped. During this lull in the action, I again pointed out that she was still very dangerous because she could kick the snot out of anyone near her rear end. Perhaps we should move the panels and pin her against the fence?

Other Half informed me that she was a former show cow and thus wouldn't kick.

Come again? In what universe? This bawling, slobbering, angry creature in no way resembled a show cow anymore. In fact, she looked very much like a wild animal plucked out of the swamps of the South Texas Lowlands.

He ignored my warning. The angry cow swished her tail back and forth. He ignored her warning. With Son holding tightly on the bull tong chain, Other Half scooched up to Angry Cow's Ass.

And she kicked the shit out of him.

The sound of ripping blue jeans tore through the night. Other Half bellowed and limped away. Son and I exchanged looks. He was putting weight on it so it must not be broken. Maybe. Hopefully. We examined the leg and it looked bad. Bad, but not broken. In the world of working cattle, that meant - get back to work.

But he had an idea. Perhaps, just perhaps, it might be easier to take panels apart and scooch one forward to press cow against board fence. I almost kicked him in the other leg.

"WASN'T THAT WHAT I SUGGESTED?"

He allowed as how that's where he got the idea.

So we did that. And wonder of wonders - it worked. The next week he bought a head gate and made a working pen with a chute. Apparently cow men can be trained but it takes getting the snot kicked out of them first.

If you want to tempt fate, tell someone you'll be somewhere at a specific time, and if you do, once everything has gone to hell in a handbasket, hope there is a

Southern Man to bail you out.

During summers, I became Dr. Frankenstein as I hooked up jumper cables between my truck and the Beast, my FrankenMower. Beast was an ancient Sears Craftsman riding lawnmower that was held together with duct tape and baling wire and had to be coaxed into life every time you needed to mow. The hood had blown off and was lost on the highway long ago during a trip back from the Lawnmower Repair Shop, so without a hood covering the engine, the bowels of the beast were exposed, giving it a cyber-monster appearance which matched its dubious temperament.

Since joining households with Other Half, he had taken over the job of keeping the Beast running. I'm sure this was a great relief to my neighbor who had painfully observed Beast and I over the years and no doubt sided with the machine. My rule for lawnmowers is simple:

"If the machine is still moving forward and grass is still coming out the side, then no matter what kind of noise or smell comes from the creature, forge onward and keep mowing!"

More than once my long-suffering neighbor had stood in his driveway and watched Beast and I mow uneven row after uneven row with a loud whack, whack, whack as the blade of the mower hit the deck with each turn. With an impatient wave, he'd motion me into his garage and perform a quick and dirty M*A*S*H surgery on the Beast which lasted until I hit the next pavement brick.

The Other Half soon tired of fixing Beast himself and saw an opportunity for freedom in the form of a For Sale sign on a used lawnmower parked on the highway. It was a shiny, newer version of Beast, so he put some money down on it and promised the seller we'd pick it up the next morning between 9 and 10 a.m.

By doing so, he tempted the gods of fate because this is

how that morning played out:

As we climb into the truck that morning, I note that it's parked in front of the horse trailer so I ask, "Why is the truck hooked to the trailer?"

"It's not. I was working in the trailer last night and needed the lights, so I had it plugged into the truck."

Okay. That's good enough for me. He knows what he's doing. So I sip coffee while he pulls the truck away from the trailer. The cord on the trailer, that big one, the really expensive one, with the really expensive plug. Yeah, that one. That cord follows the truck instead of staying with the trailer. I start to point this out when I see it in the mirror. Too late. SNAP! The plug snaps off and the cord flaps back against the horse trailer. Apparently that really expensive plug was caught up on the tail gate of the truck. Other Half leaps out and stalks to the back of the trailer. There is a lot of cussing. We have been awake for 30 minutes.

We table the major project of fixing the expensive plug because we must pick up the lawn mower. As fate would have it, the ball on the truck is too big for the hitch on the little trailer. (That happens whenever you pin yourself down to a specific time, such as "I'll be there between 9 and 10.")

So I calmly sip coffee while he is on his hands and knees at the trailer hitch. There is a lull in the cussing when he realizes the hitch on the jeep is the perfect size for the little trailer. Cussing resumes, however, when he discovers the hitch lock doesn't want to come off the truck.

He stalks away to get the Magic Man Medicine, better known as WD40 spray. A few spritzes of WD40 and the hitches are switched. The dogs and I watch all this with great interest. I sip more coffee. It is important to be properly caffeinated if you have tempted the gods of fate.

We get the trailer hitched up and head over to pick up the mower. Money changes hands and the mower is loaded. While following Other Half in my truck I notice there is a definite wobble on the right side of the trailer, so I pick up the cell phone. "You have a flat tire on the trailer."

There is a long pause. He is cussing under his breath. "How flat is it?"

This question confuses me. Flat is flat. What does a man mean when he asks "How flat is it?"

"It's flat."

"Well, we'll have to drive to a gas station."

That makes sense. So I ponder the question, "How flat is it," as I watch the trailer wobble down the road. Soon the smell of burning rubber wafts through my air conditioning vent. That pretty much answers his question. As he pulls into a gas station, I hop out and inform him that the tire is shot.

"How do you know?" he growls as he walks back toward the trailer.

"Because it's falling apart and pieces are all over the highway." What is it with the questions?

He stands over the sad little tire and there is more cussing. Then he climbs into the back of his truck and opens the tool box. There is much tossing of tools. There is mumbled cussing. Eventually a tire iron and a big-ass jack get tossed out. The big-ass jack looks like something I might want to play with. I pick it up and try to figure out how it works. Other Half is not in the mood to give me a lesson on How to Use A Big-Ass Jack. He quietly takes it away and does it himself. No problem. I didn't really want to use it any way.

He quickly jacks up the little trailer and reaches for the spare. The tire iron is too big. There is much cussing and the F-Bomb explodes. Several times.

It is hot. I think now might be a good time to head off to the convenience store to get him some snuff and caffeine. He asks me to see if the convenience store sells tire-irons.

Really? I do not say this out loud. He is sweating and his face is red. The last thing he wants to hear is me inform him that Ahmed doesn't even know what a four-point tire-iron is, much less sell them. So I flip-flop into the local Valero station. Sure enough, no tire-irons. Ahmed has absolutely no clue what I'm talking about. No problem. There is a busy gas station across the street.

Do I expect that they will sell tire-irons? No. I expect that they will have men. Southern Men. Men who have tool boxes on their trucks. Since Other Half is a Southern Man, and is as helpful and gracious as any member of the breed, I am completely shameless in my search to find help for him.

So I flip-flop my way across the street. This gas station is bustling with folks. I stand in the sun and wait for divine guidance. Where Lord, is a man who can help?

Ask, and ye shall receive. I head into the store and the door is opened for me by a Bona Fide Southern Man. (Southern Men open doors for ladies, even middle-aged ladies in flip-flops) I take a closer look at Southern Man. Yep. Here was definitely someone who could help Other Half. He was standing by the ice machine with several other men, waiting for his turn to get ice.

"Excuse me. I need some help."

The other men at the ice machine keep loading ice. (They were certainly not true Southern Men.) Southern Man looks straight at me, waiting to hear the problem. I explain that My Other Half is having a Very Bad Day. He squints into the sunlight and sees Other Half bent over the trailer. Then he walks outside.

After a minute of tossing around the tools in the back of his truck, he locates a small tire-iron and agrees to head across the street. I trot off, confident that Southern Man will be true to his word. Sure enough, he beats me over there.

He and Other Half share a Man-Moment as they stand over the trailer and examine the problem. The tire-iron is a perfect fit. Other Half's blood pressure is coming down. While Other Half gets the tire off, Southern Man excuses himself to go into the Valero station to get a gallon of milk. That's when I realize that Southern Man left the Busy Gas Station without his ice and milk so that he could come help us. Bless his heart!

Where would we be without the grace of Southern Men? Even after seeing so much tragedy life has to offer, the presence of a bona fide Southern Man does restore one's sense of goodness in this world.

"These aren't the droids you're looking for."

~

Those old enough to remember this classic line from 1977's movie *Star Wars* can also appreciate how The Force works on a farm. Just because this Jedi mind trick works on the feeble-minded, it doesn't mean these aren't the droids you really are looking for. And just because you proclaim something, it doesn't make it so.

Saying something slowly and with confidence might work in a George Lucas space movie, but not on a farm. Those could indeed be the wanted droids, and the cows really could be out. This is how Jedi Mind tricks play out on a farm:

I walk into living room and glance through big picture window to see two bull calves staring off into the distance. Something like this always earns further attention, because this is a clue. Walk to window. Note horses also staring off into the distance. Another clue. Note that the rest of the calves are missing. Curse under breath and nod to self. Yep, the calves are out. Inform Other Half that his cows are out.

"No they're not," he answers with great confidence.

I find this answer baffling and tilt my head like a dog listening to a phonograph. Really? Is that how it works? Deny the reality so you don't have to deal with it? I argue the point but he denies the cows are really out. He has to go into town today. He does not have time for the cows to be out. (This merely offers proof positive that the cows will be out. If you do not have time to deal with them, livestock will always be out. If you have all day, the missing animals will simply be taking a siesta under a tree somewhere.)

I shrug and head out to the pasture. I feed the horses. I feed the goats. I feed the sheep. I see his missing calves in the neighbor's pasture a long way away, but hey, the cows are not out, because he said so, thus, I don't worry about it.

He comes out to feed his cows and notes that he only has two bull calves waiting to be fed. His Jedi mind trick has failed him. I continue to feed my animals. His cows are not my problem. The cows are not out. He said so.

He drives up on the ATV and motions me to climb in. I decline. After all, the cows are not out and there is a cup of coffee with my name on it in the kitchen. He demands that I bring him a Border Collie when I return. Why? The Jedi Master said the cows aren't out. He is not amused by my logic.

The missing cows are now returning to our back fence but cannot figure out how they climbed out, thus they continue northward along the fence line. I see this but go inside for coffee. My caffeine level is low and his cows aren't out anyway. The Jedi Master said so. I trot inside and make coffee. That first sip goes down like nectar of the gods. Yes. Now. Now I'm ready to deal with loose cattle.

I amble to the kennels and release the Border Collies. One zooms off. One bounces at my feet while I answer my ringing cell phone.

"Bring me the f$#@ing Border Collie!"

I assure him that help is on the way as one dog races

toward the back pasture while one walks with me. Then the first dog hears Other Half shouting something and decides that perhaps he should pick up the two bull calves that are happily munching at the trough by the house. He decides that perhaps he misunderstood the situation and is needed to gather up these calves and bring them to Other Half in the pasture. Despite my screams to abort this plan, both dogs gather up these calves and begin driving them to Other Half who has called the dogs to him.

The missing calves have found the new hole that Other Half just cut in the fence and are climbing back through because they heard breakfast being served. Trace picks them up and soon all the calves are back together.

With the cows back in the pasture, I again take this opportunity to point out that announcing something doesn't make it so. For some reason, he is not in the mood to hear this. I can't imagine why. Thus I point out again and again that the cattle were indeed, out, Out, O-U-T, out.

Now he is late. He is wet with sweat. And he still has to fix the hole in the fence. But - I do note that he does not announce there is not a gap in the fence. After all, saying it doesn't make it so. So our lessons for the day were:

1) Just because you can proclaim something, that doesn't make it so.
2) If you are in a hurry, livestock will get out.
3) If you are in a real hurry, take a Border Collie.

Timing is everything. If you don't believe it, let me share this illustration. I'd been making regular visits to the Sheep Goddess for herding dog lessons. Being a crack dealer of the worst kind, she'd been stuffing me full of homemade goat milk cheese at each trip and I was beginning to look too long at her baby goats. I'd always wanted a dairy goat so after chewing on it for a while, I bought two kids over the phone. (Without consulting the husband) I wasn't picking them up for a week. That left plenty of time to drop the Goat Bomb on him. As it was, the bomb landed sooner than later.

Other Half had been working a Big Multi-Agency Operation and had been away from home quite a bit, leaving Son and me to shoulder the farm responsibilities. He was back in town but still working the detail when he called that night. I was happy to hear his voice until I found out the purpose of his call was to inform me that he'd found a litter of raccoons. Other Half is the only man I know who can go out looking for narcotics and come home with a family of raccoons, which he would leave me to care for while he jetted off again. The long and short of his excuse was that Momma and the litter were slated for death by a Pest Control Company so he rescued the litter. A Raccoon Bomb had just landed on my desk.

The explosions began. We could not keep a litter of raccoons! It was against the law. That failed to deter him. He had a pet raccoon when he was a kid. In his mind he already saw four baby raccoons bouncing around our living room with the dogs. I pulled out the big guns. I took aim and reminded him that he'd been an absentee husband for almost 3 weeks, leaving Son and me to handle his animals and there'd be a mutiny if he brought home more responsibilities. This seemed to strike a chord.

I offered to make some phone calls to find wildlife rehabbers in his area. He agreed and went back to dinner. Minutes later I called him with two phone numbers. Then I went back to my work and forgot about raccoons.

All was well until I called to let him know I was leaving the office. He then shared that he was still, 3 hours later, in possession of baby raccoons. Do what? Apparently he only called one number and they didn't return his afterhours call.

I pulled out a Giant Hissy Fit cannon. His excuse was that he was not driving the car, thus was not in control of his own destiny and everyone else wanted to eat, not deal with raccoons. (Because normal men on narcotics details don't pick up a family of raccoons.) I aimed that Hissy Fit cannon at him and shot out a volley. Those poor babies had been sitting in a cardboard box in the back of a car for the last three hours! While the raccoons were important enough to rescue, they obviously were not important enough for him to put off eating his own dinner? How 'bout that?

Other Half assured Angry-She-Bitch-With-Hissy-Fit-Cannon that he would drop Innocent Babies off at the SPCA. The Angry She-Bitch pointed out that the SPCA was not open at this hour. Other Half countered. He dropped off a baby owl last year and the facility is always manned. He then asked if we had any Kitten Formula. I went postal. He promised he would not bring home a litter of raccoons.

Sometime later a smug Other Half called to say that Precious Babies were happily snoozing under a heat lamp at the SPCA. He was quite proud of himself. The Angry She-Bitch was slightly satisfied, but since she saw the door open, she ran through it, taking that opportunity to inform him that she'd just purchased two baby Nubian goats. As predicted, he stroked, but not quite with the same steam he would have had he not tried to bring home a family of raccoons.

~

"You like that color?"

She said it in the same tone that one would say, "I stepped in a dog turd."

The sun's rays glinted off the red spots on the goat like sunlight dappling a new penny. The friendly doe nibbled my jacket.

"I love her!"

"She's for sale. And she's pregnant."

Sold! And that's how I went to pick up two dairy goats but came home with three. The weaned baby goats were cute but this bred doe was just exquisite. Not only did she have an uncommon beauty, she was gifted with a sweet and gentle nature that was very different from my goats bred for meat. With her long silky Bloodhound-like ears, this red moon-spotted doe was the perfect ambassador for dairy goats. Clover was the goat to make you love goats. She was a Julie Andrews singing in a high mountain meadow kind of goat. She needed to be, because Other Half would rather have added raccoons than dairy goats.

In time she produced a single black and gray version of herself. He sold quickly. Without the baby nursing, I soon discovered the little red spotted doe was a factory, churning alfalfa into milk faster than I could use it. I was giving the stuff away. Until one day . . .

With its creamy sensuous lather, goat milk soap is a decadent indulgence. Goat milk soap is to grocery store brand soap what the finest chocolatier's truffle is to an aluminum foil-wrapped chocolate bunny found at a drug store end of season sale.

Scented soap has always been an indulgence of mine, so when I found myself with an overabundance of goat milk, I drove three hours away to meet with a woman who would teach me to make goat milk soap. If the Sheep Goddess was my crack dealer introducing me to a world of new addictions, this woman was a witch in the forest, stirring her cauldron of intoxicating delights, each fragrance with a new and different property. I was swept into a veritable Soap Apothecary, with a different fragrance for whatever ailed you.

If your stomach hurts, and you don't know why, try this Cucumber Mint Soap. For the first day of school, or a new job, a dash of Mint Oatmeal Soap in the morning. The

Oatmeal, Milk, & Honey Soap is a comforting warm blanket, straight out of the dryer.

Ideas like bees darted in and out of my mind on the drive home. It was time for goats to start paying for themselves. Goat milk soap was my answer.

I soon began my new side job as a drug dealer. Soaping is not the quaint cottage task that you would imagine from reading Hobby Farm magazine where you can see in your mind's eye a woman in a homespun dress making soap like churning butter in a wooden crock. Soaping is a chemistry experiment, much like making meth, except you're less likely to blow the house up.

Soaping is *Hobby Farms* meets *Breaking Bad*. True cold process soap, like Grandma used to make, involves mixing lye with fats and oils. There are as many recipes as there are soapers but they all come down to mixing a variety of fats, and oils with lye, which is a very dangerous chemical and should be treated with the greatest of respect - long sleeves, shoes, goggles, mask. You can skip the goggles and the mask, and make your soap in shorts and flip-flops instead. You can. I wouldn't advise it, but you can. You can also find yourself backing away from the sink, coughing and gagging when a whiff of vapor blows your way too. And be careful not to spill it as you recoil across the kitchen with a wet spoon. That stuff burns. No children. No pets. No kidding.

Once mixed, however, the fats and lye join in holy matrimony, kiss and walk down the aisle, and a new union is formed - soap. It is a glorious marriage where the properties of the individual are no longer separate, but become one. This new something is born completely different from its parts. The chemical reaction is complete and the result is a wonderfully safe, wholly decadent, bar of sudsy indulgence. But until then, it's like making meth in your kitchen. And the fragrance, oh, the fragrance. The alluring scents grab you. The creamy suds and the lingering aroma bring you back for more.

For quite a while I was just making soap and giving it to friends. My soap sales started with a wedding. And no gift. So I packaged up a soap basket for Other Half to take to the wedding. I was at work that night when he called. "Hey, the mother of the groom works in a Western Wear store. They want to start carrying your soap."

A business was born. I was soon selling soap as fast as I could make it. The Other Half made light of my dairy goats until I crunched the numbers for him. In four months one goat brought in $1700 in soap sales. That was more than the sale of one calf. Suddenly someone who ate poison ivy and weeds earned a new level of respect in our home.

CHAPTER 12

BUMPER CARS WITH
BLIND BULLS & VELOCIRAPTORS

You haven't lived until you've played Bumper Cars with a bull. His icy eyes rolled slowly toward my perch on the side of the corral. My legs were nothing more than bumpers on a dock as the blind bull coasted in like a boat colliding with a pier. The big Angus gazed at me with blue, sightless eyes. Not what you want to see in your breeding bull. I saw him the day before and he seemed fine. Bully was standing out in the pasture. I was in a hurry so as long as he was standing, I didn't think anything more about him until the neighbor called. "Hey, your bull's gone blind."

And he had. In less than two days his eyes had changed from dark brown to pale blue and he couldn't see a thing. A call to the vet wasn't very encouraging but we opted for a desperate attempt to restore his vision by shooting him up with a high-powered antibiotic and flushing his eyes with penicillin. We'd give him a month. It would take that long before the antibiotics would leave his system so we could butcher him. Bully had a month to recover. If not, he'd go to Freezer Camp. It was not an option anyone wanted. Least of all, Bully.

The first step was to move a blind bull through the

pasture and into a corral. This was a game of Blind Bull Bumper Cars. Other Half, Son, and I worked on foot to slowly push him into the corral while minimizing damage to barbed wire fences, corral boards, the bull, and humans. One should check with one's insurance agent before playing this sport. Double check that deductible.

It's important to breed for good temperament in cattle and to routinely handle them with patience. If the bull proved too dangerous we'd have to shoot him. Fortunately for all involved, Bully was a gentle bull, not prone to violence or overreacting. Even a good bull is dangerous if he can't see, so it was a slow, agonizing journey. Other Half almost pulled the plug and called it quits but to do so was a certain death sentence for Bully, so as long as he behaved like a slowly coasting ship bumping the dock, we kept trying.

When touched softly with a sorting stick, the bull eased away from the pressure and so bit by bit and bump by bump, we moved him through the pasture and into the pens. Once in the chute, we were able to doctor his eyes. It didn't look good. He had a month.

Other Half studied the cow's ass like a college professor. He was preparing to go out of town again, leaving me with a blind bull, cows calving, a house full of dogs, and a flooded farm. I begged him, "Please! Let's move Paisley so she doesn't calve in the mud in the back pasture. Let's move Paisley to where I can more easily handle her."

His response after studying Paisley's back side like he was writing a grant proposal on it was, "Oh, she won't deliver for another week or two."

I gave his analysis some thought as the next day I stood in ankle deep mud staring at a wet calf. I had a murder trial in two hours. The drive to the courthouse was 45 minutes. There was barely enough time to do chores and get a shower. Paisley, who was as dumb as a box of rocks on a good day, apparently did not read Other Half's thesis on her lady parts. A small red calf stood in the mud and shivered while her idiot mother stared. The cow's expression said it all. "What the hell is that?"

Lovely. I whipped out a cell phone, ripped off my muddy gloves and dialed. "Are you happy now?"

Professor Cow Butt was ripped from the warmth of his bed in a hotel room to a screeching akin to a fan belt coming apart under the hood of your car. I was not a happy woman. He made some phone calls and Son was soon on his way over to help. Unfortunately Paisley was largely uncooperative. We toweled off the baby and tried to warm her up while Paisley stared at her like a teenager with a new cell phone. Son picked up the baby to carry her to the barn but Paisley refused to follow. Lovely. The baby tried to nurse but Paisley knocked her down and accidentally kicked her as she walked away. The calf shook her head to reassemble her rattled brains. She was okay. Except for the fact that her mother was a crack head, she was fine.

The rancher next door had received my panic call and climbed over the fence to assess the situation. Finally. The cavalry has arrived. He agreed to keep an eye on the little tyke while Son and I went to our paycheck jobs.

After spending four hours in court, I drove back home to check on the calf. The rancher was also returning back home and so he and I arrived in the back pasture at same time. Baby was still alive. He promised he'd check on the calf after his chores, so I drove the 45 minutes back to work.

Rancher checked on the baby that afternoon. She was okay. Son checked on baby when he got off work. She was okay. I returned home and checked on her in the dark. She was okay. The next morning I found the baby alone on the other side of the barbed wire fence — away from the rest of the cows.

I cussed Other Half and his Professor Cow Butt Proclamations again. Things would have been so much easier if Paisley the Crackhead had calved in the corral. While feeding the other cattle, I was mugged and shoved down. Wiping mud off my knees, hands and forehead, I cussed Other Half, the entire cattle industry, and beef in general.

Once the cattle settled in at the feeders, I tried to tote the baby back into the pasture. She was too heavy for me to carry in the mud so I got her on her feet and started poking body parts through the barbed wire fence. The calf was cooperative. It must have come from her father's side. Paisley had her head buried in a feed trough, oblivious to the fact that she even had a baby. As I walked through the gate to join the calf on the other side, Baby let out a cry for Paisley.

A small tank splashed through the mud toward me. Paisley finally remembered that she had a baby. Her pea brain registered that a biped had her baby and the baby was crying. The thought of running me down flashed across Paisley's small brain. This was an undeniably short trip. As the cow slopped in my direction, I darted behind a large round bale of hay to safety. Paisley joined her baby and glared at me. The biped had tried to steal her cell phone.

Paisley then sloshed off as the baby was trying to nurse. Her strides lengthened as the calf ran along trying to grab a swaying udder. She followed her mother around the pasture but finally gave up and laid down. Still hungry. Paisley stopped to examine her stalled cell phone. I watched them for a minute. Definitely time to sell Paisley. Life is too short to raise crackhead cattle.

His name was scribbled in pencil on the calendar. His

date with death. An appointment with the butcher. By then the antibiotics were out of his system. Bully's month was over.

As luck would have it, the antibiotics had worked. Eyes that had been pale blue were slowly returning to brown again and Bully was able to navigate around the corral. We'd put a Seeing Eye Cow with him for company but now we turned the rest of the cows into the pen. Bully appeared to be able to navigate his way through the herd so we turned them all loose in pasture. Because he managed to avoid falling in the pond, we cancelled Bully's date with death. The old bull still had another breeding season or two in him. But just to be on the safe side, we kept a bull calf from that year's crop to replace his father when it became necessary.

If you're in the business of breeding cattle, having a second bull shouldn't be overlooked because if one bull fails to do his job, each cow not bred is a serious loss of money. It's a sizable chunk of change and a risk we were not willing to accept. After our close call with Bully, we began keeping two bulls on hand.

There was a cow in my bedroom. Stuff like that isn't covered in *Better Homes & Garden* or *Good Housekeeping* magazines. By the time we found the calf, buzzards were already gathering. We scooped him up and drove him back to the barn where we got him revived, then gave him electrolytes and antibiotics. We then milked his mother and gave him a warm meal.

The plan was to leave him with her in a small pen. She licked the calf and seemed a bit concerned, but temperatures were dipping too low to leave him outside in his condition. Thus he ended up in our bedroom under a pile of dog blankets. If he died, at least the ants and buzzards wouldn't get him.

The dogs were appalled. Everyone except Blue Heeler. The little blue dog took a post on the corner of the bed where he could peek down and watch the calf. A canine Florence Nightingale.

We started calling the calf Norman. Not original, but then he didn't care. The calf was premature. Other Half had planned to put him down the next afternoon because he wasn't making a marked improvement but after some more research on premature calves we decided to give him a chance. The mortality rate is high, but some do pull through, so we opted to try.

On the second night. Other Half fed him around 7 p.m. and tucked him in before leaving for work. I came home at midnight. When I opened the bedroom door I found him motionless. Not surprising. Norman was still warm but he was gone. Little premature Norman had died.

Blue Heeler rushed in to attempt a canine version of CPR. It was touching. The little blue dog whined and licked the calf's face. I gave him all the time he wanted. He guarded Norman's body from the other dogs while I pulled Norman's pallet into the muck room. I left the calf there while the dog continued his attempts to revive the little guy. It was sad, poignant — Hollywood's version of what a dog is, and most aren't. And yet, there it was in front of me.

Briar was in the yard and so she came into the muck room through the back door to check out Norman's body. Blue Heeler growled but she was politely persistent. The Big White Dog had never seen Death claim someone so I called the blue dog away to let her carefully explore Norman's body. Then I went to phone Other Half. I was okay. No tears. Despite our best efforts, saving Norman was a longshot. It is what it is. Nature can be cruel. While I chatted with Other Half, I was okay. I was okay until I walked back into the muck room and saw Briar. Then I burst into tears.

Briar, who had never seen Norman alive, was lying beside his still body with her chin on her paws. Her expression was the saddest I've ever seen. Briar understood Norman was dead. She settled down beside him and waited, her expressive eyebrows shifting but her big head never moving from her paws. That's when I cried. Not for Norman. Norman was gone. I cried for the sweet nature of a good dog.

To the other dogs, Norman was a Thing. He was never a "someone." But Blue Heeler and Briar saw suffering and death for what it was, and they responded with uncanny sympathy. It touched me. Sadly, Norman joined the ranks of my other failed attempts to save the longshots. God is forever sending helpless animals my way. I have killed more baby birds than I care to remember. Their deaths leave me screaming at God,

"Why do you insist upon sending me these things? You know I can't keep them alive!"

I have a long history of shouting at God but like Blue Heeler, I have to try. And when the calf dies, like Briar, all I can do is mourn another failed attempt to cheat Death. Ranching isn't always about the cute and cuddly. Lots of times it's about the muddy and the bloody.

~

He died that same way he lived, like a real cowpony. Even though we had expected it, you are never quite prepared for that call.

"Skip is down, and I can't get him up," the neighbor said.

The old horse was approaching thirty years old now and time is cruel. He'd cheated Death twice that year already and we didn't expect him to make it through the winter. Other Half and Skip had logged many miles together. Skip had penned many a cow, carried many a child, and was that "go-to horse" that you could count on when you needed the job done right. They shared a lot together. They were co-workers, they were friends. They took care of each other. And so when he put the phone down, Other Half drew a heavy sigh. This horse, who had safely carried him through so much, this horse who had safely carried his children, now needed to be safely carried along his journey.

Phone calls were made. The vet was unavailable. His staff would give him the message when he got in but the earliest appointment would be in five hours. Death was already pulling Skip away. He was a fighter, but it was a losing battle, and Other Half refused to allow Death to toy with Skip for five more hours.

Skip laid his great head against Other Half and he cuddled that old horse like a lap dog. He stroked his eyes, smoothed his mane, and kissed his forehead. Then with a heavy heart, Real Cowboy shot Real Cowpony. We held each other as Skip fell. I've seen a lot of death and have come to learn that there are worse things — suffering and regret. Skip lay in the shade of a beautiful October morning with the blue sky over his head. The weather was good. It was a good day to die. Other Half took a ragged breath and went back to stroking Skip.

As I watched the bloody merry-go-round of sheep and dogs spin in front of me, I wondered how I got here. It was one hell of a week already and it was only Tuesday. My schedule had been turned upside down because I was in a crime scene investigation class that ran from 8 a.m. to 4 p.m. The problem was that to get there on time, I had to get up at 5 a.m. To top it all off, I'd quit drinking frappuccinos again.

Other Half was home and so I happily shoved all the care and feeding of the farm onto his shoulders. Just getting to class on time and home through rush-hour traffic was more than my feeble little, Starbucks-deprived, homicidal mind could handle.

Monday was bad. There is not enough caffeine in Texas for me to handle Houston rush-hour traffic both coming and going. Tuesday's drive was better but my entire routine was still thrown off. This is when mistakes are made. Tuesday afternoon I got out of class and called Other Half. He had just left the house and gave this word of warning, "Don't forget that the sheep are in the yard."

I assured him that I would remember. After all, they were in the yard on Monday and I remembered then. When I got home I drove into the driveway and saw the sheep in the side yard. *"Yep. Sheep are in the yard. Don't forget that."*

I stopped on the road and got the mail. Opened the gate. Briar came to meet me. I drove through, closed the gate, and drove into yard, careful not to roll over Briar's toes as she escorted me in. Once I gathered gear and brought it into house, I let Lily outside. Then I fingered through the mail before shuffling outside to let the kenneled dogs loose.

Now, a whole afternoon free to enjoy. I went to water the garden and check the hail-damaged tomatoes. Something was just not right. It was too quiet. Where were the dogs? Lily was not here. That was odd. Lily was always beside me. Where was she? Briar was here. Briar was my Gardening Buddy. My mind did a little rollback reel of events. "Oh shit! OLI!"

I had turned a Belgian Malinois out with sheep. The velociraptor was loose. I may as well have been screaming into a hurricane as I ran. Around the corner of the house, I found Oli swinging a ewe around by the tail. Oli was 45 pounds on a good day. The ewe was probably 150 pounds. I was hysterical.

Screaming. Cussing. I ran to them as the ewe's tail came

off in Oli's mouth! Her tail literally popped off. The sheep left her tail wiggling in Oli's mouth and raced to the other sheep. Oli dropped the tail and began madly circling the sheep which gathered around me and Briar.

Oli circled us in a mad orbit, searching for a way through me and Briar. She was in full predator mode and I couldn't stop her. Briar couldn't catch her. Endless frantic circling. She waited for her opportunity to strike again. Finally she burst past me and grabbed another ewe. I was on her immediately. The dog spat out the sheep who ran over Briar in her haste to get away. I dragged Oli off by the collar, a wild-eyed, panting maniac on two legs. The dog. Not me. Well, yes, me too. Breathe. Just breathe. Angry. At myself. Breathe. Breathe.

This was 100% human error. Oli was a Predator Deluxe. She did not belong on a farm. Eventually someone would screw up. The sheep paid dearly for our mistakes. Once the missile that was Oli got launched there was little anyone could do to stop her. The ewe lost about 9 inches of tail. Sawed off. Just like that. The other ewe had some tooth marks. Both survived but it was painfully obvious that juggling a predator like Oli with farm animals was a disaster waiting to happen.

There is a peace that comes with tending the flock. It is gift yielded only in the company of gentle beasts who live in the moment. The easy pace of sheep and goats forces the shepherd to slow down, lulled by the steady grinding of teeth that turn plant fiber into milk, meat, and wool. This heals and renews the soul just as the pecking and scratching of chickens rejuvenates the land.

A child knows when she is happy but it takes many years for the woman to recognize something which stirs her soul. After years of trial and error, years of experimenting with societal expectations, she finally understands the "click" —

that something which clicks into place and fills an emptiness not even realized. Since Biblical times man has been tending the animals, alone in the wilderness with his flock and his God. The world spins faster now, pulling us farther and farther away from the still quiet voice inside. Yet some of us stumble upon the answers of our ancestors — peace through the patient grinding of teeth, the pecking and scratching, which slows down our world and stirs our soul. Webster's Dictionary has multiple definitions for the word.

Tending:
1) (archaic) to listen
2) to pay attention
3) to act as an attendant, to serve
4) to have or take charge of as a caretaker
5) to stand by in readiness to prevent mischance

While on the surface we are the caretakers of our charges, I note the archaic definition "to listen." Is this not what all the quiet grazing, browsing, and pecking beg us to do?

Listen. Listen to the silent screech of pulled grass, the pop of the branch as it swings back in place, the brush of soil thrown behind upturncd feathered rears. Listen to the birds. Listen to the morning glories open. Listen to sunflowers turn. Listen to the earth. Listen to your soul. Listen to God. Just listen.

CHAPTER 13

THE QUEEN OF FOOLS

There is a point where you stop and consider that perhaps the decisions leading up to this moment were made in haste. You may choose to either wear a bag over your head or lift your chin, put tits to the wind, and embrace your poor choices.

On that particular day Other Half had already done all the morning chores for me and so all I needed to do was hike outside and release the sheep and goats after they finished breakfast. It was planned as a quick trip out and then back so I trudged to the barn in a major fashion faux pas: a bright orange "Life is Good" t-shirt, no bra, gray yoga pants that came down slightly below the knee and — cowboy boots. There was no need to get dressed. All I had to do was open two gates. What could happen? So the Farm Fashionista thumped outside in her cowboy boots and locked the Border Collie in an outside kennel before proceeding to the barnyard. Since the plan was for the sheep and goats to come into the yard to mow, I left the back yard gate open.

The goats were housed in a small pen inside the main sheep pen so after opening the sheep gate, it was then necessary to open the goat gate. I let the sheep out and then released the goats. The dairy goats followed me like puppies toward the back yard. They did this because they were dairy goats. I was the Pied Piper with my animals trailing behind me like obedient mice. It was a Julie Andrews in the *Sound of Music* moment until I realized the sheep were not coming. They had run into the goat pen to hoover up any remaining alfalfa.

The goats reached the back yard but then turned in confusion.

"Where are the sheep? We can't get sunflower seeds until everyone is together. Where are the sheep? We must go find them."

So they collectively turned and trotted out of the yard and back toward the goat pen. I stood at the gate and called. "Baaaa!!!" I yelled. They ignored me. As they passed I grabbed two goats by the collars and hauled them back into yard. While dragging two unwilling dairy goats I called to the others, "Baaaaa! Baaaaa!"

And that's the moment I felt it. Yes. Someone was watching. Like a balloon with a slow, deflating leak, I straightened up and looked around. The rancher next door was standing in his driveway watching my circus. Even through his sunglasses, I saw the slight smile. A twitch at the corner of his mouth. I can only imagine what he was thinking.

I let go of one of the goats, gave him a helpless wave with one hand to acknowledge my ridiculous condition, and then went back to wrangling stock. The sheep still wouldn't come. It was time for a Border Collie.

Lily had already assessed the situation from her kennel and thus with no instructions she moved the goats back into the yard. Then she stalked toward the sheep. They saw her and took off running away but she scooped them up and together everyone headed for the gate. I put her on down while the sheep waited impatiently for me to open it. With a Border Collie at their heels, they were ready to go in the back yard.

I passed the water tank and picked up the toilet brush which was used for scrubbing water troughs. With brush in hand, I opened the gate to let the sheep into the yard. They filed in like church ladies as I stomped behind them. I stole a glance at the rancher. He was leaning on his fence. Watching. Oh my. If it were possible to look even more ridiculous, the addition of my toilet brush had completed my ensemble.

I had two choices. I could hide my head in shame and never come out of the house again, or I could rise. Hold my head up high. Tits to the wind. Embrace the crazy. If you go outside looking like the Queen of Fools, you may as well carry a toilet brush scepter.

"When the fruit is ripe, the apple will fall."

For three weeks I'd been on Baby Watch. That's a long time to hover over a goat. The first week was because her full sister gave birth one week early so I started watching this doe like a hawk just in case she chose to follow her sister. Nothing that first week.

The second week she was due so I really watched her. And the neighbors watched her. Nothing. The last week she was as wide as a 55 gallon drum, and overdue. I was calling friends in a panic. She was a first-timer. What if there were complications? Should I induce labor?

Dear Friend Kaye (Vet's wife): "No, don't induce. Let nature take its course."

Dear Friend Sue gave this pearl of wisdom: "When the fruit is ripe, the apple will fall."

At 5 a.m. the first apple fell. The second apple fell at 5:29 a.m. Both bucklings. Since it was healthy birth with two healthy babies and a healthy momma, I wasn't complaining. As I sat in the stall attending births I gave some thought about how my life was so different from everyone else whizzing by on the highway at this hour. Earlier in the week a well-meaning co-worker heard me complain about the impending rain and said, "Why are you the only person in Texas that doesn't want rain?"

I almost shot him. He meant well. He really did. He is a highly intelligent, very well-educated, dear, sweet person who is simply out of touch with life outside suburbia, and still thought we were in a drought. Most folks don't notice rain unless it affects their morning commute. People who live in the country understand juggling animals in the rain. When the rain did come, it was torrential rain with high flooding, the kind that drowns baby goats and lambs. Farmers have to be on top of that kind of rain.

The rain came and went. The flooding receded, leaving lots of mud and happy frogs. More rain was due. Lovely. I had sheep bagging up. Such is the life of the farmer, but at the moment, I had two healthy babies on the ground, Other Half was returning home from working the Mexican border, and I could happily turn the farm over to him and go to my job-with-a-steady-paycheck.

I listened as the traffic zoomed on the highway and thought about my last 12 hours:

At 7 p.m. I check the goat. Nothing. At 9 p.m. she is talking to her belly and appears to be having contractions. At 11 p.m. she decides it is just gas. At 1 a.m. she is sleeping. At 3 a.m. she is sleeping. At 4:55 a.m. the dog in the house announces that she has to pee. I inform her that

I will check the goat then come back and get her. She can stay outside until I do morning chores.

Walk to barn. Peek in barn to see a baby flop out of the doe and land on ground. Grab doe's sister who rushes in and tries to steal baby. Escort new Aunt outside of stall where she peeks over and calls out advice to her sister. Race back to house for towels and baby stuff.

Towel off little guy. Check his privates. Yep. It's a boy. Figures. He's flashy. Get him cleaned off. Momma is really attentive until she stops cleaning him to have the next one. At 5:29 a.m. she drops another boy. She leaves him there to go back to Baby #1. Baby #2 is solid brown. By the time we are done, the babies are clean and I'm covered in amniotic fluid, sand, mud, and shavings. At 6 a.m. I call Other Half and wake him up. He is in some motel room on the Mexican border. The phone call is a slightly more polite version of: "Wake up. Babies are here. Hurry home. I gotta go to work today. You're on deck."

I feed the goats and milk the new Aunt. Brand new Cousins peek at the new arrivals with great interest until breakfast is served, then it is every kid for himself. The doe passes the afterbirth and I hurry to scoop it out and take it to the trash can on the street. Today is trash day. I wonder what my co-workers would think of this. While the rest of the world is emerging to join the Rat Race, I'm racing afterbirth to the trash can. As I return to the stall I see the rancher next door going to feed his horses. I call to him, "Justin! Two bucks."

"Oh good!"

That's it. Short conversation. Nothing more needs to be said. The watch is over. We can relax. He has been on baby watch over the fence for three weeks too. We both go back to chores and that's when I have a chance to assess my wardrobe. Once again, I am a Farm Fashionista. Uniform of The Day: Brown yoga pants & White t-shirt smeared with mud and amniotic fluid, black rubber boots

Class. Real class. Sigh. Perhaps I should take a shower before I run into anyone else. Tromp into house. Take a shower. Thank you, Lord, for warm water and rosemary mint soap! Hear dog in her crate. Oh crap! I forgot her! Dog had to pee! Climb out of shower. Hastily grab up clean clothes. Uniform of The Day: Gray yoga pants & yellow t-shirt with new mint green Clima-Cool running shoes

Rush dog outside. Step about twenty feet off porch and muddy water seeps into the ventilation holes in the soles of my Clima-Cool shoes. What was I thinking? In what universe does the birth of baby goats signify the end of a swampy yard? Trot back into house and trade mint green running shoes for black rubber boots.

Sip homemade frappuccino and watch the world wake up. The dogs do their thing as I reflect on birds, bees, butterflies, rainbows and the fact that I still have amniotic fluid in my hair. Apparently I was distracted by the dog in the crate and forgot to wash my hair. Go back inside and wash hair.

The farm is awake, time to do the rest of the chores. Check goats again. Second afterbirth has passed. Scoop that sucker up and race to trash can before the garbage man comes. That should really be an Olympic sport — running in rubber boots while carrying a sloppy afterbirth on a stall rake. Athletes must be able to open and close three gates and a large trash can without losing afterbirth. Time will start from the moment the afterbirth is scooped up until the garbage can lid flops back into place. No time is given if the afterbirth is not in the trash can before the garbage truck arrives.

I pass the test. The garbage truck comes and goes. I finish the chores. I sling a fifty pound bag of cattle feed over a fence and carry it to the feeders. A cow's tail flicks more mud on me as I slip and slide my way back from the

feeder to the fence. Those words come to mind again:
"Why are you the only person in Texas who doesn't want more rain?"

Ah, the voice of suburbia — a land of manicured lawns, paved driveways, and sidewalks. Only here, completely out of touch with the rural life, can someone wonder why more rain isn't a good thing. I finish my chores but now I'm disgusting again and decide I just cannot bear to wear that mud any longer, so I take another shower. It is 8 a.m. I've taken 3 showers already. Poor planning on my part but I chalk it up to lack of sleep.

Uniform of The Day: Black yoga pants, pink t-shirt, and black rubber boots — the uniform of the female farmer.

I can now stay clean for a while. It is 8:30 a.m. I need to leave for work in 4 hours. On the way I have to stop by the feed store for Chaffhaye and beet pulp. There will be no pass-off of the baton as my husband and I cross paths on the highway. I will head to The City to my Paycheck Job as he returns to take the reins on the farm but already the day can be measured a success. Two new lives have joined the world and I beat the garbage man to the trash can.

When farmers and ranchers are already ass-deep in mud, they do not want to hear that they need the rain because the state is in a drought. People who say this tend to be weather men and folks who aren't actually slopping their way through chores in the mud. These are people who get up in the morning, walk down the sidewalk for the newspaper and return to the comfort of their clean house. They can then get ready for work. This involves walking on clean floors in rooms with clean walls. They can select clean clothes and clean shoes. After this they may walk through the house into the garage where their car is parked. They will drive to work and be slightly miffed that their clean car has now got road scum on it. They will be even further miffed when they discover their child's afterschool sports event has been cancelled due to weather. They will return home in their climate-controlled vehicle, drive up to their mail box, open their automatic garage door, slip their shoes off onto a special "mud mat" at the door, and settle down to a nice evening in front of their computers and/or television where they will hear the weather man announce that we are still in a drought.

Now let's examine the lives of people with farms:

These people get up early to care for animals. There are no holidays, no sick days, no snow days, no rain days. Like the old donut commercial where the man staggers out of bed every morning and says "got to make the donuts," these people stagger out of bed and say, "got to feed the animals."

During heavy rains, if these people have carpet at all, the carpet is not clean. These people will always have tan carpet because that color matches dirt. It will be tan with a muddy brown layer in high traffic areas. The walls are flecked and smeared with mud at dog level. Muddy boots are stacked in the foyer. Muddy coats hang from the kitchen chairs. Muddy towels are piled in front of the washing machine. They smell slightly of wet dog.

These people fall out of bed in the morning to slide into Carhartt jackets and trip toward the foyer. They examine the strange lump in the hallway and note with satisfaction that it is not a dog turd, but a clod of mud from someone's boots. They thank God for this and continue to the foyer.

In the foyer they select the driest pair of wet boots and struggle to get them on over insulated socks. They then slide to the barn. These intrepid individuals are either sliding in mud or ice depending upon the day of the week and the hour of the day. Depending upon the temperature, the locks on the gates may be frozen shut. Much cussing and banging will be involved to open them. If it is not frozen, it will be muddy thus resulting in muddy gloves.

The sound of the gate opening will not be greeted by soft welcoming nickers but by impatient banging and screams of "Where's my bloody breakfast!"

It is at this point where the individual will be mugged. Feeding farm animals is not as simple as reaching into a clean dog food bin and tossing sterile kibble into a bowl on the kitchen floor. Feeding farm animals on a cold, wet morning is like a Walmart Black Friday Sale. Mouths will reach and grab from all directions but unlike monsters in a scripted Haunted House, they will make contact and will knock you down. Only when you have been knocked down by cattle while slinging out hay or cubes can you truly understand the meaning of the term "collateral damage."

An Olympic figure skater has nothing on the moves a sheep rancher can make when sliding in the mud under the onslaught of wooly backsides pushing at knee level. After the initial wave is over and mouths are busy then the farmer can ready himself/herself with the problem of water. Ice may need to be broken and buckets must be filled. This is not the time for multi-tasking. Doing other chores while leaving hoses unattended only results in flooding. Although this is a Law of the Farm Universe, to save time most ranchers will ignore this and thus overfill buckets which will lead to more mud and/or ice later. And more cussing.

After the livestock have been fed and watered it is now time to return to the house and get ready for work. Yes, work — because hauling 50 pound bags of feed and 65 pound bales of hay is not work. Sliding through mud or ice while carrying water buckets that slosh on your pants leg is not work. It is now time to shed those muddy clothes and find clothing that isn't muddy. It will not be possible to find shoes/boots that aren't muddy. Although the selected pants start out clean, they will be flecked with mud along the journey between the house and the truck as the now off-duty rancher leaves for the office. The running board of the truck will be slippery from either ice or mud, thus resulting in Olympic gymnast moves to get inside the vehicle and more mud on pants legs.

On the drive to work they will note the scores of farm workers at the local farmer's market removing or covering the crops for the third time in a week. People who have livestock will arrive at the office with hay in their hair, without make-up, with mud smeared on clean clothes from the knee down and from elbow to wrist. Their co-workers will be dressed in clean clothing that is not appropriate for the weather outside a climate-controlled office or vehicle. They will question the off-duty rancher about the moral issues regarding raising livestock for food as they explain that everything necessary for a good meal can be obtained without guilt, or effort, from the grocery store

To a rancher, having enough hay is like having a healthy 401k. Hay equals happy animals. Happy animals equal happy ranchers. With another cold front bearing down on us, I wanted to make sure we had lots of hay in the barn before the storm blew in so I loaded the dogs into an empty pickup and headed across town.

It was a bit of a drive, but the hay would be good, and the price was right. We loaded the truck with just enough hay to get us through the storm and then headed back home. I stopped for diesel and checked my load. Looked good. Careful not to joggle my cargo, we putt-putted on down the highway.

As I approached the railroad track crossing that went straight up and then straight down, I crept along and felt sorry for the van stuck behind me. After we crossed the tracks we slowly made our way to the house. As I pulled into the driveway, the van behind me stopped.

I expected to get cussed out for slow driving. Nope. The guy said we'd lost a bale of hay while crossing the tracks. I thanked him and resisted the urge to point out that while he was stuck behind me for 3/4 of a mile between the tracks and my driveway, he could have honked the horn to let me know I'd dropped a bale. Instead I thanked him, turned the truck around and sped off to find the lost bale.

I was only 3/4 of a mile away but by the time I got back to the tracks the bale was gone. I was furious. There was lots of cussing. I cursed the sorry son-of-a-@#%&* that stole my bale of hay. I turned back around, mad at myself, mad at the hay thief, and mad at the world. One bale of hay lost was a BALE OF HAY! This was not as simple as the loss of an expensive drink at Starbucks. That bale of hay would have meant warm bellies.

Anger boiled inside me as I unloaded the rest of the hay. That sorry so-and-so stole my bale of hay. Stolen hay has bad karma. Serves him right. Bad Karma Hay for him! Then a little voice tapped me on the shoulder to remind me that the hay would probably go to innocent animals. No. I definitely didn't want the hay to have bad karma. Erase that.

The hay was lost, and I could let it color the rest of my day cloudy or I could change my perception of what happened. Fact or fiction? It really didn't matter. Since I don't know what happened to the bale of hay anything that I imagine happened would be fiction anyway, so I let my imagination run with it. We make our own reality.

So mine went like this: *The bale of hay bounces off. The van drives around it. A Sorry Son-Of-@#$%& sees it. He sees that I don't notice and grabs the hay for himself. Takes it home and feeds his grateful animals.*

Since this scenario still left me pissed off, I tweaked it a little more: *The bale of hay bounces off. The van drives around it. A Sorry Son-of-@#$%& sees it. Has been trying* *to date a sweet country girl with horses who won't have anything to do with his sorry ass and decides that he can give this free hay to her as a way to win her heart. Gives her the hay. She feeds it to her hungry horses but knows he's an idiot, and won't date him anyway.*

This scenario still pissed me off, so I tweaked it some more. *The bale of hay bounces off. The van drives around it. A single mother is driving home from her all night job, wondering how she is going to feed her horse that she refused to give up when the Sorry Son-of-@#$%& who was her husband ran off with a Pole Dancer. She sees the bale of hay in the road and knows it's the answer to her prayers. She smiles. Picks it up and feeds it to her happy horse.*

I liked this scenario more but it still needed some tweaking. *The bale of hay bounces off. The van drives around it. A single mother is driving home from her all night job, wondering how she is going to feed her horse that she refused to give up when the Sorry Son-of-@#$%& who was her husband ran off with a Pole Dancer. She has worked all night. She is tired. She has to pick up her kids from her mom's. She's afraid she's going to lose her job. She's being sexually harassed by the manager so sends out a silent prayer to God for help. She rounds the curve and sitting in the road is a bale of fresh hay. It's more than a bale of hay. It is proof that God hears her prayers.*

Yeah, I liked this scenario even more but still the story needs more tweaking. *The bale of hay bounces off. The van drives around it. A single mother is driving home from her all night job, wondering how she is going to feed her horse that she refused to give up when the Sorry Son-Of-@#$%& who was her husband ran off with a Pole Dancer. She has worked all night. She is tired. She has to pick up her kids from her mom's. She's afraid she is going to lose her job because she is being sexually harassed by the* *manager. She sends out a silent prayer to God for help. She rounds the curve, and there, sitting in the road, is a pristine bale of the freshest hay imaginable. She scoops up the hay, happy that God heard her prayers and provided for her. She returns to work that night to find that the owner has fired the manager because he's a jerk, and she is now the new manager. She now works day shift and can be home with her children at night. She now has weekends off. So now she can enjoy a little time on the weekend with her girlfriends, riding the horse she refused to give up when the Sorry Son-Of-@#$%& who was her husband ran off with the Pole Dancer.*

Yeah, that works. I'm good with that. We really do make our own reality.

And that's the truth of it. Most of the time we really do make our own reality. Despite what television would have you believe, it takes more than a handsome homicide detective and a sexy CSI to work a murder. There is an entire cast of characters working behind the scenes of every death. Too often, the glowing accolades go to the wrong people. Instead the credit should go to people like Mr. Bartlett.

He is my hero and I give him the respect that he has earned over countless dead men. Mr. Bartlett's job is to pick up the dead bodies and transport them to the morgue. Hollywood doesn't often showcase this job. When they do, they depict a creepy, slow-witted Renfield creature — someone strong and too dumb or too weird to be bothered by this gruesome task. Mr. Bartlett is none of these things.

He is a most delightful person who sweeps into a crime scene like a breath of fresh air. Despite the fact that the corpse before him has decomposed into the carpet, is wedged behind a bathroom door, and weighs 250 pounds, Mr. Bartlett never fails to maintain his good humor. As he picks up bodies that the flesh is literally falling off the bone, he does it with a patient smile, and I marvel, even as I gag a little.

One day I asked, "You never seem to get down. You keep everyone else cheery. You are my hero. How do you do it?"

He gave me a smile and said the most profound thing. "I see fewer flies."

And with that, he went inside to pick up the man who'd been dead so long that he'd been eaten by his dog. I chewed on those words a while and decided that perhaps this was the wisest thing I'd ever heard. Perhaps the world would be a much brighter place if we just concentrated on the good around us and saw "fewer flies."

CHAPTER 14

MISSION IMPOSSIBLE

Seeing fewer flies is important but there is nothing quite like an army of maggots to bring you into the here and now. No matter what else is going on in life, maggots will take center stage. Maggots are a flashing neon sign that says, "Life goes on, get over your problems and get back to enjoying the time you have left. Nothing else is important."

Let me paint a picture for you so that when you're watching *CSI* on television and you think that I had the coolest job, please keep in mind that sometimes my job was like *Mission Impossible*. You are faced with a difficult, almost outrageous task, and no one else is going to do it.

The Problem: A loaded Glock semi-automatic pistol is underneath a decomposing body.

The Mission: Retrieve that gun and safely unload it.

Yes, I'm serious. No one else is going to do it and McDonald's doesn't pay well enough to cover your feed store bills, so put on your blue gloves and get to it.

Step One: The body is in a very small, very tight place, so you must remove door. Use a hammer and a chisel to pop the pins out of the hinges. They are painted on. Use some elbow grease. To do this your face must be approximately 16" from the face of a decomposing man. (Think about the guy who decomposed in place in front of Indiana Jones when he "chose poorly." Now add the smell that you didn't get in the movie theater. That's it. Now we're in the same place. Continue.)

There is a crunch of popcorn under your feet. What? That's not popcorn, you say? You are correct. The popping and crunching you feel under your feet are the hard casings from the various life cycles of the maggot. Little brown pellets break under your boots. Your toes curl in disgust with each crunch. The door finally comes free and we move on to Step Two.

The body car guys remove the body from the room. They must do this carefully because decomposing things fall apart. You inform them that they do not make enough money. They agree. The body is now laid out on a body bag for the exam. You do a preliminary examination prior to zipping him up and taking him to the morgue. You chart bullet holes and any other injuries. You note maggot activity. As you write on your pad, maggots are inchworming across the carpet. Try to avoid stepping on them. This is futile. Your toes curl some more in disgust.

Step Three: Crunch time. You stare at the gun sitting in a sea of maggots. Their body has been removed and they are not happy. Ponder for a moment what it takes to make a maggot happy. Shake that thought out of your head. Gingerly lean down. Wait! Stand back up. Adjust the Bluetooth in your ear to make sure it does not fall into the Maggot Pond because if the Bluetooth falls into the maggots that sucker will stay there.

Deep breath. Lean over and with two gloved fingers, pluck the loaded gun out of maggots. Make mental note to speed up retirement plans. Duck walk across crunchy maggot casings to place the gun on a towel. Maggots stubbornly cling to gun. Rub them off with a towel. Weigh out how much money you will lose if you retire now. Place gun on towel. Turn to medical examiner. She is green. This confirms that you do indeed, live in some alternate universe and normal people don't do these things. But we're not done yet. The gun must still be unloaded.

Pick up gun again. Maggots squish against your gloves. Toes have curled and you are now walking on them. Push button to release magazine. It pops loose but the clip does not come out. Slowly pull magazine. Maggots fall out with it. Glance at medical examiner. She resembles a lime at this moment. Think perhaps a margarita would be nice right now. On a beach somewhere. Anywhere. Anywhere but here. Go back to gun.

Maggots are now crawling across the towel in search of a body. Flick them off your glove. The gun is still loaded. You try to rack the slide back to pop the bullet out of the chamber. No luck. It is glued shut with dried body fluid goo. Goo cement. Inform medical examiner it is highly possible that attempts to unload gun may cause it to fire. Her color changes from lime green to slightly greenish-white. Set gun back down on towel and contemplate problem.

Time is up. No Fairy Godmother is going to materialize and unload the gun, so you pick it up again. Pray that if it goes off the damage is minimal. You have crossed the threshold. You no longer care if the damned thing goes off as long as the bullet comes out and no one is hurt. Ordinarily that would be a nightmare but the maggots have moved you to a different emotional plane. Score another one for the maggots.

Take a deep breath and give it another go. The bullet grudgingly comes out — along with more maggots. Shake them off your hand and think about retirement again. Chant. "HappyPlaceHappyPlaceHappyPlace ..."

Wipe hands and gun off with towel. Maggots crawl across the towel on their way to nowhere. It is now time to unload the magazine. Push your thumb into the top bullet and press it out of the clip. It slides out onto the towel — along with more maggots. Grit your teeth and keep pushing bullets out. With each bullet, more maggots fall to the towel.

Time for pictures. Stand the bullets up in a line. Maggots inch along in a micro-race to hide in the fort of sticky bullets. As the flash goes off they peek out and wave at the camera. Lock eyes with medical examiner. This is your first time to work together. You have now bonded over maggots. There is something about falling into the Abyss of Disgust to glue total strangers together.

"We are alive. We are disgusted. If we have nothing more in common, we have that, thus we are now friends."

The body has been removed. Maggots are still crawling out of it but the gun has been recovered. Mission accomplished.

~

Despite the maggots, television will tell you that my job is glamorous. Rarely. On the occasional blue moon. The blue moon that comes to mind was the very high profile case that my buddy, Fergus Fernandez, and I worked. I knew the call would be coming in because as soon as I walked into our downtown building, I saw that it was breaking news on the television in the lobby foyer. I paused beside the guard station to watch. Yikes! It would surely be national news in a less than an hour.

I was first up in the scene rotation so I'd be primary on the case. On the long elevator ride up I pondered how I'd work the scene. When I got into the office the television was already on but the call to go hadn't come in yet. The scene was still hot but it was inevitable; we would be going out on it. It was so big, so public, Fergus would be going too.

Fergus and I discussed our strategy as we watched it play out live on television. To our amazement and utter annoyance the media news choppers were all over the scene and we could clearly see the SWAT team at work. If we could see it then everyone in America could, including our suspect. There was nothing to be done about that so we gathered what information we could from the television screen and began a rough diagram of the scene on a Subway napkin as we ate a hasty dinner. Then the phone rang.

The scene was still hot. Even though it was still unfolding, because of the nature of the call, they wanted us to head that way now. We loaded the trucks and left. Fergus and I played phone tag with each other and with the office as we wormed our way through rush hour traffic. By the time we arrived the scene was no longer hot. It was under control. People were dead, but then we already knew that.

There was a surreal calmness. Although calls of this nature were normal for us, they weren't normally played out on national television so there were butterflies in my stomach. Fergus pulled his truck to a stop in front of mine. We both stepped out at the same time. News helicopters buzzed overhead as the afternoon rays glinted off our sunglasses while we headed into the building. It was a real Television-CSI moment.

Once inside, we got the news that the President had already called. The President. Of the United States. That's a pucker factor for you. After a quick meeting with detectives it was decided that one CSI was needed to work the scene inside the building and another was needed to work the scene outside the building. I threw Fergus under the bus and sent him outside with the news cameras.

Fergus may not like the cameras but the cameras love Fergus because he looks like Johnny Depp. It is his cross to bear. The camera loves beautiful people.

Once at work the scene played out like countless others: senseless violence, lives ruined. In the end, despite the moments of glamour, both Fergus and I wished we were somewhere else. In reality, the job isn't about the glamour, it's about the shattered lives. As the rest of the country was watching the tragedy play out in all the glitz of television, we were stepping over bloody bodies. It was not particularly glamorous.

"Can you come do a talk for a group of school children who are studying Forensics?"

They wanted me to do a 35 minute Power Point presentation with a question and answer session about my typical day, but they wanted it to be "Rated G, please."

"Do what?"

"Rated G, please."

Nothing about my job was Rated G. At the very best, it was Rated PG-13 and that was simply because I might be processing a suspect who had committed a Rated R offense. So I explained that while I did have a Power Point presentation which could be modified to PG-13, I could not modify my talk to Rated G.

The very kind teacher explained that I would be speaking to students in Grades 5-8, and yes, I could make it a Rated G presentation.

"No, I can't."

She passed me on to another teacher who promised she would "help me" modify my talk to make it a Rated G. I asked if she understood what my job really entailed.

"Just describe a typical day for me," she said brightly.

"The phone rings. Someone is dead. My job is to go out and determine exactly how they died."

There was a long pause. I let her digest how she was going to turn this into CSI Disney and continued. "I study the body and look at things like blood spatter, body position, stage of rigor, etc. to determine if the scene matches up with the story given to investigators by witnesses and suspects."

"Can you just talk to them about how much money you earn and what kind of education you need to become a CSI?"

"No, I don't have a 35 minute Power Point presentation on that."

Kids ask questions. Most kids ask really thoughtful questions and I can't cheat a child by not giving them a straight answer. I cautioned her. If a child asked an intelligent question, I planned on giving an intelligent answer. She countered. She would give the kids question cards before the presentation. They would just read the question on the card. That way they couldn't ask anything that might lead past a Rated G topic.

Color my mind boggled. This may be a common practice in some places but count me out of it. If I take my time to go talk to the kids, then they deserve to get a proper discussion and have their own questions answered. Since the school insisted on a Rated G presentation and since I could not in good faith provide one, I had to regretfully decline.

My hands were tied by the G Rating. I felt bad for the teachers because they were just trying to do their jobs, handicapped by the burden of administrative strings attached to everything they do. I know they want to educate their kids. They want to expose them to things that spark their interests. The problem swings right back to the "*CSI* Effect."

Because of television, there is a tremendous interest in forensics. That's not a bad thing because it brings new and fresh minds to the field, but it also encourages people to "mainstream" what is in essence a really dirty job.

The teachers were frustrated because I refused to accept that I could "just omit all the parts of your job that aren't Rated G," and I was frustrated because they couldn't accept that if you took out everything that wasn't Rated G, there would be nothing left but, "I answered the phone."

This was the same as asking an undertaker to come do a talk at an elementary school about embalming, but "keep it Rated G." The only difference is that undertakers have not been glorified enough by Hollywood to make every kid in America want to become one.

Over the years I gave talks to several school groups that had the maturity to handle the subject. Teachers sent home permission slips so parents and kids weren't surprised by the topics. I was allowed to honestly answer their questions. They got to see a modified version of what a CSI does without photos of dead bodies but at the same time, we never glossed over the fact that the entire job centered on a dead person. As long as everyone understands and accepts that the field is ripe for inquisitive minds of any age who seek the challenge of a good puzzle. But never forget that at the core of that puzzle are shattered lives.

~

The shadowy figure slipped underneath the gray Chevy Impala so quickly that I may have missed him if I hadn't already been scanning the parking garage for some sign. There he was, a blur of orange darting from an Impala to a mini-van.

Tigger was a skinny, scruffy little dude who was somehow managing to eek a living in the police department parking garage. I'm not sure how far the cat traveled but I sometimes glimpsed him on the 3rd floor and he was a fairly regular visitor on the 2nd floor where we parked the CSU trucks. The trucks were backed into a large bay area which allowed us a bit of privacy where we could hide bowls of cat food and bottled water from the prying eyes of the brass who may not approve of police officers feeding cats. Several crime scene investigators were feeding him and my guess is that kind-hearted people parking on other floors probably fed him too. Rarely sighted during the day, Tigger could sometimes be spotted late in the evening, after the city had gone home to televisions and take-out meals. Except for those of us working divisions which must be staffed 24 hours, the parking garage was empty after dark.

Even as I sprinkled cat food into the little dish, I worried about Tigger. Moths dancing in fluorescent lights are a poor diet for a half-grown cat. I'm sure he'd feast on a mouse from the McDonald's on the first floor if he could find one but the hip bones protruding from his lanky frame said he didn't get a lot of mice. Most likely he depended upon the kindness of strangers.

I poured some bottled water into another dish before walking back to my truck to load my gear and head out to my next call. Dead homeless man near a bus stop. My dolly was parked beside my truck, both waiting patiently for me. Like a pack mule, the dolly was loaded with tool boxes and tackle boxes, and as I hoisted the green tackle box into the truck, Winnie-the-Pooh and Tigger waved, smiled, and saluted. Worn smooth and a little frayed on the edges, the stickers were now seamlessly a part of the green box. I ran my thumb across Pooh's ample belly before slamming the tailgate.

As I climbed into the front seat, I glimpsed the orange cat slithering up to the cat food bowl. He paused to stare at me. I nodded, bid him bon appetit, and drove to my dead homeless man.

CHAPTER 15

WHEN COWS FLY

We make an adventure out of everything we do and buying cattle is no exception. The big Livestock Show & Rodeo had just begun and for us this involved looking at a lot of cattle. We had started adding Santa Gertrudis heifers to our herd. Bred to Angus bulls, they produce fast growing babies that give us little or no problems in the brutal South Texas climate. Although we were planning to attend the 7 p.m. Santa Gertrudis sale, we sat down in the bleachers for the 2 p.m. Braford sale. Just because. Because we had time to kill. Because our feet were tired. At a show that size finding a place to rest tired feet is an issue so Other Half urged me to go to the cattle sales arena and plop down. I cannot be held blameless for the subsequent results since I agreed to this.

My feet were tired and my experience has been that the upscale cattle sales work very much like Las Vegas casinos. They want you to stay. They want you happy. They will provide free food and drink to keep you there. So although these areas have limited access to the regular public, people with real cowboy hats and real cow shit on their boots are always welcome.

We sank into the bleachers and relaxed for a moment, and then Other Half started looking around. I'd known him long enough to recognize that look. Before he even uttered the words, I knew what he was going to say. "Since we're here, I might as well register for the sale. You never know. We might see something we want. You never know."

"But we came to buy Santa Gertrudis heifers . . ." My words just hung in the air. Nevertheless, I let it go. My feet were happy to be sitting there. Besides, this was an International Sale which brings in buyers from Mexico and South America. No matter how many times we bid against those big Mexican ranches they still take home the best genetics. They pay dearly for those genes because we don't let them go cheaply but the big money normally wins these things. With that in mind I was happy to sit there and preview the sales catalog.

Brafords. Nice cattle. Big red cows with large splashes of white. I liked them. But then again, I was not there to buy cows. I was there to rest my feet. He returned and happily plopped down beside me. We studied the sales catalog as if we were buying Brafords. I knew nothing about Braford genetics. I was simply looking for a nicely built, naturally polled heifer.

The sale began. The prices climbed. What we were looking for easily ran $3000-$5500 for unproven heifers. Fine, if you're planning on buying it, but not really what we wanted to spend for a cow we didn't plan to buy anyway.

Then a little cutie walked into the ring. Other Half looked at me. I shrugged. Whatever. He started bidding on her. Las Vegas has nothing on the allure of a cattle sale. In no time Other Half was deeply involved in bidding on a heifer that wasn't even part of our breeding plan. Each time he looked at me for assurance, I nodded. What the hell?

All was well and good for a while. Things were getting

excited though, and through the shouting and chaos, I noted the large calf getting more and more stressed. Her excitement grew. The little boy leading her became a rag doll. A kite on a string. She dragged him across the ring. And flew! Like a bird! She jumped out of the freakin' arena!

My mind raced backward in the bidding. Yes. Yes. It had stopped on us before her fit. Oh crap! She was quickly captured by a gang of burly ranchers who thrust her cowhide back into the arena. One of them relieved the boy and was trying to handle her himself. It wasn't going well for the grown man either. Also dragging him like a kite on a string, she climbed the podium, knocking potted flowers everywhere. Oh @*#*!

As I watched a full grown cowboy ski across the podium, the stage and back into the arena, I had two thoughts:

1) I bet that cow now belongs to me.

2) Thank God I have Border Collies.

The auctioneer continued. Yes indeed. The bidding had stopped at us. Did anyone want to pay more for this beast? No one? Really? Of course not. The gavel came down.

Some things are just meant to be. Over my lifetime, I've come to trust that God has a plan, so even though the last thing I needed was a wild cow that jumped fences, I was willing to sit back and let God drive. Other Half went to pay for the beast while I gathered up my courage and walked around the curtain to meet her.

She was standing calmly tied to the fence. No hint of the wild critter that was flattening flowers five minutes earlier. I spoke to her and she looked at me suspiciously. An old man in tennis shoes came up. I informed him that I was the new owner of his beast. He shook my hand and assured me that she was just scared. This was her first trip to town. He apparently had pulled her straight out of the pasture, given her a body clip and brought her to the show. As long as he was with her, she was calm, but she didn't know the young man who showed her and once she stepped into the sales ring, she was no longer with the other cattle. She was alone. She was scared. Without the support of someone familiar, she said, "Nope. I'm done! I'm outta here. I can fly!"

And fly she did. Other Half returned with the sales papers and the men began to negotiate for transport of the animal. In a weird twist of fate, even though there were cattle from all over the country at this sale, this particular breeder lived only two miles down the road from us. I had driven past his pasture and admire his cattle many times. I had probably watched this little calf grow up. The rancher offered to keep her, breed her to his registered Braford bull, and return her when she was pregnant.

In the end we bought a 14 month old registered Braford show heifer and a purebred calf from this heifer for less than half her value because she got scared and jumped out of the show ring and no one wanted to pay big bucks for her when other better-behaved cows were still for sale.

Since she could fly like she had wings, I named her "Delta the Flying Cow."

You don't own a farm. The farm owns you. City folk have this idyllic scene in their heads of farm life which includes sunshine and baby animals. The very worst they can imagine is the smell of manure. Country folk know better. Ranching is about blood, sweat, tears, and mud, lots of mud, sometimes bloody mud. If you have cattle, throw in some cow shit too. These scenes do not space themselves apart, allowing you breathing time to recover before you are smack with another. No. This kind of farm living is usually spaced right in the middle of being hurried to get to your full-time job that pays better than ranching, or when you have had no sleep.

Delta the Flying Cow turned out to be really nice so we

made out like bandits. She came home from the breeder's ranch, and eleven months later her calf was due. At 11 p.m. on that night I rolled into the driveway, already exhausted from no sleep the night before, and did a flashlight check on Delta. A gigantic wet calf was shuffling around the barnyard with the other heifers and a prone Delta was in the back pasture.

"Calf is alive. Delta is dead," I told Other Half as I gave him the play by play on the phone. I did a hasty check and verified that the calf was female. Oh good. At least if I was bottle feeding it, the calf was something we could keep. I patted her wet, muddy butt, took a deep breath and walked toward Delta.

She was stiff, feet extended like a board. Then I saw her ear twitch just a little when she heard my voice. Hope sprang forward with that ear. I knelt down to assess the situation. Delta wasn't dead. She was simply stuck. She had laid down beside an old hay bale to give birth and now she was stuck. Her feet were pointed uphill and for whatever reason she couldn't roll over on her back. She'd need help getting up. Someone needed to tie a rope on her back legs and pull her over. I looked around the pasture. There was no one but me. Crickets. No one was stepping up to help me. Just crickets.

I cussed Other Half. These things always happened while he was at work. So I went to get a lead rope and walked back out to Delta. While I was doing this the newborn calf was sucking on a very patient dry maiden heifer's udder.

I leaned down to loop the rope on Delta's feet. This is dangerous work since a cow can easily kick you from this position. Delta didn't. I looped her feet, stepped behind her and commenced to pull. And I slipped down in amniotic fluid and cow shit. People in subdivisions don't picture that part of farm living. I got up and tried it again at a different angle. And slid down in goo again. The next time I gave the rope some more distance and managed to get beyond the goo. I pulled and I pulled. Delta tried to help. Nothing. It was clear someone else would need to pull the front legs at the same time I was pulling the back.

Other Half had called Rancher-Next-Door. He was on vacation. Other Half called Next-Door-Neighbor. He didn't answer phone. Other Half continued to yell advice in my earpiece while I evaluated mud, blood, and cow shit. He decided to call his Best-Buddy-He-Grew-Up-With. I decided to walk next door.

Plan A: bang on the door and ask for help.

Plan B: flag down a passing motorist. In this neighborhood the odds are good someone will help you flip your cow.

I walked down the road and into their driveway. Fortunately Neighbor's Daughter and Son-In-Law had just returned home and she was happy to volunteer him to go into the dark and flip a cow.

I introduced myself with a filthy handshake and an apology. He had some cow experience and in short order we managed to flip Delta into an upright position. She took it from there. Delta walked over to her calf and announced, "This belongs to me. I want it back."

The calf walked off with her mother. The young man helped me move the rest of the heifers into an arena so Delta and Baby could bond. He was leaving just as his Father-in-law was walking through the gate. Neighbor (Father-In-Law) had been on calf watch for this arrival. He stepped into a mud puddle in the dark, shook it off, and walked on. A deep gratitude swelled inside me. There is something about country people, the kind of folk who will come out in the mud after midnight to check on a neighbor's cow.

Best Buddy and his new bride arrived. He got the phone call for help and she tagged along to see. I think this was her first exposure to mud, blood, and cow shit. Welcome to Ranching 101.

Delta was a very protective mother. She was so protective that nobody wanted to go double-check the sex of that calf. The big girl lowered her head and rolled her eyes and somehow knowing whether it was a boy or girl just wasn't as important as it seemed before.

And so there it is, the new bar from which you can measure your friends and neighbors. Can you call them at midnight and ask, "Will you help me flip a cow?"

The best day's work he ever did was smiling for his "Wanted" poster. As was our custom, Other Half and I were spending vacation time bouncing around Texas in an unspoken search for a place to retire. A travel plan for us was not chiseled in stone but merely a suggestion and that trip had us in Abilene, Texas. I was sitting in the pickup with Lily and Blue Heeler when Other Half returned from the campground office with a "Wanted" poster. Technically it wasn't a "Wanted" poster. It was a "Found poster."

Found! Male Border Collie!

Other Half thrust the paper at me. "Look!"

I scanned the smiling face of a black and white dog in a red bandana and dismissed it. "We didn't lose a Border Collie."

Not to be put off, the man stared into the imploring eyes of the dog in the poster and said, "But what if they can't find his owner and he needs a home? He should be with Border Collie people."

We were not Border Collie People, we were people who had Border Collies. There is a difference. (Apparently I was mistaken about this.) Other Half insisted upon calling the number on the poster and getting the story on the dog.

The rancher who answered was delighted with the idea that Other Half might provide a home for this little criminal. Apparently the true owner had already been located but the dog wouldn't stay there, choosing instead to roam the countryside chasing and penning cattle, so she no longer wanted him. Most ranchers take a dim view of dogs chasing cattle and so it was certain that if the dog didn't get hit by a car, he was sure to be hit by a bullet. The rancher and Other Half were so eager to meet and exchange the dog that I was powerless to stop the two magnets from sliding together. Over my strenuous objections, they agreed to meet at the local fire station so Other Half could "just see" the dog.

Who goes on a vacation with two dogs and adopts a strange, intact, stray dog? My Other Half. It was love at first sight. The dog climbed out of the rancher's truck and held his neck out at an odd angle to smile at us with a lopsided toothy grin. A large section of his back had been shaved to expose the teeth marks left from a close encounter with a donkey. The rancher had taken the dog to the vet, so he showed us x-rays of the damage. Although left with back problems that would plague him the rest of his life, the dog was lucky to be alive. The rancher paid to patch up the dog, named him Cow Dog, and attached a little red blinking Christmas ornament to his collar so he wouldn't get hit by a car on his travels. Although he was really fond of the dog, he didn't have a fenced yard, thus he couldn't keep him.

This "love at first sight" affair was getting out of hand. I insisted the dog must be able to get along with our other dogs. He did. At that moment. During his job interview. The three dogs walked around the fire station parking lot and nobody launched an attack so that was good enough for Other Half. "See? See! He gets along great with the other dogs!"

For this man, getting along great simply meant there was no bloodshed. Then. At that moment. Bloodshed would come later.

A sheriff's deputy drove up to check out the happenings and assured us that if we didn't take the dog with us, he would end up dead since no matter how cute he was, people were getting tired of him chasing cattle. Despite my misgivings, I had to grudgingly admit the dog needed another home and we were a better option. Other Half was simply delighted. He helped Cow Dog into the back with the other dogs who gaped as he called dibs on a window seat.

Imagine that you are out for a Sunday drive with your parents when they stop to pick up a dirty hitchhiker who then leers and jeers at you in the back seat when no one else is watching. Such was the position poor Blue Heeler found himself in as we bounced down the highway with the newest addition to the family.

At first no one believed that this kindly moustache-twirling dog with the ingratiating smile was really a Snidley Whiplash, Tie-The-Maiden-To-The-Railroad-Tracks-And-Poop-In-Your-Toy-Box kind of miscreant. No one, that is, except Blue Heeler. He knew it. He knew from the start. Blue Heeler knew before we'd left Taylor County.

And so it was that our vacation took an unexpected turn. Exactly how does one explore Texas with a truckload of dogs that may or may not get along? Perhaps time would better be spent getting to know the new dog in a more familiar setting. I studied the map and suggested we might head for a little town in North Texas that I'd come to love years earlier. It had hosted K9 training seminars for law enforcement officers and for several years I'd attended both the spring and the fall sessions.

It was a sleepy little town, a community of cattle ranchers and oil field workers. It didn't appear to offer much except a town square around a courthouse and a scenic state park. The state park was a perfect place for us to camp while we figured out how to fit this new dog into our family.

On our drive over I told Other Half about the town and the wonderful couple who hosted the seminar each year. Twice a year this couple, and in fact, the whole town, opened up their homes, their businesses, and their ranches to people who trained dogs for mantrailing, cadaver, and narcotics. My Bloodhound had been in the hardware store, the video store, and even the courthouse itself. Any place that had that kind of love for law enforcement and dogs was definitely our kind of town.

When we finally arrived at the park, I sat in the truck with the dogs while he went inside to get a campsite. A few minutes later a large bear of a man loped out with open arms. After all these years? Could he even remember me? The crushing bear hug said he did. Other Half has never met a stranger and while checking into the state park, by happy coincidence, he ran into Leo, the male half of the couple I'd been telling him about, so he made a point of letting the man know that I, longtime seminar trainee, was sitting in the truck. With dogs.

I don't think Leo has ever met a dog he didn't like, even Cow Dog, who by that time had been re-named Cowboy. Would we come to dinner that night? Well sure, sure we would. And thus a breath was blown on the spark of a friendship which ignited the flame. Dear Friends Ruby and Leo welcomed us into their home and into their hearts. By the time our vacation was over we no longer needed to bounce around Texas in search of a home. We'd found our town.

CHAPTER 16

THE PEARL OF GREAT VALUE

The single hawk's feather lying at the foot of an oak fluttered in the breeze just enough to get my attention. It waved at me and confirmed what I suspected. Here was the sign I'd been searching. This was the place. A place to call home after we retired.

Like a piece of string in a little boy's pocket, a creek flowing around a distant mountain folded and curved, and almost crossed itself along a winding path through the property. Giant Post Oak trees flanked the banks like watchmen standing in silent guard. A platoon of boulders squatted in the creek, stone soldiers guarding the land in rugged defiance as the water ambled along its rambling journey. High sand cliffs stood tall where the creek had its way with the land and cut deep in those areas without benefit of rugged rocks to stand firm against the current.

The creek was a living, breathing part of the land, bringing both life and death. Even in the drought, the ponds were still holding water, encouraging a forest rich in deer, turkey, and feral hogs. This chunk of land was a place we could live. It was just far enough away from civilization to be private, but close enough to enjoy at least the simplest conveniences of society.

We had to be sure though. In order to buy this new ranch, I had to sell my precious Failte Gate Farm. It was a leap of faith. Once sold, I couldn't get it back. Was this primitive property worth it?

I took one last walk down the red dirt road, deep into the forest, looking for a sign that this place was worth losing what I'd already built. And that's when I saw the red feather waving at me, assurance from the land itself that if we took care of it, it'd take care of us. So filled with a little dread and a lot of hope, we drove back south.

For quite some time Other Half and I had been bouncing between both of our farms. But in order for us to purchase the new wild ranch, my Failte Gate Farm and his Rocking RL Cattle Company had to co-exist on one piece of property so we could sell the charming little home that had been my farm. This meant making painful decisions. What could be pared down? Who could be sold? Who could you not bear to sell?

Sacrifices had to be made with no promise that this wild ranch would still be on the market by the time my farm sold. I was giving everything up for just a dream. And as deadlines loomed the stress mounted. I was still juggling two farms and a full time job even as I packed to get one farm ready for sale.

The alarm clock jarred me awake each morning to remind me that I must rise early to either/or/and: pack boxes, sort yard sale items, oil paneling in the house, scrub floors, take down fencing, put up fencing, meet with the realtor, meet with contractors, and meet with customers buying livestock.

I'd packed the coffee maker so no homemade frappuccino was in the bare refrigerator, but each morning

I still checked. (Perhaps this would be the day the Frappuccino Fairy will leave me a present.) I was on a rapidly spinning carousel that threatened to lift off like a space ship.

Each morning I stepped out the door to the sound of sheep screaming, goats hollering, and horses neighing. Dogs barked as they raced the fence line, escorting sheep to the barn. Their combined shrieks echoed in my head, bouncing off thoughts that already crowded my mind like commuters on a bus.

"Am I giving up everything for nothing? Will that ranch still be available? If I sell this place it means all my animals will have to fit on his farm. Can they do that? Even if we buy that ranch, can we bounce between North Texas and here once a month for years until we retire?"

I shoveled grain to the horses, flipped some token alfalfa pellets to the sheep and tossed goat grain into troughs. My dairy goat climbed onto her stand, thrust her head in the bucket and suddenly there was peace.

I straddled the bench behind her and placed the bucket underneath her udder. Her teats were warm in my hands and soon the rhythmic squirt-squirt made its metallic ring. For a short time there was peace. Throughout the barn screams had been replaced by the soothing sound of grinding teeth. I laid my head against her flank, thankful for a moment of peace among the crashing waves of insanity. While moving an entire farm may drive you crazy, milking a goat can bring you back into the now, and remind you why you keep all these animals. They are cheaper than therapists.

The triumphs and tragedies of life are well illustrated in the confined cosmos of a barn yard, and there is no greater therapy than a farm. In this renewed age of homeschooling, I would also argue there is no greater classroom than a barnyard either. Perhaps that is what this world needs — fewer mood-altering drugs, and more time spent fixing fences, less time spent on a therapist's couch, and more time spent in the pasture, less time learning about life on television, and more time experiencing the circle of life on a farm. Perhaps.

I will never own another vehicle equipped with a car alarm. If you have dogs, you don't need a car alarm anyway. If you have a vehicle as ratty as mine you don't need a car alarm. I had an old Toyota 4Runner which had logged countless miles trucking dogs around Texas so it smelled like a Bloodhound. There was hay stuck in the weave of the carpet and there were always dog noseprints on the windows.

Years ago I read the tale about a very rich man who never failed to stop and pick up a penny. When questioned about why a wealthy man like himself would bother picking up stray pennies, he explained that each penny is engraved with the words, "In God We Trust," and so he didn't look at it as picking up pennies but that each penny was a reminder to trust in God. Each penny was a little blessing, a smile from God, if you will.

It was still dark when I packed up the Border Collies and drove to House #1 for some pre-dawn packing. I stopped for caffeine at a local convenience store bustling with petrochemical plant workers starting their own day. The dogs noted a shifty-looking young man sitting in the car beside me and threatened him. Since he just looked like a scruffy guy on his way to work, I stepped out of my truck and saw the dime on the pavement. I passed it up to go inside but as I did the little voice in my head said, "That dime is ten times the blessings of a penny! Go back and get that dime!"

So I did. Even as I picked it up I wondered what the scruffy man must think of me, but with a shrug, I passed it off and went to the cooler for a bottle of frappuccino. Two. One for now. One for later. At the counter I opened my wallet and saw exactly $1 where there should have been $121. Helpless to explain this I accepted that one cannot argue with an empty wallet and put a bottle back in the cooler. Adding some change to that dollar, I had just enough money for one bottle of caffeine. The dime was still nestled safely in my pocket.

So with frapp in hand I headed to the car. The windows were both fogged up and slobbered up by Border Collies who'd been raging at groggy petrochemical plant workers. Waving them back I sank into the seat and popped open that frapp as I put the key in the ignition, and nothing happened. The car was dead.

While banging my head against the steering wheel I heard it — the very weak ringing of a car alarm. The dogs had bounced the car enough that they had bounced the positive terminal off-kilter. I popped the hood and jiggled the battery terminal. Nothing.

I jiggled battery again. This time the car alarm went off loudly and blasted all over the parking lot. The Border Collies had apparently jiggled the battery loose and activated the car alarm. Now that the battery was connected the truck was loudly informing the entire parking lot of plant workers that I was trying to steal it.

I leaped into the truck and dug around for the key fob clicker thingy that would deactivate the alarm. Once I got it stopped, I jiggled the battery and turned the ignition again. Nothing. Still dead. Tears of frustration were bubbling below the surface but just as there is no crying in baseball, there is no crying in a parking lot full of strange men either. Besides, I had a dime. Ten times the blessings.

While I was contemplating blessings that weren't appearing, Trace climbed into my lap and stepped on my phone, which butt-dialed somebody. The tell-tale ring of a phone dialing echoed through the darkened truck so I snatched it up to see who Trace was butt-dialing at 5 a.m. Trace had called Daddy.

A sleepy Other Half answered. I informed him that my truck had broken down and I had no money. He was unconcerned about the money. He did not take it and no one could steal money from my purse without walking through all those damned dogs. (His exact words.) He assured me that money was still in the purse. Angry, I looked again. There it was. Oh well, I was still stranded in a parking lot at 5 a.m. He instructed me to jiggle the battery terminals. (As if I had not already tried that) It didn't work that time either but it did attract the attention of three large men in a big pickup.

"Do you need help?"

"Yes, I do!"

Soon two very large, corn-fed plant workers were staring at my engine. Some channel lock grips, a piece of metal, and a few minutes later, the engine started. I was cautioned to buy a new positive terminal and not stop the engine until I got home. Oh, and don't run the headlights too long! This advice concerned me slightly because it was still dark.

They were happy they had helped a damsel in distress. Other Half was happy he didn't have to get out of bed. I was happy the engine was going. And the Border Collies were happy to be on the road again. I thought some more about the dime in my pocket and how things have a way of working out if you just have some faith, and how out of a hundred other available telephone numbers in my phone Trace butt-dialed Other Half.

Life trudges on, and whether we participate in it or not, the wheels of change will continue to grind. Life had overtaken me and like a child caught in the surf, I was pounded into the sand, almost drowned and then released, a bit shaken, and a bit wiser.

My beloved Failte Gate Farm sold. The grass was returning with the recent rains but the new owners had no livestock to appreciate that. They seemed like nice people, a young family fleeing suburbia. I watched their children gathering flowering weeds for makeshift bouquets and was charmed. Later, after the handshakes and paperwork, the charm wore off. I drove up to find that they'd taken a chainsaw and cut my favorite climbing rose to the ground. I was devastated. I was reduced to crying over a plant.

The papers had not even been signed and they were already tearing my farm apart. I came to pick up packed boxes and was greeted by empty spaces and sawdust where beautiful plants had stood. I sat in the truck and cried. It wasn't the roses but the loss of the farm itself — my cute little house with foundation problems, my picturesque board fences that were falling down, my 5-stall barn, my flock of sheep that had reduced to a mere core of breeding stock now, and my calico cats.

I missed my calico cats. Twice I tried to move them to House #2. Twice I was forced to reluctantly return them to their old farm. The new owner wanted them. I refused to give them up. My mother still lived close enough to feed them and so she slowly coaxed them over to her place permanently. My mom would oversee their care. I hadn't lost them. I'd done the responsible thing and tried to do what was best for them. But still, it hurt.

Life for me moved forward. And so it was that I found myself in a big chain used book store to sell or trade four boxes of books. I didn't want to part with them but I had no room and someone else could love them. I had resigned myself to that. The books had been in a vacant house for six months and we were down to the wire. The new owners were moving in. My boxes of books had to go.

I unloaded them up front and browsed the store while the clerk tallied their worth. What is a lifetime's library worth anyway? I had barely started poking around, thinking about my Christmas shopping for books, when the clerk doing the inventory called me back. Thus began my meltdown.

"I found a bug!" he cried, wringing his wrists. "We cannot take dirty books! I need to WASH MY HANDS!"

"A bug? A single bug? One bug?"

"One bug! But that's all I need to see! It looks like you have a wonderful collection of books here, but I simply cannot take any of it because I FOUND A BUG!"

I stood there, waiting for this to sink in, as he explained that I would have to toss all my books or leave them in a Good Will box. Apparently their standards are lower than his. One silverfish was enough for him to trash an entire lifetime of books. This simply did not compute for me. My mother raised me to cherish books. A book is a treasure.

"There is no frigate, like a book."
Emily Dickinson

After his humiliating public display, I shamefully packed up my boxes of books and drove out of the parking lot. I didn't want to get rid of the books anyway but his public shaming sent me over the edge. The tears caught me. I called Other Half but was crying so hard that he couldn't even understand me so it was just easier to hang up and sob. The roses. The cats. The books. The farm.

Then my phone rang. There are certain friends who will drop everything at a moment's notice. Dear Friend Maxine is one of these. I answered but the sobbing made me incoherent.

"Stop driving. Pull over! I'm coming to get you!"

And she did. It took a while before she could

understand my week through the sobs. In a nutshell:
Overtime at work. Deaths that shatter families before the holidays. Food poisoning. Lots of throwing up. No sleep. No food. Loss of farm. Loss of books. Loss of cats. They cut down my favorite rose. ("They did WHAT?!!") No time for Christmas shopping. None. No presents. No Christmas tree. Nothing but Christmas carols on the radio.

She listened and then she did something that friends do. They talk you off the ledge. We finished crying together. She proclaimed the clerk an idiot. She took all my books. We went through the boxes. Never found the bug. She packed my treasures away in her car and they became her treasures to keep or sell as she wished. And she proclaimed the clerk an idiot again. We went back to the House #2 and life slowed down. The few ewes I had left were lambing and she admired the babies. I showed her pictures of The Promised Land, the ranch we would buy if it was still for sale, the ranch that had to be for sale because I'd already given up so much to buy it.

Once again I was reminded of what another dear, dear friend told me as I was finishing up trial on the murder that haunted me.

"When the trial is over and everything done, you must do the Arapaho thing. You must turn your back on it, walk away and say 'It is finished.'"

Wise words. It is finished. That week was finished. And life moved on. So I took the Arapaho way, turned my back on that week and said, "It is finished." (That is quite calming by the way, you should try it.) All through this ordeal, I had faith that God would lead me to a much better place. Even as doubts whispered, "You're gonna lose your farm and your dream ranch will already have been sold to someone else," I held tight to the faith that if that were the case, an even better ranch was waiting in my future.

As fate would have it my ranch was still there. The realtor had other properties listed too and I grudgingly agreed to look at another place in the area before we put money down on what I was certain was my ranch. The other ranch was set up for cattle, offered good hunting, a well, and had a cabin that we could actually live in while building our house. The problem was, it wasn't my ranch, and even as I drove around it I was impatient to go see my red feather ranch again.

The sun was beginning to creep down as I climbed into the back of the ATV and we drove off to take another look at the ranch I've dreamed of, had given up so much for. It was wild. It was remote. It was beautiful. It was mine if I wanted it.

A peace washed over me. I was home. As I rode through it again I let the place soak into me. This was it. I needed this place. This place needed me. It was a piece of history. It needed protection. It needed someone who would appreciate its wild beauty and not see it as merely a resource for stripped timber, oil, and future ranchettes. I could take care of this place. This place could take care of me.

The realtor asked, "Do you want to sleep on it overnight and let me know something tomorrow?"

"No."

He asked again.

"I want it."

"Don't you want to sleep on it overnight?"

"I've slept on it too many nights already."

Finally Other Half said, "If this is what she wants, then we'll get it. Let's start the paperwork."

And so it was that I signed my name, threw the money from the sale of my little farm at him, and bought a dream.

~

Recall the parable of the man who found a pearl of great value and sold everything he had to possess it. The ranch had become my pearl. At the first opportunity we packed up the kids and the grandkids and as the Beverly Hillbillies in RVs, we descended upon the ranch.

Behind an obscure front gate the drive leads the traveler deeper into the forest and into another time. Tree branches on either side reach toward each other and threatened to scrape the walls of trailers being towed down the mile long red dirt road. We arrived before dusk and made a hasty camp in a large meadow that swept down with a scenic view of the mountain. Two ancient pecan trees stood in the center of the pasture like ushers, their arms beckoning us welcome to this new place.

I awoke the next morning to a frozen wonderland. The sun had barely peeked over the treetops and not yet cast its rays on the mountain when four dogs and I stepped out of the camper and crunched across the frosty ground for a morning walk while the rest of the world stayed under the covers. The dogs bounded in and out of the forest as I walked down the red dirt road which led us deeper and deeper into the bowels of the ranch. Where the road crossed the creek the banks panned out to a bed of small pebbles over flat rock. Clear water gurgled over the rocks and moved on toward a cluster of large moss-covered boulders. As I trudged in, the dogs splashed through the creek and up the sandy bank on the other side to gallop up the hill and out of sight. Except for the Border Collie by my side.

I paused to photograph Lily as gazed at me with eyes full of wistful adventure. To truly appreciate a guttural taste of life, take a walk with a dog and see the world reflected through her eyes. Since I'd filed no flight plan before scaling the uphill bank, I left my empty frappuccino bottle on a boulder on the opposite side of the creek to show my family that yes, yes, she did cross a frigid creek on a frozen morning. I could pick it up on my way back.

As we crested the top of the hill, the sun's fingers crept over the trees to touch the earth brushed with sugar. Rays of light refracted through ice crystals and burst with radiated colors in my lens. An old church hymn that I didn't even know I knew sprang into my head. I hummed the bars to "Oh Happy Day" as we wandered through this glorious world and words could not express how profoundly grateful I was that God had placed this land in my hands.

In this age of cookie-cutter houses and McMansions it's easy to lose track of the history of land. Few people know the story of their land, and even fewer care, but like Scarlett O'Hara's father, I feel a kinship with land. For many, *Gone with the Wind* was a story of ill-fated love, but to me, it was a story about love of land. Gerald O'Hara spoke for my heart when he explained the Irish and their kinship to the land to young Scarlett.

With more than just a drop of Irish blood in me, I also feel strong ties to land. When we were looking for land in North Texas, we found many other pieces of property, tamer places that were already developed, but they didn't speak to me. I was looking for something — a connection. I was listening for something. The drumbeats of Jumanji. Something calling to me. Wild as it was, this property still called to me.

Our ranch was part of a much, much larger ranch that was carved up a generation ago. We were blessed in that one of our neighbors, Miss Junebug Jones, was part of the original family that owned the ranch in the 1800s. She was able to give us an oral history of the property that we couldn't find in the history books. We bought the ranch knowing that the local fort had been built to protect settlers from the Indians that were living on what would later become our land. The wild creek which ran through the property prevented significant development of roads in that area. Then we met Junebug Jones.

Miss Junebug Jones painted the history of this place with colors the black and white text of history books left out. She showed us where the old schoolhouse used to be and told us about how the old homestead where we are building our house used to belong to a lawman whose wife was a seamstress. One day she made a suit for the postman. He came to pick up his suit. He stopped to change and was riding back to town wearing his new suit when he was attacked by Indians and killed. They took his new suit.

Another family gave up this area because of the Indian attacks and moved farther south. Miss Junebug said the family was later killed by Indians in their new home. Their baby was left alive and Miss Junebug's grandpa went to get the baby and bring it back.

I listened to her stories and marveled. She is of true pioneer stock. While driving her around the property I once cautioned her to let me check an area for snakes before she got out of the truck to walk around in sandals, and Miss Junebug barked, "I used to walk around this place barefoot!" I do not doubt that old girl could shoot the eye off a rattlesnake without breaking stride.

Like all places, this land is rich in history. We were blessed that we had someone like Miss Junebug Jones to share it with us. She told us where the babies were buried, where the big house with the columns burned down, and where she fished as a child. I still think about these things as I walk the dogs down the red dirt road. This is the same path the postman rode, the same path Junebug Jones walked barefoot as a kid; the same path that I plan to walk as an old woman to the mailbox.

A land rich in history is alive, a thing of its own. One of our favorite parts of this ranch is the history surrounding it. This area was thick with Indians and the resulting conflicts between the natives and the new white settlers. Even with our modern conveniences, the land is harsh, giving us a greater respect for the people who scraped a living here. We saw signs of them everywhere. Old hardware from wagons in the sand. A large draft horse shoe hanging in a tree. An old homestead was hidden in the trees above the pecan meadow, its crumbling chimney supported by the tangled limbs of low-growing cedars. The old cistern sat north of this, its yawning mouth beckons a peek into the dark mystery of its bowels.

As if we wiped the dust off a dirty window and peeked inside, the old homestead slowly emerged with the change of seasons. Time weathered the land to unveil hidden treasures. Some items were a mystery, their identities only known when someone older and wiser educated us. A long flat funnel shaped metal turned out to be a flattened well bucket. Who knew?

Most items were metal trinkets, pieces of farm equipment and such, but one day Other Half stumbled upon a piece of whimsy with a more personal note. We were poking around the homestead in search of wild plum trees when we noted a large rock peeking out of the grass. Since this area can also be thick with copperheads, I'm not given to just reaching down to follow my curiosity but Other Half had no such inhibitions. He hoisted the odd rock up to eye level and upon closer inspection we found that it wasn't a rock at all, but mortar that had been fashioned by hands into the shape of a sourdough bread boule. We could even see the grooves in the rock where hands had shaped it. This naturally begged us, and later others, to place hands onto the rock in a quest to fit fingers into the very place that someone from another time touched. But like the Glass Slipper, or the Sword in the Stone, no one got it right. It could be forced to fit, but wasn't quite right. Close, but no cigar.

Other Half brought the curiosity back and used it as a door stop, a piece of history which reminded him of the people who settled this land. And it sat there. For weeks. Visitors came, picked it up, tried their hands, and marveled at the oddness of it. One day something strange happened.

Miss Junebug Jones came to dinner. Other Half could not resist showing Miss Junebug his curious rock. Just like everyone else, Cinderella placed her hand on the rock but this time her fingers settled into the grooves exactly. The rock was a perfect fit. It was creepy but in a good way, as if you recognize something unexplained but wonderful just happened. Other Half gave the rock to Miss Junebug as it clearly belonged to her family and had found its way back home. Some things you just don't question.

CHAPTER 17

ANNE FRANK MEETS DIRTY HARRY

When you play Twister over dead men for a living, you have very few social skills left. Normally I hide this pretty well but from time to time, the raw beast emerges. And so it did when my new ranch was threatened. After we bought the place we drove up at least once a month. It was a day's drive. We would spend two days there and then drive back the fourth day. Every month. For years. During that time we were building a home.

Before I was a police office, I was a 6th Grade Science teacher. Pause and let that sink in. To help illustrate the problem of deforestation of the rain forest, I showed the kids the animated movie, *Ferngully*. In this delightful cartoon, a young man driving a giant tree shredder machine, is shrunk to the size of a bird, and gets up close and personal with all the lives he is about to affect if he takes down the trees in the rainforest. I hadn't thought about the movie for years until the Evil Oil Company Tree Shredders threatened my ranch, my beloved Ferngully.

It started innocently enough, as things like this always do. They sent a letter asking permission to do a seismic survey on our property. We were told they simply came through, walked along with cable, and then brought thumper machines which thumped the land and they read the seismic thumps. They offered to pay $10 an acre. We lost the letter. But one day we went to the ranch, and wonder of wonders, the Survey Company has already been on our land without permission. They had put survey flags out.

When we returned home we called the Evil Oil Company. They were eager to chat with us since they haven't received our letter as yet. They started haggling.

"Ten dollars an acre just to go on your land!"

"But you've already been on our land!"

"No, we haven't."

"Yes, you have."

"No, we haven't."

"We have pictures of your flags."

"Oh . . ."

"So now that you have trespassed on our land, what are you going to do for us to make us happy?"

"We're paying $10 an acre!"

"Ten dollars an acre? To just walk on our land? And thump?"

"Yes Ma'am!"

"Will you help improve the dirt road in?"

"Yes Ma'am!"

So we agreed but we still hadn't sent the agreement letter in when the phone rang a few weeks later. Other Half answered it. Just listening to his end of the conversation raised red flags.

"Permission to cut trees? Why do you need to cut trees?"

The long and short of it was that the Seismic Survey Company must cut a 12 foot swath running east to west on the north side of the property and another 12 foot swath running east to west on the south end of the property.

"Come again?"

The man patiently explained this once more. Apparently our property had a lot of trees and they needed to cut them down. He was calling to ask for permission.

Other Half looked at me. I shook my head. "No!"

Thus the 3-way conversation began as the Permit Agent tried to explain where he needed to cut and Other Half relayed this to me. He hadn't had as much sleep and was more easily confused so he finally gave me the phone. I listened and relayed this back to him:

"They want to start at the north pond and cut a 12 foot road all the way through the forest, across the creek, and through Moss Bluff!"

"Oh, hell no!" he barked.

The Permit Agent explained that they would only cut trees with trunks that were less than 6 inches in diameter. He assured me they wouldn't take out big trees. I didn't have a lot of faith in his promise. Absentee landowners leave their property vulnerable to corporate predators and so we told the Permit Man that we were on our way to supervise them. The Permit Agent took that opportunity to share the fact that they had already cut down some trees.

"Do what!"

"But they were only mesquite."

I like them but others argue that mesquite can be a troublesome trash tree. It has thorns and is said to suck up a lot of water. Most ranchers want them eliminated. The fact that they chopped down mesquite trees was supposed to make it easier to swallow. Although I didn't mind the loss of some mesquite, I didn't want them all eliminated and I was very concerned about what else had been cut. What damage had already been done before the trees in their path got so big it forced a phone call?

In a race to protect my own beloved Ferngully, we loaded up the truck and headed north. We arrived shortly before dark so there was no time to scout around the ranch for damage. The Permit Agent was supposed to arrive early in the morning, so as soon as the sun rose the dogs and I loaded up in the ATV and went to survey the damage. Other Half stayed at camp to wait for the Permit Agent.

Everything looked okay at first but we soon found the mesquite trees. What was so frightening is that we didn't find the mesquite trees. They were gone. Reduced to just shreds of fine mesquite mulch. An entire road of mesquite mulch. The dogs and I drove down this new road with our mouths open. What kind of machine did this?

And why? Why cut this new road at all when the old road was right beside it? At most they were barely 20'-40' apart. The only thing I could figure was that the old road wasn't along the exact route of their survey ribbons. This didn't bode well. The ribbon route was headed toward my big trees. I pondered that as I drove toward the north pasture and found the reason for the phone call the day before.

Like a Native American staring at a field of slaughtered bison, I gaped in sick amazement at the bodies of shredded oak trees. These were the kind of trees which make for pissed off landowners with guns. Chewing through these trees was a bit more of a feat than chewing mesquite.

But they tried. And apparently their Tree Chewing Beast broke down. The hulking yellow machine stood in the forest, waiting. Guilty. I walked around the carnage for a while then followed the new trail of ribbons toward the next intended victims, straight through my giant hardwoods toward Moss Bluff where two people joining hands cannot reach around the girth of some trees. I wanted Other Half to see this before he spoke to the Permit Agent. The sun was high in the sky and the Permit Agent would be there soon. Things were about to get ugly.

~

"Despite everything, I believe that people are really good at heart."
Anne Frank

In many ways I'm a schizophrenic, for like Anne Frank, there is a curious part of my nature that wants to believe that deep down, people are basically good and if given the right information they will choose good over evil. Yet the cop inside reminds me of what happened to Anne and the countless other victims that I've stood over myself. Therefore I end up with a warped personality, one where I will extend the olive branch, but am just as quick to hit you over the head with it.

And so I was reserved and cautious when the Permit Agent drove up before I could show Other Half what the company had already cut. The experience of others has taught us that big corporations and/or governments will do what they want in the end with little or no regard for the lives they crush in their path. On the other hand they don't like trouble. They don't want to end up in court, on the news, or at the end of a gun barrel. They may win the war, but they'd like to avoid the battles. Although we might not be able to stop "progress" we might be able to de-rail or deflect it.

The Permit Agent stepped out of his truck, cautious, yet friendly. He had a kind smile and an easy manner. He looked like a man who'd been shot at before. We shook hands and after an exchange of pleasantries loaded up in the ATV for a tour of the ranch. We warned him about the snakes. He smiled and allowed as how everyone warns him about snakes but in all his years doing this he'd never had a run-in with a snake. That's fine. We were the ones wearing the snake boots, so off we went.

As we drove he explained that the initial ground crew surveys the property on foot and puts out stakes and ribbons. The blue ones are where men will walk with cable. The orange ribbons lead to orange stakes.

The stakes are where the Thumper Trucks must access to "thump." Although in theory they want to cut a path in a straight line, geography and the size of trees forces them to "zig-zag." He explained that the shredders couldn't cut down big trees.

"You can't sling a dead cat around here without hitting a big tree," I said.

Apparently he was unfamiliar with this phrase because it flummoxed him a bit. Our goal for the day was simply to find the orange stakes on his map, locate them on the ranch and agree upon a route to get the Thumper Truck to the stake while minimizing damage to the property. Since he reportedly came from a family of tree farmers, he sympathized with our cause.

As we drove I got the distinct impression that he was the person who stopped the cutting in order to call the landowner. Clearly the men doing the cutting were not the same men dealing with the ranchers. It became apparent that the workers were simply given a map and were cutting dot-to-dot. He was, in essence, their boss and had the authority to alter their path. We were making some progress.

So we drove around the ranch showing him easier access to his stakes so that we could protect my trees. We were actually getting along fine. He seemed reasonable. I was feeling comfortable until I saw a flurry of stakes at Moss Bluff around a tree that leaned over as its top reached for the ground. It was one of my favorites.

"Oh, hell no!" I stomped off into the forest toward my tree. As I surveyed the proximity of the stake to my tree and calculated a possible route to it, they walked up. This man simply had to understand that his shredders could not damage my trees and I could think of only one way to sum up the situation.

"Sir, I play Twister over dead men for a living so I have very few social skills left. That said, I will not hesitate to go bat-shit crazy on the company that cuts down my trees."

He blinked. My bluntness caught him off guard. But he recovered and we soon had mapped out a quite reasonable route to access Moss Bluff without damaging my boulders or big trees. After we finished mapping out all his points and agreeing upon cut-routes, Other Half made a request.

"Since the shredders were already here, and since your company trespassed earlier without permission, and since the company has already cut some trees without permission, would you have the shredders clear some mesquite from the front pasture and the back pasture?"

Other Half argued his point: the company had started work without permission and we had not even received a check for the $10 per acre (which as I pointed out was laughable if they thought it could buy the right to cut my trees.) Our request would cost them something in time and labor, but if we pulled the plug on the whole deal it would cost a lot in time and labor too. The Permit Agent agreed. It looked like we were all on the same page.

I thought of Anne Frank. Maybe there is some goodness in everyone. And that's when I saw the copperhead.

"Look, there's a copperhead."

Both men jumped. "Where?"

"Right there."

Then I reached under my shirt-tail, into my back pocket, pulled out a gun, and said, "I am so sorry about this, but my dogs aren't safe with you here."

BANG.

I'm not sure if it was the snake four feet from his leg, the fact that I had a gun he didn't know about, the fact that a woman casually shot a snake, or the fact that she apologized to the snake first, but the Permit Agent was visibly shaken. I didn't bother to explain. I'm a crazy bitch. Dirty Harry. Now he knew that. And as we would soon learn, he needed to know it.

The Permit Agent left so we packed up the dogs and went to town for supplies. It was hot. Texas in June is a dry brutal heat that scorches everything in its path. We didn't dare leave the dogs in the camper while we were gone. If the generator ran out of gas or if the air conditioner quit, that camper would become a hot tin box and our pack would become roasted hot dogs. On our way out the front gate we ran into the Tree Shredder guys on their way in.

Other Half stopped them on the dirt road. I expected crusty old men, what I saw were young men who look to be about 12 years old. They were friendly enough. I asked them if the Permit Agent had squared them away about what and where to cut.

"No big trees," was the driver's reply.

"No big trees?" That summed up our morning ride through the ranch? "No big trees?"

Since the Permit Agent took careful notes and spent a great deal of time out there, I doubted their only instructions were "no big trees." On the other hand, having taught 12 year old boys for 10 years, I'm sure they condensed a thirty minute long lecture into "no big trees."

Okay then. Well hopefully they wouldn't make much progress before we returned. One beast had broken down and another one had to be moved onto our ranch. We should be back before they got going. We left them and headed to town. The closest town is fifteen minutes away and boasts a cafe, a pizza place (only open on weekends), a steak place (only open on Friday and Saturday), a gas station (just one), a post office, a bank with the original brass bars around the teller window just like an old Western, and a grocery store.

We stopped at the one-room grocery store. Morrows Grocery was much like Henry Ford's original car. You can have any color you want as long as it's black. At Morrows, you can get anything you want, as long as it's on the shelf.

The choices were limited, but the people were friendly and after all, too many choices makes for a longer shopping experience. That isn't to say you don't spend as much time in Morrows as in the big chain stores, it's just the time spent is in gossiping with the staff instead of actual shopping. And the meat, oh my, the meat. The butcher shop in the back of the store carried the finest cuts in North Texas.

After the required time spent gossiping and shopping we headed back to the ranch with steaks, pork chops, Frosted Flakes (because when all else fails, Tony Tiger will come through for you.) and ice - lots of ice. I had forgotten the cooler at the camper so my ice was melting fast in the truck.

While in town, we saw the Tree Shredder truck pass us on the street. "Were they our Tree Shredder boys?"

"Surely not, they haven't had any time to do anything."

"Maybe it was another truck from the same company."

We didn't think any more about it until we arrived back at the ranch with melting ice and rapidly warming meat. I tried to open the gate and discovered the Tree Shredder boys had locked us off our own ranch!

The Survey Company had asked if they could put a lock on the gate. When we arrived on Friday night we had seen their shiny new key lock threaded through our combination lock. The young men had failed to thread their lock through our lock. They simply locked their company padlock, effectively locking us off our own ranch.

There was our lock, dangling uselessly on the end of the

chain. There was their lock, effectively locking us outside of our own ranch. And my ice was melting. The cussing began. I unleashed a flurry of cuss words as Other Half speed-dialed the Permit Agent. He explained the problem as a veritable 4th of July fireworks display went off in my mouth. I was livid.

"How, (I shouted loud enough for the Permit Agent to hear) can people who don't understand how to LOCK A GATE, be trusted with a GIANT TREE SHREDDER?"

The Permit Agent was deeply apologetic. The boys were no longer at the ranch. Other Half advised the man that he would be cutting their lock off the gate. The Permit Agent profusely apologized assured us that he would be back tomorrow morning to replace the lock and give us a key so that it didn't happen again.

Since we didn't have bolt cutters Other Half used a police entry tool to break the lock. I didn't ask why he didn't have bolt cutters but did have a long pole SWAT entry device in the tool box of his pick-up. Ours is a bizarre household.

The Permit Agent did add one interesting tidbit to the story. Both Tree Shredders had now broken down. One had a broken fuel line and the other had a flat tire. It was interesting fuel for thought. Perhaps our own Ferngully had fairies too. Or perhaps the spirits on our ranch have a working knowledge of modern machinery. Or what is more likely, 21 year old men have a remarkable ability to tear up giant Tonka Toys when chewing through trees.

The next morning the dogs and I rose with the sun and sure enough, a silver pickup drove up. It was the Permit Agent bearing a bag of ice in each hand and a bag of doughnuts. Clearly unsure of his welcome, he almost poked his peace offering at me with a stick. I happily accepted his gifts. No hard feelings. Good help is hard to find these days. He explained that the boys meant well but didn't have a lot of experience with ranch etiquette. Despite myself, I liked the Permit Agent. He had a hard job. I'm sure being a liaison between ranchers and oil companies is tough. Not only did he have to juggle the oil company and the rancher, but he had to juggle the survey company and the tree shredders. On the other hand, I've had downright pleasant conversations with known murderers before too, so no matter how personable someone is, you still have to stay on your toes.

Getting cozy with big business (or the government) is like the story of the old woman who found a rattlesnake freezing in the cold. She picked it up and put it in her shirt to warm it. Once warm, the snake bit her. She cried, "But I saved you from freezing!"

The snake replied, "You knew I was a rattlesnake when you picked me up."

I liked the Permit Agent but there was still a healthy distrust of him. Before he drove away he assured me the boys wouldn't be able to cut until the shredders were repaired and that wouldn't happen until Monday. We were supposed to leave on Monday morning. Other Half and I discussed it that afternoon. We needed to stay until they finished cutting on our land. Too much was at stake. We called our bosses and took Tuesday off. Nothing happened on Sunday. On Monday, they came and got one of the shredders. On Tuesday morning all hell broke loose.

The sun rose Tuesday morning just as it had every other morning during our stay. The dogs and I took our morning drive. I took pictures of sunflowers. On the surface all seemed well, but there was an air of ominous expectation. The forest was quiet. Waiting.

After our morning ride I returned to the camper and picked up Other Half. The boys had arrived with the repaired shredders. The engines idled while the young men stood on the giant tires and studied their maps. Other Half walked up and introduced himself.

I sat in the ATV and waited with the dogs. The machines were idling and dogs with high prey drive don't mix well with machinery that contains rolling blades. A few minutes later Other Half brought one young man over and asked if I'd show the boy the creek crossing to see if his shredder would fit through the narrow gap. I agreed and the young man loaded up. You'd have thought he was climbing in with a grizzly bear. Clearly the Permit Agent had briefed him. I did nothing to change his opinion, but drove silently. We went through the crossing and he decided his Beast would fit through the gap. The young man then surprised me by asking if I would drive him around the ranch and show him where I wanted him to go, where I didn't want him to go, what he could cut, and what he couldn't cut. Like the Grinch That Stole Christmas, my heart grew a little bit that day.

As we drove, he talked, and my heart grew a little bit more. This man was not much more than a boy, but he had dreams. He dreamed of buying land like this. He came from a place with no trees and he wanted land with trees. As we drove, he became a person and so did I. This boy was not the Evil Oil Company, he was simply a young man, with a low-paying job, miles away from home, trying to do the best he could. The Border Collie riding in the back got hot and climbed into the front seat, right into the boy's lap. Wonder of wonders. Lily liked him! She is shy, and rarely friendly with strangers. He started to pet Blue Heeler. I advised him against it. Ranger smiled at the boy anyway to assure him that he was a harmless little blue dog. Will wonders never cease? I returned the young man to his Tree Shredder, confident that he would take care of my land. There I met his boss.

~

Remember this: Not all snakes crawl on the ground.

It's rare that I take an instant dislike to someone but as I drove my young friend back up to his Tree Shredder I knew at a glance that I didn't like his boss. From his expression, he didn't like me either. Because the shredders were still idling, I stopped the ATV at a distance.

The boy walked back to his shredder and after a few brief words, Other Half climbed into the ATV. On our drive back to the camper, Other Half shared that the Boss was "an asshole." Of course he was. I knew that. I've seen men like that before, men with small minds and too much power. He was arrogant, a man who believed that time is money, and money can buy anything. He lives by the Golden Rule. He who has the gold makes the rules. But he isn't the man who has the gold, he simply works for the man who has the gold. He basks in the glow of borrowed power. Landowners like us just get in the way. Other Half had already chewed him out because he was the man who trespassed initially, he was the man who cut trees without permission. He was our problem.

Other Half said that when the Boss Man drove up and saw the shredders idling, he got out of his truck, tapped his watch, and gave the other boy a hard time because the shredders weren't already cutting a path. Other Half had some words with him and the guy backed down a bit. Other Half is used to confrontation.

I gave it some thought and realized that by driving off with me, my new friend, the person responsible for the safety of my trees, had put his job in jeopardy. Men like the Boss Man enjoy lording whatever power they possess over their underlings.

An ugly anger rose inside me. Not only would I not allow my trees to be cut, I would not allow this young man to get in trouble because he wanted to clarify my wishes before he started cutting. I had a thought. I dropped Other Half off at the camper and drove back out to the work site to confront The Boss Man. We had a "Come to Jesus" meeting in the forest.

You cannot believe how liberating it is to not concern yourself with social niceties. When I first started patrolling the streets I tried to be nice to everyone, but guess what? You just can't. Some people don't understand "nice." Some people don't respect "nice." And with the wrong people, being "nice" can get you killed.

I'm not saying you have to live your life being rude, but you must find and develop that part of your personality that allows you to speak your mind and get confrontational without getting emotional. It is a skill. Find it, use it. It's how I developed my olive branch principle, extend the branch, but be just as quick to beat them with it.

The Boss saw me coming and stepped out of his truck. I saw the look of impatience before he was able to slide his mask of politeness back on. There is no point in polite, ice-breaking, chit-chat with someone like this so I got to the point. "I do hope that young man isn't getting into trouble because he went off with me."

"Well Ma'am, he's not in any real trouble. It's just that we're already behind schedule . . ."

"My husband told me you were giving the other boy a hard time because they hadn't started shredding."

"Did he? Well I's just kiddin' a bit."

I'm familiar with this tactic too. Feigned submission. They are not apologetic, they just want you to go away. "That young man wasn't holding up work because he was taking a joy ride; he was with me because I was showing him better routes to his stakes."

And that's when I saw what I was looking for, the flash in his eyes which betrayed his anger. I saw it and he knew I saw, so it was time to pull off his polite mask. He said, "What you people don't understand is that we have certain ways we have to do things. We have to cut a straight line from point to point. We can't just zig-zag through the forest to make you people happy. All this is taking too much time. This costs a lot of money."

"It's going to cost this company a lot more money if they cut down the wrong trees!"

He gave me a smile and shrugged. "They got plenty of money."

"If you think for one instant that you're cutting my big trees, you are sadly mistaken. The Permit Agent told me you could do a zip-zag path to spare my trees."

"Well he shouldn't have. These contract guys don't really know much. Most folks just get the check and don't worry about it. And besides, we don't cut down the really big ones. We can't. The machines can't."

"Bullshit. If you think that stupid check can pay for my trees, you have another thing coming."

"Well, you already accepted it."

"Wrong! I haven't! In fact, I haven't received any money yet. We would never have allowed you on our land if we'd been told you were cutting like this. That was not in any agreement!"

"You mean you haven't received your check yet?"

"No! No money. No improved road. Nothing. So no deal!"

"Well, if that's the case, we should leave until you get the check."

He said this like it was a threat, as if somehow I wanted the money enough that the threat of them leaving would make me beg him to stay. The joke was on him when I barked, "Exactly! No check. No agreement. Pack your shit and get off my land! If you think that stupid check bought you the right to cut my trees, you were wrong!"

"Well that's where the Permit Agent dropped the ball. He should have told you. Most folks don't mind. Besides, it's hard to tell what people want. Some want the mesquite out. Some want the cedars out. Some want the oaks out. We don't have no way of knowin'."

"If you talk with the landowners before you start cutting, then you'd know!"

"Well, that's the Permit Guy. He should have . . ."

He was backing down. He wasn't prepared for me to call his bluff and throw his Tonka Toys out. I left him in the forest. It was a good time to call for reinforcements. Before I called the sheriff to try to evict them, we called the Permit Agent. Other Half told him about Boss Man's attitude and Permit Agent assured us he would be right over. True to his word, he showed up pretty quickly. I relayed the conversation and he acted surprised. This Boss Man had never behaved in such a manner with him. The Oil Company hired the Permit Agent and the Permit Agent's Company hired the Survey Company and the Tree Shredder Company.

"So really, you're his boss."

Permit Agent hemmed and hawed.

"No, in the grand scheme of things. In this food chain, you're his boss. That's why he's nice to you."

Permit Agent reluctantly agreed that if one looked at it from that angle, I was correct. He might like to know how quickly this guy threw him under the bus. Long after they left our ranch, this man would be causing problems with other ranchers by setting fires that the Permit Agent would have to put out. And blaming him.

While I felt that he and I were on the same page and the boy and I were on the same page, the Boss Man and I were at odds and as soon as he left, Boss Man might make the boys do it his way. Permit Agent assured me that he would supervise all cutting on our ranch. Those shredders would stay on the path I had agreed upon, or they would be leaving my ranch. Permit Agent would see to it that the shredders stayed on course.

While we were chit-chatting, the guy from the electric company drove up. We all made polite chit-chat for a few minutes before Permit Agent excused himself to go recalibrate Boss Man. Meanwhile, the forest was abuzz with the rumble of giant machinery.

The Electric Company Man was a welcome sight. Soon we would have electricity and our dependence upon the generator would end. It was heavy and loud but nevertheless, I always thanked God each and every time it started up with the mere push of a button. As much as I love my wild land, I do enjoy the modern comforts of lights and air conditioning. There was troubling news though. We wanted to run power poles past the proposed homestead site to the pasture where our travel trailer was parked. While it wasn't far from our intended homestead, it was a few hundred yards and that was far enough for a gigantic leap in cost.

If we ran power to the homestead lot it would cost approximately $700. If we ran it just a few hundred yards more to the travel trailer, the cost would be approximately $7800! I almost choked. Maybe we should move the travel trailer to the proposed homestead site?

Problem: That site was still pretty wild. It had lots of old growth mesquite trees and the remnants of the original homestead which included an old fireplace and a cistern. It also hosted copperheads. This made the idea of clearing the lot in the summer less than appealing.

Other Half, always the wheeler-dealer, decided that since the giant shredder machines were already on his ranch perhaps they could be employed to clear this lot of mesquite. It couldn't hurt to ask. As if on cue, The Permit

Agent drove back up in his silver truck.

Other Half wasted no time in asking for the moon and the stars. The Permit Agent didn't say 'no,' but said he'd talk to the Boss Man about it. On cue, the Boss Man came driving up. Since the Boss Man and I were only one step away from reducing ourselves to fence-fighting dogs, it was a good time to check on my own dogs in the camper. My presence was not needed in these negotiations. It was easier for Other Half to convince them that he was the only barrier between them and his crazy bitch of a wife if she wasn't there.

I returned about thirty minutes later to find the Shredder Boys had brought their beasts in to cool them down. The Boss Man was gone. Other Half handed Permit Agent and I some ribbon. Believe it or not, while under the scrutiny of his supervisor, Boss Man had agreed to let the boys clear the homestead. He had even given other Half two spools of ribbon. Yellow ribbon meant cut the tree. Red and white checkered ribbon meant do not cut.

Well, wonders never cease. I didn't for one minute believe Boss Man did this out of the kindness of his heart. The Permit Agent and I busied ourselves marking trees. My young shredder friend came over to supervise our tree marking and look for copperheads. The young man was a snake lover. I was ready to send him home with every poisonous snake he could find. Other Half encountered a rattlesnake in the tall grass but wasn't able to pin-point the location. In that case, discretion is the better part of valor. Back away slowly. Snake wins.

Soon the trees were marked and the Permit Agent left. The boys were back in the woods on their beasts. Other Half was sitting in the Electric Company Man's pick-up truck while they did paper work to set up service. Everything seemed hunky dory. I should have known better.

I checked on the dogs again and then went back to check on the men. As I walked up Other Half and the Electric Company Man were shaking their heads in disbelief. Apparently my shredder friend had just received a phone call from the Boss Man. There would be no free shredder work.

"Do what?"

"No free shredder work," Other Half reported.

"But he already agreed to do it."

"I know. The boy feels so bad that he offered to do it in his off time for free. He just asked if we'd let him come hunt a deer later. I told him we would."

I smiled. It was nice to see that I wasn't wrong about putting my trust in the young man. I was still baffled by the audacity of the Boss Man's about-face. I turned to the Electric Company Man.

"Did you see The Boss Man agree to clear the homestead?"

He assured me the lying bastard (his words, not mine) agreed to do the work while in front of his boss and even gave Other Half the ribbon to mark the trees. Electric Company Man then pointed out that in this part of the country if you give your word, you stand behind it. The Boss Man guy was giving the term "snake in the grass" a bad name.

Okay then. Regroup. We haven't lost something we didn't have to begin with. The more pressing problem was that once again, the Boss Man had proven he couldn't be trusted. Whether the homestead was cleared or not wasn't as big a deal as whether or not he would abort the agreed upon plan of zig-zag cutting in favor of his straight line swaths. He was the kind of person to do it just to prove that he could.

Even if I had to sit in the cab of that shredding machine, I would make sure my trees were safe. It was time to call

The Lone Ranger & Silver. A few minutes later the Permit Agent drove up in his silver truck.

I gave him an ear full. I'm sure the poor man was sick of the drama on our ranch but he listened politely and nodded. Then he assured me that he would take care of it. An hour later two shredder machines showed up in our homestead lot. While they worked I took the opportunity to take a long walk around the property to survey what the machines had already accomplished.

I was amazed. True to his word, the young man did exactly what he said he would and more. He protected my trees and still cleared a fire line down my south fence line to reach his stake. He could have driven straight through my forest. Instead, he chose a route that minimized tree damage.

As I walked through the ranch, two fawns sprang out in front of me. They are why I fought so hard to retain the forest. This land is more than just trees. It's habitat, a home for a multitude of little lives. And it's my responsibility to speak for them, to fight for them.

I returned back to the homestead to find the shredders still hard at work. The Lone Ranger sat in Silver, supervising their progress. He saw me walking and drove over to get me. I thanked him for the ride and for all he was doing to stand behind his word. He dropped me off at the camper and I crawled in bed to snatch a bit of shut-eye before our long drive back south that night. I peeked out the window once to check on their progress and saw a shredder hard at work, clearing mesquite from the front pasture. Not only had the Permit Agent kept his word about saving my trees but he had saved us thousands of dollars in dozer work around the ranch. They finished hours later. We packed to leave as the sun was sinking. The only roar across the ranch was the sound of our generator. The Shredder Beasts were silent. Their work here was done. We walked around to survey the final product and we were pleased. It had been four days of battle and an emotional roller coaster, but we'd come through it. I still believe that you cannot trust big business or the government, for they are only as good as the people in charge. Thank God for good men who stand by their words.

"Nearly all men can stand adversity, but if you want to test a man's character, give him power."
Abe Lincoln

CHAPTER 18

MY DRINKING PROBLEM

The shredders had cleared enough of a spot for us to build a small cabin. Our next order of business was to start moving some of the cattle north. This was no easy feat. We were supposed to leave for the ranch at 3 a.m. on Wednesday morning. That didn't happen. On Tuesday Other Half called the kennel to inform them that his Patrol Dog would be coming for an extended stay. No problem. Bring her on. For weeks I had reminded him to call the kennel. And he did. He called. He lined up her visit. He did everything but remember to drop off the dog.

On Tuesday night I walked around the corner of the house and saw an extra dog in the outside kennel. He'd forgotten to drop off the patrol dog and now the boarding kennel was closed. We would have to wait until the kennel opened on Wednesday before we could leave.

That didn't turn out to be the only problem. After spending Tuesday putting new tires and new fenders on the cattle trailer, Other Half discovered that goats had chewed the wires to the trailer lights thus there were no lights on the trailer.

This may not have been a bad thing. Wednesday morning while I took the Patrol Dog to the kennel, Other Half repaired the trailer lights. It was lucky we didn't leave according to plan because the morning news reported that a tractor trailer had turned over on the highway and there was a chemical spill which blocked traffic for hours. We could have been smack in the middle of that traffic chaos. Score one for the goats.

After the dog was dropped off at the kennel, the trailer had new tires and new fenders, and newly repaired lights, we were on our way at 3 p.m. Other Half pulled the cattle trailer loaded with cows and I followed towing another trailer.

Don't ever follow a cattle trailer down the highway. That is not mist on your windshield. It's cow piss. All was well until midnight, the Witching Hour. We stopped at a gas station for fuel, ice, and potty breaks for everyone — except the cattle, because they'd taken potty breaks on my windshield for miles. While loading ice in the cooler, with a Slim Jim still hanging out the side of my mouth, I saw that one of the tires on the cattle trailer was leaning to one side. That can't be good. Imagine a cattle trailer loaded with cows and slimy cow poop and a broken axle in a strange town in the middle of the night.

Think about that. I thought a lot about it. I had plenty of time since I was going anywhere. I thought Other Half was gonna cry. I was past it though. This was beyond my scope. I had already mentally written the problem on a little yellow Post-It Note and stuck it on God's desk. It was beyond my pay scale. God could handle this one. And He did.

In this world there are friends, and there are Dear Friends. Dear Friends are people you can call at 1 a.m. to say you are stranded on the highway with a loaded cattle trailer. Dear Friends will climb out of bed and drive 2 1/2 hours with an empty cattle trailer to come rescue you. Dear Friends Ruby & Leo are those people.

The young attendant who worked in the gas station was gracious. He talked with us most of the night. Weird things happen in the middle of the night. Really weird things. He and I were chatting and I discovered that he was from the same small town as Dear Friend Leo. Wonder of wonders! So I told him that a Dear Friend coming to rescue us was from that very same little town. He inquired as to who this person was, so I told him it was Dear Friend Leo.

"That's my uncle!"

Shut the door! What are the odds? That's when you know everything will be just fine. A coincidence is simply the stroke of God's paint brush. Clearly He had read my sticky note.

So at 5 a.m. Dear Friend Leo arrived and we moved cattle into his trailer. Because his wasn't big enough, we left three cows in our trailer. By 5:15 a.m. we were back on the road and limping the 2 1/2 hour journey to our ranch on three wheels with three cows in the trailer. A wheel for each cow.

I tried not to imagine the conversation I might have with Allstate later. On the other hand, we didn't have too many other choices, so with a wing and a prayer, we drove onward. We approached Fort Worth at pre-rush hour. This is that time of the morning when traffic is zipping along like a flock of birds. Our 3-wheeled trailer was doing about 45 mph while the traffic around us zipped in and out at 65-75 mph. It was the stuff of nightmares. A white-knuckled journey. Even Other Half was scared. I was beyond scared but then I have a better imagination. I could easily imagine the other axle breaking, the trailer lurching to one side, digging into the pavement, and the subsequent chain of events that would follow. Dead cows all over the highway.

I didn't relax until we pulled onto our red dirt road. The

sun peeked over the horizon as the cattle stumbled out of the trailer and ambled off toward the pond. We'd made it. In the grand scheme of things we should consider all the positives.

We hit a pot hole in the gas station parking lot which broke the axle but we found it before we got on the highway thus there was no damage to the hub or the tire. We ended up in a well-lighted parking lot that hosted food, drink, and a bathroom. The cops in that town were wonderful and quite helpful. The Shell clerk was a relative of a dear friend. We have friends that will drive out in the middle of the night to help us. No one died.

Few things are more beautiful than a sunrise over the pasture after a night like that. The next day when we limped to a repair shop with the empty cattle trailer, I spotted a field painted with clumps of purple flowers. As the long spires waved in the breeze of passing vehicles I gave a nod and a wave back. Sometimes bad things aren't. Sometimes God reads the sticky note you hastily tack on his desk in a panic.

"I learned that courage was not the absence of fear, but the triumph over it. The brave man is not he who does not feel afraid, but he who conquers that fear."
Nelson Mandela

I've seen a lot of stuff, and frankly, it's just plain hard to impress me anymore but that night did it. In the middle of another 10 hour drive back home from the ranch in North Texas, we received a text from the neighbor who'd been farm-sitting for us down south.

Other Half's Border Collie, Cowboy, was missing. Since storms had moved through the area earlier, we assured the farm-sitter that the dog was merely hiding under the house, scared of the thunder. We weren't concerned until we arrived home to blue skies, a setting sun, and no dog.

I called the dog and there was a distant answering bark from under the house. I called again. He barked. I searched inside the house. Perhaps he had broken a window during a storm and was now inside the house. Nope. Husband and I got down on our bellies with flashlights to check under the house. Didn't see him there. But then he barked again. Oh no. The dog was stuck under the bowels of the house. The horror began to sink in. The dog was stuck under a pier-and-beam house that only had about 8 inches of crawl space. Where was he? How do we get him out? Had he managed to tear through the floorboards? Was his collar hung on something? If we didn't get him out, he would die in the Texas heat. Stuck. Under. The. House.

I burst into tears. I burst into prayer. This was definitely beyond our scope. It didn't take long to make the leap into a hysterical, shaking, blubbering mess. Cowboy wasn't even my dog but the thought of him dying under the house simply because we couldn't help him sent me into a tailspin.

We couldn't leave him there. His barks were strong but later as he got weaker would we even be able to hear him? We couldn't isolate his location. The barks were sporadic. Sound echoed under the house in weird ways. Is he under the kitchen? Absolutely! Flashlight there! No. Not under the kitchen. Maybe he crawled into the wall. I was having a panic attack. Okayokayokayokayokay. Just breathe.

How do we get him out? My plan? Go into the kitchen and start ripping the floor out. Husband's solution? Other Half decided to put on a Tyvek suit and G.I. Joe like a Tunnel Rat in Vietnam to get his dog.

Do what?! DO WHAT?!! The very idea made my throat tighten. Even as the walls closed in on me, he zipped his plastic suit up, slipped on some rubber gloves, got down on his belly and slid underneath the house.

Color me impressed. The crawl space was only eight inches deep. Because of the rains, there was standing water under the house. Once you factor in rats, snakes, spiders, and whatever the hell else lives under a house, it takes real balls to crawl under that house in search of a dog. But he did. Never underestimate a man's love for his dog. He crawled under the house and he promptly got stuck. The beam on his flashlight was fading. Mine was beginning to flicker.

Hysterical, I called a friend. That's what police officers do. They don't immediately call the fire department. They call each other. They call their friends. Then, only when police officers are helplessly stuck, then and only then, will they call the fire department for help. (It's a sibling rivalry thing.) I called a former cop who does search and rescue work. He and I used to work on a SAR Team together. He is your go-to person when life bitch-slaps you or you make questionable decisions and need the cavalry to come with flashlights, saws, jacks, and moral support.

By the time he picked up the phone I was crying so hard that he couldn't even understand me. This was a new experience for him. Cop Friend had never seen me hysterical. It doesn't happen often but there it was. I was a puddle. I needed advice. I needed help. I needed somebody to stand in the dark with me.

It took a few minutes to relay the situation but without hesitation, he offered help and assured me that he would gather his toys and head my way. Neither he nor I had any idea what we were going to do, but it made me feel better just to know that he was coming. God bless him!

There are friends, and then there are the kind of friends you can call at any hour and they will come because that's the kind of fabric they're made from. If you have people like that in your life, hang on to them. They're precious.

I stood in the dark, wiping tears, waiting on Cop Friend, when happy barking erupted from underneath the house. Other Half had managed to find Cowboy and free him. I called the dog. I could see him. He was dancing around the husband, wagging his tail and licking him. He wasn't under the kitchen though, he was deep under the bowels of the house. I called him again. Nope. He wouldn't leave the husband who was stuck again. Lovely.

It was shaping up to be a fire department call. This is how people end up on the 5 o'clock news. This is how people end up on the yahoo news feed. Given some time and slick mud however, the husband managed to inch-worm himself free too. Like a wet calf being born, Other Half slid out from underneath the house. Cowboy followed him. My prayers had been answered. It was time to give the husband a wet rag and a cold beer. It was time to hug a muddy dog and a muddy man.

Sometime later I was in the courthouse talking to an officer that I worked a case with five years earlier. We met briefly on a murder and hadn't seen each other since. At the time she'd been working patrol in a particularly active part of the city, so I asked if she was still there.

"Oh no! I needed a rest. I got tired. I'm in a desk job now and I love it. It's so relaxing. I don't miss the action one bit!"

I chewed on this for a minute, mulling it over in my head. Before I became a crime scene investigator, I'd been working on a very active team, running narcotics and felony warrants. The Crime Scene Unit was a physical rest for me too, so I understood where she was coming from. Then I thought about my normal day off.

Other Half worked a 12 hour shift Saturday night. He got to bed at 6:30 a.m. At 7:30 a.m. my mother called to inform me that a water pipe on her well had burst and water was spewing from the pump house like a geyser. Thus the day began.

It took longer to drive to her house and Home Depot than it took to fix the break in the pipe, but nonetheless, it wasn't on my list of things I wanted to accomplish that day. We returned to his house and while giving the dogs a potty break, I heard the water well pump kicking on and off.

No one was doing laundry so that was a bad sign. Apparently the very thing to relieve boredom of a horse is the red float valve bobber of an automatic waterer. When a horse pulls the red bobber out, not only is the resulting geyser enjoyable, it has the added benefit of flooding the pasture, which brings out humans who gesture and cuss, and provide further entertainment.

Even on a good day, Other Half wasn't fond of that horse. On a day with no sleep, I didn't even want to tell him that Montoya flooded the pasture again. I just turned the water off and decided we could fix the float valve later.

Back in the house, Other Half was settling down in his recliner to watch a horse race that he'd recorded earlier. With fried chicken in one hand and a remote control in the other, he was a man wearing a Do Not Disturb sign. I got my plate and settled on the couch to watch the horse race as if I didn't already know who'd won.

Beside the television set was a large 3-paned picture window. It was entirely possible to watch the pre-race show and also note that Cowboy, the Slightly Deranged Border Collie, was racing back and forth along the fence in the back yard. He was running after horses in the pasture that not only were not moving, they didn't even know (or care) that he was there. I went back to the horse race.

Pretty horses. Pretty colors. Outside the Deranged Border Collie raced back and forth past the window. The pre-race show gave all the interesting behind-the-scenes stories on the horses and I got quite involved. But something was wrong. I couldn't put my finger on it. Wait. Deranged Border Collie hadn't passed the window in a while. Should I even care? Something, some niggling something in the back of my head moved me off the couch. I peeked out the window. What I saw was a scene from some absurd Disney movie.

Cowboy must have smacked right into the water spigot and snapped the PVC pipe in two. Water was spewing out and Cowboy was playing like a city child in a summer fire hydrant. Leaping in the air. Biting the geyser. A mermaid. A Mer-Mutt.

Oh. My. Gosh. I glanced at Other Half, happy with his remote and his fried chicken. A completely insane thought crossed my mind.

"Dear God, Thank you that it was his dog, and not one of mine. Thank you that it was his dog and not my horse. Thankyouthankyouthankyou."

After a quick under the breath amen I called Other Half to the window. He stood there, mouth slack, watching his dog play in the spray. Cowboy is lucky that Other Half was holding a fried chicken wing and not a gun.

It took almost two hours to repair the pipes that Cowboy had snapped off. One pipe was above ground and the other was under a foot and a half of sloppy mud. It was ugly. I think we both deserve gold stars for not beating the crap out of each other with shovels. It says something about our self-control.

So on that morning, as I sat across the table from a police woman who told me about how life was so much less stressful now that she had a desk job. I pondered that for a moment and reflected. A desk job probably wouldn't do much for the stress in my life. I still want a gold star for not smacking him in the head with a shovel.

As has already established, I have a drinking problem. Frappuccinos. Starbucks Frappuccinos in little glass bottles. Shaken, not stirred. They are sinful. They are addictive. They are expensive. They have 180 calories each.

I decided on Sunday night that once again, I would quit drinking frappuccinos. Monday afternoon Other Half brought home a 4-pack. I'm not sure if it was for me or him. It didn't matter. I'm weak. I drank them. One day I'll whip this caffeine addiction. Just not today. And tomorrow isn't looking too good either. Other Half's patrol dog, Oli, was limping. He dropped her off at the vet's office and went to work alone. When she was ready, he called for me to go pick her up.

The verdict was in. Oli had a career-ending bum left knee. Great. Just great. I called Other Half to let him know that I had picked up his dog and he dropped the bombshell on me that Son's truck has just been stolen. Then like a bad infomercial, he said, "But wait! There's more! All his police equipment was inside the truck!"

Son had just joined the police department and picked up all his gear that day. He and his sister then stopped in The Big City to buy more gear that he would need in the police academy. His truck was stolen out of the parking lot. Great. Just freakin' great. An entire Policeman Starter Kit was in that truck.

The phone rang again. Wonder of wonders. More drama. Paisley the Problem Cow was out again. This time she was out of a lease pasture. It was the cherry on the sundae of my day. I had to pack up Border Collies, drive to a lease property, round up a stupid cow and get back in time to go to work. After I called Other Half to scream about Paisley, I loaded up dogs and a sack of cattle cubes. Then I drove through front gate and locked it behind me.

On the highway I passed a police car. There was a moment when we both paused. Then the cop turned around. Never good. There is not enough caffeine for this kind of day. I called Other Half to cuss because I was about to be stopped for speeding because of his stupid cow.

Yes, indeed. I was being stopped by police. The police officer was a tiny female. Was I ever that young? Was I ever that tiny? I felt old and fat. Many years ago, at the beginning of my career, I was that young and tiny. I think. Maybe. She introduced herself and told me I was going 40 mph in a 30 mph as she glanced at my FBI Academy sweatshirt. I took that opportunity to let her know there was a gun in the truck but that I was a police officer. There was so much barking I couldn't hear her answer. I yelled at the dogs to shut up. The deputy introduced herself. She shook my hand and took my word that I was a cop. Maybe it was the shirt. Then she asked for my driver license. Happy to oblige, I opened the truck to reach into my bag and get it. At that moment my routine traffic stop turned into a horror movie. The only thing missing was the Psycho soundtrack music — and a Border Collie.

There was only one Border Collie in the truck! Where. Was. Cowboy? This was much bigger than a traffic stop. I'd lost a dog!

I jumped on the running board and climbed inside to search for a dog that wasn't there. The deputy didn't stop me. She may have been a bit worried. Her simple traffic stop was getting out of control. Distracted with my search, I babbled about a loose cow and losing a Border Collie from the inside of a truck. She looked ready to leave. This was not covered in her police academy. That much was clear. I wasn't a real criminal and I was a tad nutty. As such, I was not worth more of her time, so she gave me back the license and bid me farewell. I gave a quick wave and drove off in search of Cowboy.

Either he hopped out of the truck when I was loading cattle cubes or he hopped out when I closed the main gate.

I sped home. Apparently I had not learned anything from my first traffic stop. There were no cop encounters on the way home so I bounced into the driveway to find that Cowboy was in the yard wondering why I had left him.

Grateful, I loaded the old dog up and raced back the other direction. The deputy was gone. Too much crazy in this neighborhood. I was about to arrive when I got another phone call. The neighbor just got Stupid Paisley back inside. This news clearly disappointed both Border Collies. Their help was not needed but I still had to fix the fence. While I was working, Cowboy snuck off and bit Paisley. It was the high point of my day.

With the fence finished, I roared back home. Only thirty minutes to do chores and take a shower before heading out to my real job, the job with an actual paycheck. I stepped into the house and was greeted by trash all over the kitchen floor. One of the dogs had a party in the garbage can. I kicked the trash in disgust and left it for Other Half. I was running late for my job because I was doing his chores while he was at his job. He could deal with this mess himself.

After a fast shower, I climbed into my uniform, hopped back in my truck and turned the key as I glanced at the gas gauge. Empty. Figures. I called the office to advise them that once again, I would be late. It surprised no one. This is why I have a drinking problem. When the day heaps trouble with a shovel, a cup of coffee can be your life jacket.

After the diagnosis, Oli was medically retired from her job as a police dog. This gave her plenty of time to plot ways to kill sheep. After several close calls and much heartbreaking deliberation, Other Half decided to place her in a home without livestock or children. The sheep gave a sigh of relief.

CHAPTER 19

YOUR WORST NIGHTMARE IS MY WEDNESDAY

Domestic arguments in our household took on a whole new level. One evening Other Half was berating me for not setting out the new patrol dog's shot record where he could find them. I sat in my office, typing a homicide report, while he snapped and snarled into the phone about how he needed those dog papers now. Not yesterday, now!

Carefully and with great detail, I told him again where I thought he could find the papers. When he couldn't immediately put his hands on them, he snarled louder into the telephone.

I snapped. "HEY! You can lose that tone with me, Mister! I just cut down a dead man with my own pocketknife! I don't wanna hear about your damned dog's papers!"

Silence. End of discussion. Score for the CSI. Point and match.

~

He ran into the street as I pulled up. With tears in his eyes the old man gestured wildly for me to hurry as I stepped out of the truck. He was polite, respectful, and desperate. This was puzzling. Mine is not a job of hurry. In broken English he explained that I must hurry. I must cut him down. The old man gestured CPR. Was there a language barrier? No. The horror of the situation dawned. He doesn't know. With a sigh and a determined, steady gaze, I met those tearful eyes and told him. His grandson was dead.

"No! Hurry!" He gestured CPR again.

I hate my job. I hate my job. I hate my job. If someone called me, then his grandson was dead. I tried to explain that. He shook his head and begged me to cut the boy down. Begged me to start CPR. Begged me to try. I could not look into those eyes and refuse him. So I lied. I told him I'd go cut the boy down. I put a hand on his shoulder and promised that I would check his grandson again. I left him with a tiny glimmer of hope. And I hated myself for it.

And in that moment I hated the asshole who told the old man that they couldn't cut his grandson down because they had to wait for me to do it. Which is most cruel? To show the old man that the boy is dead? Or to give him the hope? He believed he had to wait until some person with the authority to cut the boy down did so. He thought that after that we could try CPR. How was it possible that no one, no fireman, no police officer, no one, had taken the time to explain the situation to a desperate old man?

They couldn't cut the boy down. The boy was already dead. They did have to wait for me, but they could have explained that the boy was dead and no amount of CPR would bring him back. Or maybe they did, and in his grief he simply couldn't accept the reality. Nevertheless, someone had punted the ball to me and now I had to crush the old man.

My stomach was a tangled mass of briars as I walked into the garage. I nodded at the officer guarding the door and went inside. No. There was no doubt. There wouldn't have been. By the time my phone rings there is never a doubt.

I stared at the boy for a while. Took in all the details of death. He was a beautiful child. But he was dead. I didn't cut him down. The Medical Examiner would need her photos too. Instead I took a deep breath and walked back outside. Back to the old man. Back to those eyes.

Years ago all the officers in our department had to take a mandatory class on Post Traumatic Stress Disorder at the Police Academy. The class was required for all officers but was aimed primarily at officers who were soldiers returning from combat. While they touched on the fact that some "regular" officers see horrific scenes on duty from time to time that can also result in PTSD, they skipped the Crime Scene Unit entirely.

"Your worst nightmare is my Wednesday."

This quote could be a CSI motto. The class video began with a warning about the "graphic" and "disturbing" images which I was about to see. I was more disturbed by the fact that I was not in the least bit disturbed by any of the graphic images revealed. In fact, most of them were just a typical week in the Crime Scene Unit.

I'm not trying to make light of the images but merely point out that we are expected to stomach daily what psychologists have already agreed is too much for the human mind to emotionally handle. The class outlined the causes, signs, and symptoms of PTSD and all of it was familiar. There was another CSI in the class with me. We discussed their list of symptoms and he summed up the entire class with each bullet point. "Got it. Got it. Got that too. Don't have that yet. Got that one . . . ."

The whole point of the class seemed to be this:
Recognize PTSD in your friends.
Recognize PTSD in yourself.
Seek help.
Don't self-medicate with alcohol or we'll fire you.

We recognized it all right. We all had it. The group of us sat around our cubicles later and talked about it. Evening shift and Night shift sat together. According to the class definition, we all had PTSD. Without fail, all of us.

Exactly what do you do about it though? Unlike combat, there was no end to our deployment. Another stressor was simply a phone call away. They couldn't just shuffle us out of the unit and replace us with new officers. Replacing us wouldn't solve the problem because we would never be able to un-see the years of things we'd seen, or un-do the years of things we'd done. Most of us were too close to retirement to quit. We had become quite specialized. What else would we do? Besides, except for the whole PTSD thing, the job is a relatively good job and as a friend once said, "We have to do this job, because no one else can."

We are both blessed and cursed with strong stomachs. As a group we explored the problem further. The class didn't go into much detail about the treatment for PTSD but it appeared to be drugs and counseling. None of us planned on taking drugs and because of the nature of our job, counseling was out too. You can cuss and discuss the horrors you've seen with a counselor all day long, but it doesn't change the fact that you were fingering through coagulated blood and brain matter last night in search of a fired bullet. That kind of life is "effed up" any way you cut it. Talking about it with someone who has never done that isn't going to help much. Sleeping pills won't change it either.

So we talked with each other. Only someone who also has blood and brains stuck to the bottoms of their boots can understand. With them, you aren't a freak. You aren't alone.

One night I stumbled upon a new technique for coping. After 50+ trips around the sticky body of a decomposing man, I'd had enough. I was already sick when I arrived on the scene so after hours in a house with no air conditioning and a decomposing body under a ceiling fan, I'd reach my critical mass. I could no longer hold back the tide of disgust. I was hot. I was tired. I didn't feel good. I wanted to go home. I let my mind take me away.

"I'm not really here, playing Twister over this rotting dead man. I'm really — a florist! Yes! That's it! I'm a florist! I work in a flower shop. I arrange flowers. I smell the freshness of each bouquet. I put them in the refrigerator. I tie bows. Yes, that's it! Dirty flower water gets stinky but not like this. Nope. I'm not really here. I'm arranging flowers in a flower shop. I'm bringing smiles to people's faces."

And so it continued, this little mental game. I had a beautiful arrangement of sunflowers, and spikey blue-purple flowers in a dark brown vase with horses etched on the side. (Since my reality is quite detailed, my fantasies are quite detailed too.) Then I worked on some pink roses in a heavy crystal vase. I put in more spikey flowers, both white and purple. I didn't know the names of my flowers. I just knew the color and shape, because you see, I have never been a florist.

It was an effective coping technique. I used it whenever I became overwhelmed by rotting flesh or a sticky floor under my feet. I could simply step into my flower shop. Stand in front of the glass case with the door opened. Feel the cool air. Smell the flowers and the foliage.

> *"Everything you can imagine is real."*
> *Pablo Picasso*
>
> ~

The job of a CSI lends itself to the surreal. In time I came to accept those surreal moments of the job. Most of these were experienced alone in the dark so it was easy to pass them off as interesting fancies of the imagination, inadequate caffeine, and lack of sleep. From time to time however, one of these episodes of weirdness catapulted itself to the forefront and like a pig wearing a tutu, captured my attention.

This was the case during a particular memorable courtroom testimony. I photographed and videotaped murder scenes to allow the jury to experience it years later. The videotape is meant to be a silent journey through the crime scene. A sound plug in the video recorder is meant to insure this silence. Because I am a technophobe with little or no confidence in the obedience of electronic devices, I didn't talk to anyone while filming, lest the ill-mannered contraption record me begging a patrol officer to go to a local convenience store and buy a Dr Pepper and a Butterfinger for me. I just didn't trust the machine when it said it wasn't recording sound — for good reason.

Two years later I found myself sitting in a courtroom assuring the prosecutor and the jury that yes, indeed, I did videotape the crime scene as I found it. After a bit of fumbling with the computer it spat out my video and the jury followed me into the scene of a homicide.

As soon as the video started rolling I realized the damned sound was on. The wind rustled the crime scene tape as officers called for Gatorade. I was thankful I had maintained a habit of silence. The camera walked down the driveway and silence resumed as the garage provided a buffer against the wind. Slowly the camera picked up the blood droplets on the sidewalk.

The viewer focused on this trail of blood as the silence was broken by the tones of an ice cream truck rolling in the distance. With those tones, the viewer was thrust into the surreal. The lonesome notes of Brahms' Lullaby, the Cradle Song, echoed through the courtroom as the camera moved along the blood trail to her body behind the front door. The all too familiar children's lullaby continued as the camera moved up her legs and panned over her bloody body. I was in shock.

In my mind I heard the words often paired with this quintessential bedtime tune.

"Lullaby, and good night . . .
Close your eyes, now and rest . . ."

The camera moved over her permanent slumber as I sat in stunned silence. I had not planned this. I had not even been aware of the ice cream truck as I shot the video, but there in the courtroom, the painful notes of Brahms' Lullaby played an eerie tune as the viewer stood over her body. I scanned the jury and locked eyes with a woman old enough to be the victim's mother. She knew. She knew that song. Perhaps she had hummed that song to her own child. I thought about the young victim's mother sitting in the courtroom but coward that I am, I refused to look at her.

The ice cream truck faded into the distance as the camera moved away from the body and into the house.

Silence resumed and I breathed again. But there, in the back of my mind, the mournful tones of Brahms' Lullaby, a child's song playing in the music box inside my favorite teddy bear, will forever be paired with a mother's last sight of her sleeping child.

Over time I grew weary with my waltz, my "Danse Macabre." Each night Death would bow and extend a boney hand in invitation, and each night I was obligated to perform. I had moved from excited wonder, through appalled hopelessness, into resigned acceptance, and now I was moving toward irritated emptiness.

The elevator doors slid open with a ding and I rolled the cart forward into the quiet parking garage. My truck sat in its corner like a patient donkey tied to a rail. One by one I hefted the boxes off the dolly and into the cargo bay with a grunt. The Tigger sticker caught my eye. He was smudged with fingerprint powder stains and his tail had been wrinkled and torn but it was his smile that captured my attention.

It looked like . . . . Perhaps. Just perhaps. His smile looked like it had faded just a tad. I spit on my finger and rubbed it across the sticker. A bit of the print powder came up on my fingertip. I wiped this on my pants, hoisted Tigger and his tackle box into the truck, and slammed the tailgate.

~

One more dead baby. Two more grieving parents. I eased into the driveway and cut the engine. With a quick check inside the metal clipboard to verify it had the right papers, I stepped out of the truck. Showtime. Wipe the face clean of emotion. No suspicion. No concern. Nothing but the facts.

Long flowering crepe myrtle branches pushed their way

into the sidewalk and dangled in my face as I shoved past them. It was too early for flowers. I pulled my coat closer as the fingers of a late cold front reached for me.

I stumbled. There was a cloaked body on the porch. There, sitting in the dark at the edge of the patio, was a black shrouded box on a gurney. Was the medical examiner here already? Had they moved my body? I didn't get my photos! I pushed away another teasing branch as it swung across my nose. The police officer standing guard moved aside and opened the door for me. As I passed him I asked, "Where's the medical examiner?"

"Not here yet."

"What?"

"Nope, you're the first one."

I shut the mouth that was gaping open and excused myself to step back outside again. Yep, a dead baby. Covered on a gurney. I flicked out a flashlight to check it out. Nope. It was a barbecue grill. A barbecue grill with a black plastic cover. When you see bodies that aren't there, it might be a sign that you've been doing the job for too long.

First come the tears, then comes the hollow emptiness. Then you climb into a shell, numb to the world outside the camera. Running case after case, like a fiddler crab, you carry a protective shell around. It becomes so much a part of you that you forget it is simply a borrowed shell. It is not who you are.

I looked at the stained hollow faces around me and almost burst into tears. The tragedy was so immense we were all in shock. The chaos outside was muffled as I climbed through the rubble to get inside the scene. I could hear nothing but my heartbeat. Overhead the news choppers circled like giant vultures feeding on our pain, and like the news cameras, my eye was drawn to the

American flag draped across the debris near the center. That flag and the others like it would unite a community.

I stumbled through the water and scaled across the bricks to reach the flag. Why was I here? These deaths were no mystery. My camera could do no more than document what we already knew. I glanced at the pinched and pained faces standing around me and crawled into my camera before I could break into sobs. I did what I always do, I retreated into my otherworld behind the lens and photographed the scene.

The camera caught their shock, their hollow eyes, and their tearstained and soot-covered faces. Hours later I would stare at these faces on my computer screen as I stumbled through my report. Then the sobs would come, great heaving sobs that could not cleanse the smoke and soot from my soul. But there in the moment, I stared through the camera and snapped away while the hoses still watered down the fire.

I just wanted to do my job and stay out of their way, out of their pain. They waited for me to finish so they could collect their dead. That damned news helicopter. Hovering over a crumpled American flag. I fought the urge to hurl a sooty brick into the air at it. Instead I walked in wet boots back to my truck. I closed the door and fought the tears again. As I followed the parade of ambulances on our way to the morgue, citizens lined the street and saluted as we passed. Some good came from that damned news chopper. The people of this city knew and they came out, not to gawk, but to silently line our path. To show their respect. A man stood on the street corner with bagpipes. The mournful tones of "Amazing Grace" drifted in the breeze. Locked inside my truck, staring through the tinted window at the people, young and old, who raised their hands in silent salute as we passed, I could finally cry.

~

I drove back to the office with the smell of decomposition clinging to my clothes, my nose, and my mind. The sweltering heat of summer came in with a vengeance, bringing with it the tide of the dead. Everyone was mentally and physically exhausted, but the dead, mindless and faceless as toy soldiers, the dead kept marching toward us.

The sun was still up and more dead bodies were already on my horizon. I was hungry. Tired. Ready to hurl my truck keys across the street and walk back home, leaving the dead and their responsibilities behind. Instead, I took a quick detour through the city. In this land of concrete and steel they were my cup of water in a desert.

The cost of these extra few minutes paid off as he ambled across my path. I rolled down my window and the steady clip-clop of hooves entered. The big white horse patiently plodded across the intersection towing smiling tourists. Flowers decorated his carriage. The young black man at the reins nodded and waved as they passed.

For a moment I could forget the stench of death. There was nothing but the smell of that horse. The smile and wave of a stranger. The steadfast beat of solid feet, bringing me home. And as they passed, so too did the moment. I no longer had the urge to fling car keys blindly across the city and walk home.

I wheeled slowly down the street and saw more carriage horses. They patiently waited. They patiently pulled. And that day, they pulled me back, and grounded me once more.

~

"Can I see another's woe,
And not be in sorrow too?
Can I see another's grief,
And not seek for kind relief?"
William Blake

Those words are as true today as they were when William Blake wrote them some two centuries ago. Grief is part of the human condition. When asking about the nature of my job, people always comment, "That's so gross. How do you deal with the bodies?"

It's not the bodies, it's the grief. Dealing with the body is the easy part. Dealing with grieving family members is far more difficult. Grief takes many forms and much of the time, the display of grief is a cultural thing. While some scream, flail, and pass out, others stoically stare with a vacant, hollow look, and still others, appear to have no emotion at all. Over time, however, I've learned not to judge these things.

Does the mother, who collapses into the arms of her husband, love her child more than the father, who stares at me with silent tears while I place his daughter's tiny earrings in his outstretched hands?

The public is fascinated with murder. True crime headlines tease and titillate as John Q Public plops into his recliner where he remains from the evening news, through a crime drama, and well into a crime documentary, leaving his seat only long enough to make himself a sandwich during the commercial break. He is fascinated with all facets of murder and the murderer. But can he recognize the real deal? Are not the eyes the mirror of the soul? Everyone wants to believe the eyes will betray him. Surely a murderer has the cold, dead eyes of a shark or perhaps the crazed expression of Jack Nicholson in *The Shining*, but I would argue the truth is far more disturbing.

The truth is, he is your boyfriend. Your husband. Your neighbor. The young man your daughter dated last week. He is the man who installed your new energy-efficient windows. He is the dentist you've used for ten years. He is your son. Your grandson. She is your wife. Your girlfriend. Your boyfriend's ex. Your wife's new lover.

The eyes are not the mirror of the soul, and a killer wears no brand. There is no "M" for "murderer" monogrammed on their clothing like the scarlet letter. They can sit across the table and carry on perfectly reasonable conversations. In fact, by the time you have finished photographing and taking a DNA sample, she has explained why, because he took her car keys, it was a perfectly logical thing to chase her husband 368 feet down the street and stab him in the heart with a pair of scissors. You will listen to her, and you will nod your head in agreement, put the lens cap back on the camera and walk out of the room.

My job not only required attention to detail but it demanded that I be able to recall these details, under oath, one to three to five or more years later. Since I can't recall what I had for lunch yesterday, without a good report, remembering details from a case last year becomes difficult. This is further complicated by the fact that many of these cases are the same. The names change but the details have a glaring similarity.

Most of the time, a glance at the report and my photographs will jog my memory, but in time, even that could fail me. I was called by the prosecutor on a dead baby case. Her attempts to jog my memory over the phone were fruitless.

"This is the dead baby case from 2010 at Wandering Oaks Apartment Complex."

"Not ringing any bells."

"The baby was murdered."

"Let me guess. Mom's boyfriend was babysitting. He said the baby was fine when he fed it. He put it to sleep, but it rolled over and fell off the couch/bed and he put it back. He came back later to find the baby not breathing, so he called 911. Hospital said x-rays show extensive skull fractures. From falling off a couch. Onto carpet. Autopsy shows baby was beaten to death."

"Yes! That's the case!"

"Don't remember it."

"What?"

"They're all like that! I need to look at my report before I can remember which case yours was."

She was confused as to why I couldn't remember this case, so we agreed to meet after I had looked at my report and photos. Sadly, my report didn't joggle my brain either. This case was like so many others. I scanned the photographs. It was the same apartment I'm in every week, year after year. I was getting frantic, worried I was coming down with early on-set dementia. Nothing about this case was different from all the other dead baby cases. So I went to the meeting. It unfolded as follows:

With the details of the case right in front of me, I am still unable to recall exactly which dead child this is. It bothers me. There are so many, they are so similar, but still, each child deserves, no, demands, to be remembered as an individual. As I stare at countless photos, no bells are ringing in my head. Grief and guilt flood me. How could I let this little guy down? He was more than just a number at the Medical Examiner's office.

Then I see it — one little detail. One tiny detail that opens the dam of memories. And with that one detail, I remember his case. I remember him. I remember the pinched faces of the nurses in their desperate attempts to get him stabilized enough for transport to another hospital. I remember that I couldn't take detailed photos of his body because he wasn't dead yet and I surely wasn't going to make the medical team stop their work so I could photograph his injuries. I finally remember him as something more than words on paper.

And that's when my cell phone rings. Our meeting will have to wait. I am being dispatched to another case. The prosecutor politely waits and listens to my end of the conversation.

"You have another dead baby for me. Mom's boyfriend was babysitting. Fed the baby and put him down. Baby fell off the bed. Boyfriend called 911 . . . ."

Now she understands. Her eyes tear up a little as I say goodbye and walk out toward yet another dead baby.

It all came back to me as I sat in the courtroom and watched the video that I made so many years ago. The January rain blew out of the darkness and fell on her body as I counted the bullet holes. At that moment, I hated this godforsaken city. Tired of death and the senseless killing, she was the statistic that pushed me over the edge. I would remember her because with that cold rain came the dawning of a realization. No matter what I did, the dead would just keep coming. One moment you are a vibrant, contributing person, and in the next, you are lying dead as the rain turns to sleet.

And now here we were, back in the rain. I watched the jury as they walked through the scene from seven years ago. There were enough monitors placed around the courtroom that everyone had a good seat. I'd seen it before, so my time was better spent watching faces. I scanned the courtroom. Every eye was riveted to a screen. The camera lingered over her bloody body and they winced. Then I noticed him.

He smirked at me from across the room. For a moment, my eye met his gaze and then continued on. I refused to give him the satisfaction of getting any more of my attention. He is not the bad-ass he thinks he is, merely one more idiot with a bad temper. Even as my gaze passed him by, I analyzed his smirk. He feels no guilt for what he's done. It was his right. In fact, he's surprised we make such a big deal about it in this country.

My gaze landed on him again as I left the courtroom. His eyes smiled at me. The court gave him 80 years. Welcome to Texas.

~

His crime was so heinous that even the seasoned closed our eyes and shuddered at the details. By the time he came upstairs for us to process him, investigators not involved in the case wanted a glimpse of the man capable of doing such a thing.

"Did you go see him?"

"No, I didn't want to."

This clearly puzzled my young colleague. The suspect was already a bit of a celebrity and here he was, in our office. There would be justice after all. For this I was glad. I really was. But I've seen enough through the years that I really didn't want to see the face of evil again. It wasn't my case but the horror of it affected us all and I wouldn't let it go any further than that. I didn't want to be touched with the brush of evil. There is enough of that in my own cases. I do not borrow someone else's.

Evil spreads like a toxic ooze in a cartoon, leaving ugly snapshots in the photo album of your mind and angry stirrings in your soul. Pick and choose your photos wisely.

"Battle not with monsters, lest ye become a monster, and if you gaze into the abyss, the abyss gazes also into you."
Friedrich Nietzsche

I had already spent too much time gazing into the abyss, too much time battling monsters. My clock was ticking. It was time for a change.

CHAPTER 20

KNOW WHEN TO PUT DOWN YOUR CHISEL

In spite of the blood rapidly staining my shirt, I pressed forward. If you're looking for sympathy, look outside a family of cops, or ranchers. We've seen it all, so copious amounts of blood just aren't that impressive unless your arm is actually lying in the dust.

And so it was that despite the rapid drip of blood all over my shirt and the seat of the 4wheeler, I pressed onward. Being a crime scene investigator brings with it a certain skill set. As I crashed through the brush, I glanced down from time to time to check the bleeding. Nope, no arterial spurting, just the steady, heavy flow of dripped blood. No worries there. "Just a flesh wound!" But I'm getting ahead of myself. As all bloody adventures begin, this one began with cattle.

Regarding building fences, it is said that if you can throw dishwater through it, a goat can get through it. The same can be said for keeping cattle on a large piece of property in North Texas. Since everything they need and more is provided on the ranch we own, one would think they have no reason to wander but cows don't reason like that. They also have two great allies in their quest for adventure: the creek and the feral hogs.

A lazy little creek meanders through our property like an anaconda in the Amazon. Most of the time the creek is bone dry but when it rains, the creek can turn into a raging force of nature, capable of moving large trees which crash through fences like battering rams. Then you add the feral hogs. These hogs can grow to enormous numbers and proportions. They use the dry creek beds as highways and consider the fences across the creek as mere speed bumps. In time these Porky Pigs create holes in a fence big enough to drive a truck through, or at least a large heifer.

As was my habit, each morning we were visiting the ranch, the dogs and I drove the property on the 4wheeler. On that weekend each morning I saw fresh evidence of cattle: tracks and cow patties, but no cows. Each afternoon would find the whole group of them chewing their cud under the pecan trees by the big pond in the pasture. Since the property is so wild, it's entirely plausible that we could lose a whole herd of cows, or lions, tigers and bears, and never find them. It wasn't until we were packing to leave that we realized we had a problem.

Other Half happened to look across the fence at the neighbor's property and saw a couple of our cows staring back at him. Since the property they were on was bigger than ours, and just as wild, finding everyone and getting them pushed back onto our ranch was a massive undertaking which would have been impossible without the Border Collies. Fortunately most of this group started life as show cattle and were tame so we started shaking feed sacks and calling them like puppies. The biggest chow hounds emerged from the brush. Next we had to convince them to follow us down a fence line, down a deep dry creek, up a deep dry creek, and down acres and acres in the opposite direction of the feeder trough. It was an arduous task which required patience, a great deal of acting, an empty feed sack, and dogs. The carrot. And the stick.

When we discovered the cattle were out we just had Trace the Troll and Ranger the Blue Heeler in the pickup. I raced off on the 4wheeler to open the north gate so we could call cattle to that open gate. Once they walked all the way to that gate, they would then have to retrace their path on the opposite side of the fence (our side) to return to the exact same spot they had just left but on the other side of a field fence. It is difficult to explain this to a cow.

I did manage to get one old girl in that way. Another one petered out about half way through the journey and announced that, "Fat girls can't walk that far."

I almost cried when she turned back around but I continued on with the one greedy chow hound who was convinced the empty feed sack would produce goodies if she just walked a little farther. I got her to the feeder where she was rewarded with actual cattle cubes. Then I returned for the other one. She was well on her way back to where she started, and that's when I saw a little red streak. Other Half had deployed the Heat-Seeking Missile.

Trace the Troll/Norman Bates the Psycho Ranch Dog had been jettisoned. He raced through the brush so far away from both of us that he was a mere red dot in the distance. He found the cow, picked her up, and headed her back toward Other Half, then turned her into the creek where the water gap in the fence was down, and his job was done. Just like that, she was back on our property. He was huffing and puffing and proud of himself. Blue Heeler had also been deployed but he apparently had only run part of the distance before announcing, "Little Fat Blue Dawgs don't run this far!" He returned to the truck where he was benched for the rest of the game.

In time the rest of the adult cows threaded their way through the brush and came home. Everyone came in except for five calves. Five calves, four small calves born that summer and Little Bully, a bull calf born the previous winter. He was destined to be a replacement bull for his half-blind father who had died the winter before. We had no idea where the calves were. There were hundreds and hundreds of acres to cover, in land rich with cactus, briars, brush, heavy forest, feral hogs, copperheads, and rattlesnakes. We had nothing but a pickup truck, a 4Wheeler and three Border Collies. Thus, we had everything we needed.

We went back to the ranch house and traded in the Benched Blue Heeler for Cowboy. I picked up Lily and we bounced off in search of calves while Other Half cut a hole in the water gap fence so we could drive the calves through it when we did find them.

So Lily and I drove and drove and drove. We followed the trail of fresh cow poop and in time found the calves bedded down in the forest not far off a gas pipeline easement. We then returned for reinforcements. There was a wide range in ages. The youngest calf was two weeks old. His momma was Paisley, the crackhead. What other crackhead would leave a two week old baby alone in a forest with coyotes and cougars?

Paisley is a dumbass. Forgive me, but she is. She is a crack momma with little or no maternal instinct and needed to be cut from the team. She left her infant in the care of a teenage boy. It was sale barn time for Paisley. Little Bully really stepped up to the plate. He assumed the role of babysitter for an infant and three toddlers. After watching him with the Border Collies, there was no doubt in my mind that Paisley's calf was still alive because of this large bull calf. He was very serious about protecting calves, serious enough to go bowling for Border Collies. He rolled Cowboy for getting too close to the calves. Other Half scooped up the old dog and put him in the safety of the pickup truck where he supervised the rest of the mission.

We soon worked out a suitable method for moving the calves. Lily and I rode on the 4Wheeler just outside their flight bubble. The bull calf kept himself between the infant and the dog. As long as they were moving in the right direction, we just rolled behind them. When they stopped, Lily hopped off the bike and stalked forward. Once inside their flight bubble, they would start moving and Lily would back off and hop back on the bike. This was successful while the gas pipeline easement had heavy forest on both sides, but once it opened up to heavy brush with scattered trees, the calves decided they were going to make a break for it.

I couldn't lose what we'd already gained so I took off on the left flank to head them off before they scattered. There was no trail, just brush. I gunned that engine through the brush, saw a small opening, and took it.

The vines draping over the opening turned out to be briars. The tree turned out to be a thorny tree. The 4Wheeler was caught like a rabbit in a snare. I gunned it and pushed forward before we lost the cows. And that's when the blood started flowing.

Lots and lots of blood. I think I left part of my face hanging in those briars. The important thing is that we caught the calves and turned them around. As the blood flowed down my face and dripped across the front of the bike, I left a blood trail in the sand. Unfortunately the calves overshot the hole in the fence and walked all the way down the fence line to stand across the fence from their mommas. Since the pickup couldn't go down the steep bank of the creek to help retrieve calves, it was up to Lily and me.

Imagine trying to push tired, irritated calves away from their mothers and down the fence to an obscure hole in the fence. It was a seemingly impossible task and yet that little dog did it. Every time they stopped moving, Lily hopped off the 4Wheeler, entered the bubble, and held her ground patiently while waiting for Little Bully to decide to move forward. It was a dicey game. Push him too much and he'd bow up on the dog. Get too close to the infant calf and he'd bow up on the dog. So acre by acre, Lily pushed the calves away from their mothers and toward the gap in the fence. Once Little Bully found that gap, he led the calves through it and back toward their mothers.

Later, as we fixed the hole in the fence, Other Half stared at my face and shook his head.

"How bad is it?" I asked.

"It's bad."

"How bad?"

"Bad."

"So what would you have me do? Save my face or not lose the cows?"

Without hesitation. "Not lose the cows." True rancher, that man.

Ordinarily having a face full of long scratches wouldn't have been a problem, but I had a job interview when we got back to Houston and my face looked like I'd been fighting a bear.

I knew I had the job the moment my chair broke and I almost fell to the floor. I'd had that chair my entire career as a crime scene investigator. In fact, I bought the chair at an office supply store and had it mailed to my office. My mentors put the chair together for me. Time was marked in that chair. Years of peeling juicy oranges left discolored patches on the seat cushion. Bits of chocolate were ground into the fabric. In hindsight, perhaps a black loose weave wasn't the best choice. I was fond of the chair and in some lopsided way, it had come to represent my time as a CSU, thus I wasn't surprised when I leaned over to reach for the phone and the chair broke. This wasn't a little break that you could fix with some screws. This was a break so irreparable that it's a wonder I didn't hit the floor. The weld holding the chair to the swivel base just gave up. Perhaps like me, the chair had just had enough. Ironic.

I scan my files and marvel at the death I've walked with through the years. Boxes of manila folders. Each file a life. A story. I used to try to organize the march of the dead. The first year it was easy. Each case was unique in my mind. Each death had a voice, but by the second year the cases began to run together. The same apartment complex. The same furniture. The same dead baby. The same blood. Instead of being able to glance at the photographs to remember the case, I was forced to delve deep into the file for details that made this death different. And then, beginning my ninth year, I no longer felt guilty when I couldn't remember their faces and their stories.

I was in a sandwich shop when a prosecutor called to discuss an old case. I stood there, a bag of potato chips in hand, with no access to my files and tried to remember the case due for trial. It is not enough to hear the suspect's name. Most of the time I never knew the killer's name anyway. Tell me who he killed. Nope. That didn't help. The victim's name no longer rings any bells either. This time I was lucky. The events of his case were dramatic enough that even in my stacks of manila folders, he stood out. Yes, I remembered that case. But it is the exception now.

The new investigators come, eager to wade into death investigation and make a difference. It's a hard job. The hours are long. The responsibility is great. The job does bring with it a delayed sense of satisfaction though. It takes years to bring justice to the victim. Nothing can wash away all the blood but a life sentence goes a long way. I see our young investigators come into the office, happy to begin their journey on this road of discovery. With just a few files in the box, they are still excited about each case. I'm excited for them, but I have a hard and fast rule I've learned over the years. CSU Rule #9: "NEVER ARM-WRESTLE ANYONE OVER A DEAD MAN."

If someone else wants to go out on that call, let them. Don't fight over a dead man. Your case file boxes will grow in time. You don't have to go out every time the phone rings. On the other hand, we were all that eager at one time. At least the good ones were. Crime Scene Investigation is not a job for someone just looking to do the minimum and then go home. Young, eager faces want to absorb every kind of death investigation detail they can. They want to learn it all, right now.

Fergus, Seamus, and I were the same way so many years ago. We bounced from dead man to dead man, absorbed in the details of death, eager to ferret out the facts that would bring us closer to justice. But just as our chisels carved bullets from sheetrock, other chisels were at work on us. Time in this job chisels away at your soul. If you're wise, you realize when it's time to stop carving. CSU Rule #10: KNOW WHEN TO PUT DOWN YOUR CHISEL.

Set it down before you give in to the urge to hurl your truck keys onto the bloody pavement and walk away from your responsibilities. Fergus left first. He waded through the waters and came to the bank on the other side. Fergus was the first of us to discover there is a life after Homicide. Still floating along in the rapids, I saw Fergus on the shore, happy, and for the first time, I gave serious thought to wading out too. It would be nice to come home at the end of my shift instead of staring at another six hours on my feet. It would be nice to have a reliable schedule. It would be nice to go into retirement free of more years of murder trials. It would be nice to not play Twister over dead men. To not hear their mothers' cries.

And so I took the plunge. After years of dancing with the

dead, I put in a transfer and I put it in God's hands. What would be, would be. The interview went well but it wasn't until days later when my chair broke that I knew I had the job. After all, that chair had been with me for my entire career and if it broke, it was because I didn't need it anymore. Three days later the phone rang. The job was mine if I wanted it.

Fergus had been promoted to Sergeant Fergus. He'd coaxed me away from my position as a Crime Scene Investigator to come work for him at the Command Center. His promise of a place in the sun proved to be a good one. The work was stimulating and enjoyable as I was trained to fight crime from behind a computer screen. My job could be summed up as follows: *101 Ways the Police Can Find You*. It was a fun job, but one that wouldn't last for long. Nine months later the phone rang again.

"I just sold the house!"

"You did what?!"

I'm glad I was sitting down. After 34 years in police work, Other Half had just pulled the plug on his career and decided to retire. We started looking at our finances and it just didn't make sense for us to keep two houses with two farms on two different sides of Texas, so we bounced around the idea of me retiring early and selling the farm in South Texas. We were just tossing around the idea. I didn't take him seriously. Until the phone call. I hung up and just sat there in stunned silence. Not only had he pulled the plug on his own career but by selling the house, he'd pulled the plug on mine too. Apparently the rancher next door got wind that we might be putting the farm up for sale so he swooped in and bought it. Just like that. It was three days from the time Other Half announced that he was retiring, to him selling the house with a handshake.

Stunned doesn't begin to describe it. I have stood over more dead men than I can remember and it has changed me. I came to the job of Crime Scene Investigator from a very active and fairly dangerous position on a Tactical Team. We hunted narcotics and ran felony warrants. The Crime Scene Investigator position was much more cerebral, and a definite drop in the adrenaline rush, because by the time I arrived on a scene, the dust had settled and they'd counted the dead.

The bulk of my career as a police officer had been spent trying not to get killed, and playing Twister over people who were already dead. That much time spent both avoiding death and then staring death right in the face, changes your perspective on life and here's what I've learned:

1) When things don't work out the way you want, don't get discouraged. Just have faith. If that door closed, there's a reason for it. Quit knocking. If you're in a place in life where you don't want to be, quit fighting it. Be patient. Maybe there's a reason you're there. Maybe you need some polishing yourself, or maybe you need to help someone else along their journey. Have patience. When your time is ready, the exit door will open.

2) When things that don't normally work out suddenly fall into place like a child's block puzzle, it's time to sit up and take notice. Don't question it. Just have faith.

That said, I was still completely unprepared for the final puzzle pieces of my career to plop into place so quickly. I didn't really believe it until we went to the title company to sign papers. And it was done. The house was sold. He turned in his retirement papers at work so I made the phone calls to begin the end of my career and the start of a new chapter.

Back at the office I sat at my computer screen in quiet

disbelief. One of my co-workers helped me put things into perspective.

"You seem a little sad."

"I guess I'm just a bit overwhelmed. It's what I wanted, it's just happening so fast."

"But is there really anything else you still want to do in this job? I mean, you've had a pretty interesting career. It'd be hard to top what you've already done. Is there still something you want to do here?"

How profound. I gave it a blink of a thought. "No."

And with that, I was free. I was ready to embrace the new change with no regrets. He was right. If I stayed, it would just be for the money and I've never been one to follow the money. I never take the safe route. I follow my heart. And my heart was leading me down a red dirt road.

The only person who enjoys working cattle at 4 a.m. is a Border Collie. That said, in order to stack the deck in our favor before hauling the last load of cattle north, Other Half and I decided to make it easier on ourselves and "pre-train" the cows so they'd be more willing to load.

South Texas had been getting rains just often enough to make loading cattle in the pasture too difficult. Even with 4-wheel drive the big truck might not crawl through the mud once the trailer was loaded with cattle. We were on a strict timeline and Mother Nature was not cooperating. Other Half had the brilliant idea that we should back the trailer up to the pasture gate, take pipe panels and create a funnel between the pasture gate and the opened doors of the cattle trailer. Once inside the funnel, we could close the pasture gate and trap the cattle against the back of the trailer. Then it would be a short matter to just push them into the trailer.

To stack the deck even further, we did a test run the afternoon before by showing the cows a bag of feed, and luring them inside the cattle trailer where they would be fed. The heifers were like kindergarteners in a school cafeteria. Cattle filed in and we didn't shut the door. The cattle trailer was a happy place to be. Ten minutes start to finish. We were so pleased with ourselves our hats could barely contain our swelling heads.

At 4 a.m. the following morning it was a different story.

I am wearing dirty clothes and rubber boots. Other Half takes a shower. He puts on clean clothes and good boots. He has no plans to do anything but shake a feed bag and toss out feed while I shut the door on eager cattle who push and shove to load themselves.

I slog out into mud with a sorting stick. I leave the Border Collies in the house because I have no desire to drive across Texas with wet dogs. After all, we don't need Border Collies, we have trained the cattle.

Flip on barn lights. Sleepy sheep and goats blink in the bright light and call a weak good morning. I inform them that they will eat when it is their turn to climb into their trailer. They go back to bed. Other Half grabs a sack of feed and heads to cattle trailer while I wake cattle.

The cows slowly make their way up out of the mist. Where have our eager kindergarteners gone? They have been replaced by sullen teenagers who shuffle in the dark and bitch about the hour. Like elementary school teachers, we gamely play on, resisting the urge to throw sorting sticks at cattle who take an eternity to finally complete their lesson. Eventually they all do — except one.

She sees the writing the wall. She's smart enough to know that bipeds never feed cattle at 4 a.m. unless something is up. Oh yes, something is definitely "up." I slop through the mud with a sorting stick to move her toward the trailer. She is in a three acre trap which contains a small pond, a goat pen, a round pen, and a barn. *As cagey as any hunted elk, any time I get close to her, she manages to slosh through the mud and put herself on the opposite side of one of these many barriers.*

Other Half joins our ridiculous game. As soon as he begins he wants a dog. I refuse. I don't want to put clean Border Collies in six inches of sucking mud and then ride 7 hours north with them, so for an hour the three of us play this stupid game. The clock is ticking but the heifer is not concerned about the rising sun. She has all day. She has opted out of this field trip.

Other Half calls for a dog multiple times. I stubbornly refuse. The heifer continues to taunt us. I announce that we should just leave the bitch alone here and take her to the sale barn later. Other Half refuses. As I pass by the arena gate once more, the mud sucks off my boot.

Other Half pleads for a Border Collie. Lily is barking at the window. She has been watching this fiasco from inside. Okay. Get a dog. Get two dogs. I curse the cow again as the sun creeps over her back. Other Half returns with Lily and Cowboy. The mood in the pasture changes. The Law has just arrived. The Law glances at the cattle trailer with its load of pooping cattle. The Law then looks at the single white-faced cow staring at us from across the pond. Lily slowly raises a paw to her forehead in a silent salute. She has acquired the target. Let the games begin.

Two Border Collies race off into the mist. There is much splashing and the sound of sucking mud. We had played with the sly beast for almost an hour and a half, and in that time the cow learned quite a few tricks. She tries all of them on the dogs, but unlike humans who couldn't keep up and gave her plenty of time to rest, the black & white ninja dogs never stop. They are everywhere. They are nowhere. In less than ten minutes they have her in the trailer.

Most of that ten minutes was spent with her going

through the bag of tricks she had learned with us. I have to admit it. If we had gotten the dogs as soon as Other Half called for them, we'd have been on the road in fifteen minutes.

Afterwards I hosed off the dogs, and gave it some thought. Like everyone with livestock and a bucket of feed, I had boldly proclaimed that we didn't need a dog because our cows were trained. I know better and yet I still did it. I have four Border Collies and I still staggered around in the moonlight for an hour and a half chasing a freaking cow. That has got to be a new level of stupid.

The muddy, panting dog smiled as I hosed off her tummy. There was no hint of smugness, just the happy satisfaction of a job well done. And thus is story of the stockdog — muddy, panting, earnest, and forgiving.

With a wistful sigh, I glanced at the dumpster in my rear-view mirror as I pulled the trailer out of the driveway. We couldn't take everything. Two households of acquired "stuff" had to be condensed into one apartment inside a barn, our barndominium.

We packed the essentials. We gave away a lot of stuff. For the rest of it we rented a rollback dumpster to park in the front yard. Slowly, load by agonizing load, we filled that dumpster.

The afternoon before we left I sat in the spare room on a stack of boxes and sorted through my career. It was crunch time. Sunlight filtered through a dusty window as I sifted through what was left of my gear. Exactly what does a retired CSI need? Winnie-the-Pooh and Tigger smiled at me as I picked up the green tackle box and sorted through what was left after I had let colleagues run through it like a Black Friday "scratch and dent" sale. I made a small fingerprint kit to take with me. And a buccal swab kit. Because . . . well . . . I have no clue why. What the hell, you never know when you'll have to lift fingerprints and take DNA samples. Once a CSI, always a CSI.

White sheetrock dust still clung to the hammers and chisels that were lovingly packed into other toolboxes with their country cousins who had not led such an exciting career. There would be no more bullets to dig out of walls.

And the tape measure? How many murders had this humble tool seen? How many bodies? I tucked it beside a chisel and closed the lid. Another box empty. That left the green tackle box itself.

I considered cleaning it up and taking it, but had neither the time nor the space, so with slow steps I walked Winnie-the-Pooh and Tigger to the dumpster. I didn't have the heart to sling them onto the heap so I gently set the green tackle box on the side of an overturned couch which had seen its better days. That way it was still in the dumpster but if I changed my mind at the last minute, if I found some obscure use for an old tackle box that was stained with sooty fingerprint powder, I could save it. I walked back in the house to finish packing.

Several hours later friends came over to help pack and pick through our stuff. There were great deals to be had if you were willing to sort through piles and piles of crap. You never know what won't fit on the U-Haul truck.

I found Dear Friend Maxine digging through the dumpster. She hauled out the green tackle box as if it were a prize in the Cracker Jack box. I cautioned her. "You know the drawers of that thing are coated in black fingerprint powder dust, right? It'll take forever to clean it." She didn't care. This tackle box had character. It had a story.

Yes, it did. It really did. Winnie-the-Pooh and Tigger waved at me as they walked away to start their new lives. I smiled and waved back. I'll miss them but they'll be fine without me.

The next morning, I pulled the green dolly up the ramp

and into the U-Haul for the last load. No longer shiny and with the gum still firmly cemented in place on the wheel, the cart wobbled with its lopsided whack-whack. Once inside the U-Haul, I relieved my faithful green donkey of its burden, stood it in the corner, and I slammed the door shut.

~

The mist rises over the pond to mingle with the rays of sunshine peeking over the trees, and there, in the reverent silence of daybreak, I give some thought as to why sunrise in the country can be such a religious experience.

I sip my coffee in the mist as the turkey calls. A woodpecker gives a tentative rat-a-tat-tat on a tree before flying to another. The first rays of sunlight warm my cheek. It is God's touch, a reminder that each sunrise is the gift of another day. I reflect on this moment. Perhaps this is why people in the country are often more openly religious than our city cousins. While there are those who point to our rural roots and claim that a lack of travel, a lack of education and a lack of world experience leads us to cling to a mythical god, I would argue against that.

Daybreak in the city is no less miraculous but like the wave of a starting flag, it signals the beginning of the maddening rat race, whereas here in the country, surrounded by the creations of God and not the creations of man, the country mouse can pause and reflect.

With dirt under foot instead of cold concrete it's easier to feel the heartbeat of the earth, to see the hand of God. Like a cheerful spirit, the red flash of a cardinal swoops among the trees. The armadillo shuffles through the leaves, so intent on his task that he fails to notice me. Perhaps that is what separates the non-believing city mouse from his simple country cousin. Perhaps the armadillo is like the city mouse, with his head buried, so busy moving along his journey, deafened by his own actions in the fallen leaves, that he does not see the world around him. Wrapped in his world of digging holes in the forest, the armadillo can claim there is no God. He doesn't see because he doesn't look.

I mull this in my mind as day breaks over the trees and spills into the pond. A horse standing by the fence notices me and calls a morning greeting. This sets off a chain reaction as sheep and goats now clamor for my attention. Cattle in the distance hear this and begin to bawl and wade through the forest in my direction. The starting flag has just waved on morning in the country. With a contented sigh, I raise my camera, and take a picture of the sunrise over my pond. Then I head to the house to start morning chores.

You cannot truly appreciate life until you've been up close and personal with death. Time chisels away at your core, for you cannot wade through this amount of death without being changed and rose-colored glasses were never part of the uniform. Years of brushing shoulders with Death changed my perspective on life.

Like every day in the barnyard, every crime scene I walked into had a story, and it wasn't always the story I expected. Every morning, the moment your feet touch the ground, your story begins. Often you decide whether the tale is a comedy or a tragedy, for the story is simply in the perception. A comedy perceived, is a comedy achieved. In the end, I hope that something I have shared makes you laugh, makes you think, or makes you thankful for the gifts the Good Lord has given you.

"The tragedy of life is not that it ends so soon, but that we wait so long to begin it."
W.M. Lewis

ABOUT THE AUTHOR

Writer, rancher and retired CSI,
Sheridan Rowe Langford lives in North Texas where she and
her husband raise cattle and sheep as their Border
Collies plot world domination.

Made in the USA
San Bernardino, CA
02 September 2019